DELEUZE AND GUATTARI

The philosopher Gilles Deleuze and the psychoanalyst and political activist Félix Guattari have been recognized as among the most important intellectual figures of their generation. This is the first book-length study of their works in English; one that provides an overview of their thought and of its bearing on the central issues of contemporary literary criticism and theory.

From Deleuze's 'philosophy of difference' to Deleuze and Guattari's 'philosophy of schizoanalytic desire', this study traces the ideas of the two writers across a wide range of disciplines – from psychoanalysis and Marxist politics to semiotics, aesthetics and linguistics. What emerges is an essentially Nietzschean philosophy of becoming that complements and challenges the work of such French theorists as Derrida, Foucault and Lacan in revealing and surprising ways.

Professor Bogue provides lucid readings, accessible to specialist and non-specialist alike, of several major works: Deleuze's *Nietzsche and Philosophy* (1962), *Difference and Repetition* (1968), and Deleuze and Guattari's *Anti-Oedipus* (1972) and *A Thousand Plateaus* (1980). Besides elucidating the basic structure of Deleuze and Guattari's often difficult thought, with its complex and sometimes puzzling array of terms, this study also shows how theory influences critical practice in their analyses of the fiction of Proust, Sacher-Masoch and Kafka.

Ronald Bogue is Associate Professor at the Comparative Literature Department, University of Georgia

Deleuze and Guattari

RONALD BOGUE

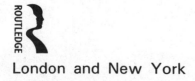

London and New York

For my father
Cameron Bogue
1919–1988

First published in 1989
by Routledge
11 New Fetter Lane, London EC4P 4EE
29 West 35th Street, New York NY 10001

Reprinted 1990

© *1989 R. Bogue*

Printed and bound by
TJ Press (Padstow) Ltd, Padstow, Cornwall.

British Library Cataloguing in Publication Data

Bogue, Ronald, 1948–
  Deleuze and Guattari. — (Critics of the
  twentieth century).
  1. Literature. Criticism. Deleuze, Gilles,
  1925– Guattari, Félix, 1930–
  I. Title   II. Series
  801'.95'0922

Library of Congress Cataloging in Publication Data

Bogue, Ronald, 1948–
  Deleuze and Guattari / by Ronald Bogue.
    p.   cm. — (Critics of the twentieth century)
  Bibliography: p.
  Includes index.
  ISBN 0–415–02017–4. — ISBN 0–415–02443–9 (pbk.)
  1. Literature, Modern — 20th century — History and criticism.
2. Deleuze, Gilles. 3. Guattari, Felix. 4. Criticism.
5. Philosophy, Modern — 20th century. 6. Psychoanalysis and
literature. 7. Deconstruction. 8. Structuralism (Literary
analysis) I. Title. II. Series: Critics of the twentieth century
(London, England)
PN94.B64   1989
801'.95'0904 — dc19

Contents

Contents

Part Two: Deleuze and Guattari

Editor's foreword

The twentieth century has produced a remarkable number of gifted and innovative literary critics. Indeed it could be argued that some of the finest literary minds of the age have turned to criticism as the medium best adapted to their complex and speculative range of interests. This has sometimes given rise to regret among those who insist on a clear demarcation between 'creative' (primary) writing on the one hand, and 'critical' (secondary) texts on the other. Yet this distinction is far from self-evident. It is coming under strain at the moment as novelists and poets grow increasingly aware of the conventions that govern their writing and the challenge of consciously exploiting and subverting those conventions. And the critics for their part – some of them at least – are beginning to question their traditional role as humble servants of the literary text with no further claim upon the reader's interest or attention. Quite simply, there are texts of literary criticism and theory that, for various reasons – stylistic complexity, historical influence, range of intellectual command – cannot be counted a mere appendage to those other 'primary' texts.

Of course, there is a logical puzzle here, since (it will be argued) 'literary criticism' would never have come into being, and could hardly exist as such, were it not for the body of creative writings that provide its *raison d'être*. But this is not quite the kind of knock-down argument that it might appear at first glance. For one thing, it conflates some very different orders of priority, assuming that literature always comes first (in the sense that Greek tragedy had to exist before Aristotle could formulate its rules), so that literary texts are for that very reason possessed of superior value. And this argument would seem to find commonsense support in the difficulty of thinking what 'literary criticism' could *be* if it seriously renounced all sense of the distinction between literary and critical texts. Would it not then find itself in the unfortunate position of a discipline that had willed its own demise by declaring its subject non-existent?

But these objections would only hit their mark if there were indeed a special kind of writing called 'literature' whose difference from other kinds of writing was enough to put criticism firmly in its place. Otherwise there is nothing in the least self-defeating or paradoxical about a discourse, nominally that of literary criticism, that accrues such interest on its own account as to force some fairly drastic rethinking of its proper powers and limits. The act of crossing over from commentary to literature – or of simply denying the difference between them – becomes quite explicit in the writing of a critic like Geoffrey Hartman. But the signs are already there in such classics as William Empson's *Seven Types of Ambiguity* (1928), a text whose transformative influence on our habits of reading must surely be ranked with the great creative moments of literary modernism. Only on the most dogmatic view of the difference between 'literature' and 'criticism' could a work like *Seven Types* be counted generically an inferior, sub-literary species of production. And the same can be said for many of the critics whose writings and influence this series sets out to explore.

Some, like Empson, are conspicuous individuals who belong to no particular school or larger movement. Others, like the Russian Formalists, were part of a communal enterprise and are therefore best understood as representative figures in a complex and evolving dialogue. Then again there are cases of collective identity (like the so-called 'Yale deconstructors') where a mythical group image is invented for largely polemical purposes. (The volumes in this series on Hartman and Bloom should help to dispel the idea that 'Yale deconstruction' is anything more than a handy device for collapsing differences and avoiding serious debate.) So there is no question of a series format or house-style that would seek to reduce these differences to a blandly homogeneous treatment. One consequence of recent critical theory is the realization that literary texts have no self-sufficient or autonomous meaning, no existence apart from their after-life of changing interpretations and values. And the same applies to those *critical* texts whose meaning and significance are subject to constant shifts and realignments of interest. This is not to say that trends in criticism are just a matter of intellectual fashion or the merry-go-round of rising and falling reputations. But it is important to grasp how complex are the forces – the conjunctions of historical and cultural motive – that affect the first reception and the subsequent fortunes of a critical text. This point has been raised into a systematic programme by critics like Hans-Robert Jauss, practitioners of so-called 'reception theory' as a form of historical hermeneutics. The volumes in this series will therefore be concerned not only to expound what is of lasting significance but also to set these critics in the context of present-day argument and debate. In some cases (as with Walter Benjamin) this debate takes the form of a struggle for interpretative power among disciplines with sharply opposed ideological viewpoints. Such controversies cannot simply be ignored in the interests of achieving a clear and balanced account. They point to unresolved tensions and problems which are there in the critic's work as well as in the rival appropriative readings. In the end there is no way of drawing a neat methodological line between 'intrinsic' questions (what the critic really thought) and those other, supposedly 'extrinsic' concerns that have to do with influence and reception history.

The volumes will vary accordingly in their focus and range of coverage. They will also reflect the ways in which a speculative approach to questions of literary theory has proved to have striking consequences for the human sciences at large. This breaking-down of disciplinary bounds is among the most significant developments in recent critical thinking. As philosophers and historians, among others, come to recognize the rhetorical complexity of the texts they deal with, so literary theory takes on a new dimension of interest and relevance. It is scarcely appropriate to think of writers like Derrida as a literary critic in any conventional sense of the term. For one thing, he is as much concerned with 'philosophical' as with 'literary' texts, and has indeed actively sought to subvert (or deconstruct) such tidy distinctions. A principal object in planning this series was to take full stock of these shifts in the wider intellectual terrain (including the frequent boundary disputes) brought about by critical theory. And, of course, such changes are by no means confined to literary studies, philosophy and the so-called 'sciences of man'. It is equally the case in (say) nuclear physics and molecular biology that advances in the one field have decisive implications for the other, so that specialized research often tends (paradoxically) to break down existing divisions of knowledge. Such work is typically many years ahead of the academic disciplines and teaching institutions that have obvious reasons of their own for preserving the intellectual *status quo*. One important aspect of modern critical theory is the challenge it presents to these traditional ideas. And lest it be thought that this is merely a one-sided takeover bid by the literary critics, the series will include a number of volumes by authors in those other disciplines, including, for instance, a study of Roland Barthes by an American analytical philosopher.

We shall not, however, cleave to theory as a matter of polemical or principled stance. The series will extend to figures like F. R. Leavis, whose widespread influence went along with an express aversion to literary theory; scholars like Erich Auerbach in the mainstream European tradition; and others who resist assimilation to any clear-cut line of descent. There will also be authoritative volumes on critics such as Northrop Frye and Lionel Trilling, figures who, for various reasons, occupy an ambivalent or essentially contested place in modern critical tradition. Above all the series will strive to resist that current polarization of attitudes that sees no common ground of interest between 'literary criticism' and 'critical theory'.

CHRISTOPHER NORRIS

Acknowledgements

I am deeply indebted to my colleagues Mihai Spariosu and Richard Unger for having diligently and cheerfully reviewed and commented on the entire manuscript. Professor Spariosu has illuminated many thorny issues in contemporary theory, and Professor Unger has lent me his unerring ear and insisted throughout that clarity and directness be maintained in the presentation of this rather abstract material.

Hubert McAlexander also read portions of the manuscript and offered timely encouragement and support, for which I am sincerely grateful.

I would like to thank as well the many colleagues, especially Betty Jean Craige and Joel Black, who have indirectly assisted me in this project through years of intelligent and informed discussion of the key issues in literary criticism.

Charles J. Stivale generously supplied several bibliographical references and directed me toward many secondary sources that have proved essential in the development of my argument.

My gratitude also goes to Len Tennenhouse and Nancy Armstrong, without whose early assistance this project would not have been possible.

I would also like to acknowledge the generous support of the Georgia Research Foundation for summer research funds in the early phases of this project.

Finally, I must thank my wife, Svea Bogue, for her constant and much-needed encouragement, and her cheerful and selfless assistance, at every stage of this endeavour.

R. Bogue

List of abbreviations

Whenever possible, I have cited translations of works by Deleuze and Guattari, providing my own translations of those texts that remain available only in French. When citing translations, I have included the page numbers of both the English version and the corresponding passage in the French edition, the latter in italics. (Translations of *Kafka*, *Dialogues* and *Mille plateaux* only became available after I had finished my manuscript and hence have not been cited.)

By Gilles Deleuze

NP *Nietzsche and Philosophy*, tr. Hugh Tomlinson, Minneapolis: University of Minnesota Press, 1983. *Nietzsche et la philosophie*, Paris: PUF, 1962.

PS *Proust and Signs*, tr. Richard Howard, New York: G. Braziller, 1972. *Proust et les signes* 4th edn, Paris, PUF, 1976.

M *Masochism: An Interpretation of Coldness and Cruelty*, tr. Jean McNeil, New York: G. Braziller, 1971. *Présentation de Sacher-Masoch*, Paris: Minuit, 1967.

DR *Différence et répétition* [*Difference and Repetition*], Paris: PUF, 1968.

LS *Logique du sens* [*The Logic of Meaning*], Paris: Minuit, 1969.

D *Dialogues*, with Claire Parnet, Paris: Flammarion, 1977.

FB *Francis Bacon: Logique de la sensation* [*Francis Bacon: The Logic of Sensation*] Vol. 1, Paris: Editions de la différence, 1981.

EN 'Ecrivain non: un nouveau cartographe', *Critique* 343 (Dec. 1975).

S *Spinoza: philosophie pratique*, Paris: Minuit, 1981.

List of abbreviations

By Félix Guattari

PT *Psychanalyse et transversalité* [*Psychoanalysis and Transversality*], Paris: Maspero, 1972.

By Gilles Deleuze and Félix Guattari

AO *Anti-Oedipus*, tr. Robert Hurley, Mark Seem, and Helen R. Lane, Minneapolis: University of Minnesota Press, 1977. Preface by Michel Foucault. *L'Anti-Oedipe: capitalisme et schizophrénie I*, Paris: Minuit, 1972.

K *Kafka: pour une littérature mineure* [*Kafka: For a Minor Literature*], Paris: Minuit, 1975.

MP *Mille plateaux: capitalisme et schizophrénie II* [*Thousand Plateaus: Capitalism and Schizophrenia II*], Paris: Minuit, 1980.

By Franz Kafka

DF *Dearest Father: Stories and Other Writings*, tr. Ernst Kaiser and Eithne Wilkins, New York: Schocken, 1954.

T *The Trial*, tr. Willa and Edwin Muir, rev. E. M. Butler, New York: Modern Library, 1956.

PC *The Penal Colony: Stories and Short Pieces*, tr. Willa and Edwin Muir, New York: Schocken, 1948.

D1 *The Diaries of Franz Kafka: 1910–1913*, ed. Max Brod, tr. Joseph Kresh, New York: Schocken, 1948.

D2 *The Diaries of Franz Kafka: 1914–1923*, ed. Max Brod, tr. Martin Greenberg with Hannah Arendt, New York: Schocken, 1949.

LFF *Letters to Friends, Family and Editors*, tr. Richard and Clara Winston, New York: Schocken, 1977.

Introduction

... and perhaps one day, this century will be known as Deleuzian.

— Michel Foucault[1]

In 1972, the philosopher Gilles Deleuze and the psychoanalyst and political activist Félix Guattari published *Anti-Oedipus: Capitalism and Schizophrenia I*, a full-scale attack on the doctrines of psychoanalysis, particularly as formulated by Jacques Lacan and his followers, which had become so pervasive in Parisian intellectual circles of the late 1960s and early 1970s. In *Anti-Oedipus* many saw a philosophical expression of the spirit of the May 1968 student revolt – some, because the book offered an exuberant and iconoclastic synthesis of Marxist and Freudian motifs within an anti-structural, Nietzschean thematics of liberation; others, because it seemed to enunciate an irresponsible and anarchistic politics of libidinal self-indulgence. The book enjoyed a considerable success, serving for a time as the focus of widespread and animated debate, and it remains the best-known work by Deleuze or by Guattari. Its popularity, no doubt, stemmed in large part from the timeliness of its irreverent radicalism and its critique of psychoanalysis. Yet *Anti-Oedipus* was neither a spontaneous effusion of May-'68 irrationalism nor an opportunistic exploitation of the cult of Lacanism. Rather, it was the result of nearly twenty years of investigation in philosophy, psychoanalysis and political theory on the part of its authors; hence, it was as much a response to intellectual currents spanning decades as a reaction to the May insurrection.

When *Anti-Oedipus* appeared, Gilles Deleuze was already well established as an important French philosopher. Born in 1925, he attended the Lycée Carnot in Paris and began studying philosophy

1

at the Sorbonne in the mid-1940s, passing his *agrégation* examination in 1949. He and his fellow students were steeped in the rationalist tradition, introduced to the rigours of Hegel, Husserl and early Heidegger, and trained to regard the history of philosophy as the essential foundation of their discipline. 'At the time of the Liberation', remarks Deleuze, 'we were strangely trapped in the history of philosophy. Quite naturally we entered into Hegel, Husserl and Heidegger; we threw ourselves like young dogs into a scholasticism worse than that of the Middle Ages' (D 18). After leaving the Sorbonne, Deleuze embarked on a series of studies in the history of philosophy, but he chose to concentrate on writers whose thought was consonant neither with academic rationalism nor with post-war Hegelian, existential or phenomenological philosophy. He turned to what he saw as an anti-rationalist tradition that included 'authors who seemed to form a part of the history of philosophy, but who escaped it on one side or in all directions: Lucretius, Spinoza, Hume, Nietzsche, Bergson' (D 21). He published his first book on Hume in 1953, an essay on Lucretius in 1961, and books on Nietzsche in 1962, Bergson in 1966, and Spinoza in 1968.

Of these philosophers, the most important for Deleuze was Nietzsche, to a large extent because Nietzsche offered Deleuze an alternative to the Hegelianism that so permeated French thought during the 1940s and 1950s. Through the Russian emigré Alexandre Kojève, whose seminars on Hegel from 1933 to 1939 had been attended by a number of important Parisian intellectuals, an anthropological, atheistic reading of Hegel had been introduced into France, one that treated the dialectic as the history of the successive forms of human consciousness and that regarded Spirit as 'nothing but the negating (i.e., creative) Action realised by Man in the given World'.[2] Kojève's emphasis on the dialectic as the history of consciousness, on freedom as negation, and on action as transformation of the world appealed to post-war phenomenologists, existentialists, and humanistic Marxists. But what was most fundamentally attractive and vital about Kojève's thought was that it forced philosophy, in Vincent Descombes' words, 'to traverse areas of existence on which it had not impinged until then: political cynicism, the virtue of massacre and violence, and in a global way, *the unreasonable origins of reason*'.[3] To Deleuze and many of his generation, however, the Hegelian dialectic only *seemed* to engage the non-rational; its logic of negation and contradiction was based ultimately on a logic of identity, within which the non-rational

2

'other' could only be conceived of as the shadow of the rational 'same'. What was needed, according to Deleuze and others, was a philosophy of difference *as* difference, irreducible to the concepts of identity and representation. Deleuze found the inspiration for such a philosophy in Nietzsche.

Throughout the 1960s Deleuze developed various aspects of a Nietzschean philosophy of difference, presenting the most detailed formulation of this thought in *Difference and Repetition* (1968) and *The Logic of Meaning* (1969). In many ways, Deleuze's work on difference paralleled the deconstructive enterprise of Derrida, itself of Nietzschean inspiration (via Heidegger). Both Deleuze and Derrida challenged the metaphysical presuppositions of traditional philosophy and the representational model of thought, and both found in difference (or differance) an 'aconceptual concept' or 'non-concept' that undermined the certainties of Western rationality. Deleuze, like Derrida, also maintained a divided interest in the structuralist vogue of the 1960s, accepting the more radical and unsettling aspects of the movement while rejecting its claims to scientific objectivity.[4] Structuralism had served the useful purpose of dethroning the sovereign subject or *cogito*, which had remained unchallenged in French thought from Descartes to Sartre and Merleau-Ponty. Structuralists like Lévi-Strauss saw the subject not as a source or ground of knowledge, but as a function of structures – social, mythical, linguistic, and so on – that escaped the subject's control. Deleuze welcomed this attack on the *cogito*, but he questioned the epistemological status of those impersonal structures that regulate subjectivity. His response to structuralism was similar to Derrida's: just as Derrida accepted the terms of the Saussurian analysis of linguistic structure and then used them to decentre the very notion of structure, so Deleuze incorporated a mathematical model of structure within his philosophy of difference, but through a theory of 'singular points', 'metastable states', and 'nomadic distributions', thoroughly problematized that model.

The anti-rational, post-structural orientation of *Anti-Oedipus*, then, although in tune with popular sentiments inspired by May 1968, had been evident in Deleuze's work for some time. *Anti-Oedipus*'s assault on the 'tyranny of the signifier' simply intensified Deleuze's attack on structuralism. The work's characterization of desire and the unconscious merely extended the Nietzschean concept of 'will to power' that Deleuze had outlined in *Nietzsche and Philosophy* in 1962. And its critique of Lacan's theory of desire was but a continuation of Deleuze's long-standing opposition to post-

3

war Hegelianism. (Lacan attended Kojève's seminars in the 1930s, and the influence of Kojève's Hegel may be discerned at several points in Lacan's work.) What one cannot attribute directly to Deleuze is the strong political focus of *Anti-Oedipus*, and in particular its concern with the interrelation and interpenetration of the social and psychological spheres of experience. This aspect of *Anti-Oedipus*, however, reflected less the influence of May 1968 than the preoccupations that had inspired Félix Guattari's work for a number of years.

From an early age, Guattari had been active in Marxist political movements. Born in 1930, he grew up in the working-class suburbs of north-west Paris and participated in various Communist youth groups as a *lycéen* and later as a university student in pharmacy and philosophy. In 1950 he joined the Communist Party, but soon formed alliances with various leftist dissidents and eventually was 'suspended' by the Party. During the early and mid 1950s, he worked within the PCF (Parti Communiste Français), assisting in the publication of the opposition newspaper *Tribune de discussion*. In 1958 he broke with the Party and began editing and contributing to the dissident newspaper *La Voie communiste*, whose frequent articles in support of Algerian independence led to its repeated seizure and the extended imprisonment of two of its directors. By the time *La Voie communiste* ceased publication in 1965, Guattari had already become active in the Opposition de Gauche (OG), an alliance of non-Party leftists, and it was from within the OG that he played a major behind-the-scenes role in the events of May 1968.

For a number of radicals, May 1968 was a disillusioning experience. Students and intellectuals had called not only for a new political order, but also for new forms of social relations that were open and free from domination. The PCF, instead of joining the students and workers, supported the government. And as the May rebels increasingly focused their attention on the structures of social institutions, it became apparent that the PCF, in its internal organization as well as its external policies, functioned largely as a force of repression. For Guattari, May 1968 exposed little about the PCF that he had not already recognized. He had witnessed the Party's periodic expulsion of its leading intellectuals, its betrayal of the Algerian liberation struggle in 1956 and the years following, and its intransigent resistance to de-Stalinization in the 1950s. He had long been critical of the PCF's limited conception of legitimate political action as the seizure of state power, and for years he had denounced the repressive structures of institutions such as the PCF.[5]

Guattari had become particularly sensitive to the political dimension of social institutions through his experiences at Dr Jean Oury's experimental psychiatric hospital, the Clinique de la Borde at Cour-Cheverny, where he had been working since 1953. Following the liberation, Dr Oury and several other psychiatrists had begun to question the structure and function of traditional mental hospitals, whose resemblance to concentration camps seemed all too apparent after the war, and they sought to establish in hospitals like the Clinique de la Borde more humane and creative forms of treatment and less hierarchical modes of interaction between patients and staff than those found in conventional institutions. At the Clinique de la Borde, Guattari began to develop a theory of the relationship between psychological repression and social oppression, and he became active in a series of groups dedicated to the study of power relations in institutions.[6] In 1960 he helped form the Groupe de Travail de Psychologie et de Sociologie Institutionnelle (GTPSI), which was superseded by the more broadly based Société de Psychothérapie Institutionnelle (SPI) in 1965. Also in 1965 he helped found the Fédération des Groupes d'Etudes et de Recherche Institutionnelle (FGERI), an alliance of some 300 psychiatrists, psychologists, teachers, urbanists, architects, economists, film makes, professors, and others, dedicated to a general analysis of institutional forms of oppression. The FGERI in turn gave birth to the Centre d'Etude, de Recherche et de Formation Institutionnelles (CERFI), the sponsoring organization of the interdisciplinary journal *Recherches*, which Guattari edited during its first decade of publication.

Also crucial in the development of Guattari's thought on the psycho-social dynamics of institutions was his training in Lacanian psychoanalysis. Psychoanalysis had initially suffered a hostile reception in France, and it was only in the 1960s that Freud became an important force in French intellectual life. The figure primarily responsible for this belated surge in Freud's popularity was Jacques Lacan, whose abstruse reading of Freud virtually transformed the Viennese doctor into a Parisian philosopher. Lacan's assimilation of the insights of Saussurian linguistics and structural anthropology within psychoanalytic theory brought Freud a large following in the heyday of structuralism, and Lacan's concept of the decentred subject continued to strike a responsive chord in French intellectuals into the 1970s. After May 1968, the popularity of psychoanalysis

5

mushroomed, and Lacan's teachings figured prominently in theoretical discussions across several disciplines, especially in those focusing on the possible fusion of Marx and Freud within a radical politics.[7]

Guattari's interest in Lacan antedated the rise in popularity of psychoanalysis by some years, for he had been attending Lacan's bimonthly seminars since 1953. From 1962 to 1969 he underwent analysis with Lacan, and in 1969 he joined Lacan's Ecole Freudienne de Paris as an analyst member. At the Clinique de la Borde during the 1950s and 1960s, he tried to extend psychoanalytic techniques to the treatment of psychotics. In his essays on institutional psycho-politics written during the 1960s he made generous use of such Lacanian concepts as the *objet petit-a*, the Imaginary, and the phallus as master-signifier. By the time he met Deleuze in 1969, he had been working for a decade on possible syntheses of Freud and Marx, and he had begun to formulate a theory of the social and political unconscious in non-Lacanian terms. He and Deleuze together developed that theory and a complementary critique of psychoanalysis, which they presented in *Anti-Oedipus*.

The popularity of *Anti-Oedipus* secured Deleuze and Guattari a certain renown, but one with unfortunate side effects. They became symbols of anti-psychiatry and the spirit of May, and as a result the broader concerns that informed *Anti-Oedipus* were often ignored. *Anti-Oedipus* was often taken as a manifesto of 'naturalism' or 'spontaneism', a view that could not have been seriously maintained if the book had been situated in relation to Deleuze's earlier works, whose importance the *Anti-Oedipus* controversy had tended to obscure. Also, Deleuze and Guattari's efforts after *Anti-Oedipus* received less attention than they deserved, since they were often dismissed as simple continuations of an outmoded style of thought. This was unfortunate, for in Deleuze and Guattari's *Kafka: For a Minor Literature* (1975) and *Thousand Plateaus* (1980), as well as in Guattari's *The Molecular Revolution* (1977) and *The Machinic Unconscious* (1979), a sophisticated theory of the interrelation of desire and power was developed, one that provides an important complement to Michel Foucault's influential studies of power and the politics of the body (a point I shall develop in the second half of this book). Happily, interest in Deleuze and Guattari is reviving. Deleuze's two-volume *Cinéma* (1983 and 1985) and his *Foucault* (1986) have been widely and favourably reviewed, and Guattari's indefatigable efforts on behalf of various radical causes and his trenchant social and political essays (many of which are gathered in

Introduction

his *The Years of Winter: 1980–1985)* have gradually established him as an important spokesman for the radical left.[8]

I have found it useful to introduce Deleuze and Guattari by considering the intellectual currents informing their best-known work, but *Anti-Oedipus* is not the sole or even the central subject of my study. I have endeavoured to offer a general introduction to the works of Deleuze and of Guattari, with particular emphasis upon Deleuze's writings from the 1960s and upon Deleuze and Guattari's collaborative efforts from 1972 to 1980. One of the objects of this book, as a contribution to the series 'Critics of the Twentieth Century', is to demonstrate the importance of the work of Deleuze and Guattari for the study of literary theory and criticism. Neither Deleuze nor Guattari is primarily a literary critic, but both have written at length on literary figures – most notably, Proust and Kafka – and both have made extensive use of works of literature in all their writings. They have also engaged a number of philosophical issues with which literary theorists have been especially preoccupied recently, such as the nature of representation, the status of interpretation, the structure of the sign, and the relation of language to social institutions and non-discursive reality. They have articulated a critique of psychoanalysis that poses a serious challenge to any Freudian or Lacanian literary criticism, and they have proposed historical models that offer several possibilities for a major reorientation of literary history. Finally, they have developed a particularly cogent form of the post-structural assault on the distinction between literary and non-literary discourse, one that treats all thought as artistic creativity, and all writing as scientific experimentation.

The larger aim of this study, however, is to provide an overview of the general development of Deleuze and Guattari's thought, within which these specifically literary issues may be situated. At present, there exists no basic introduction to their work, and it is hoped that this study may be of use not only to literary scholars, but also to readers interested in the many non-literary disciplines that Deleuze and Guattari discuss. Such an overview is no mere desideratum, for without a firm grasp of the fundamental principles and concerns that orientate their thought, one can hardly avoid misunderstanding the involved arguments and the multifarious terms and concepts with which they assault a particular problem. Deleuze and Guattari have much to say about individual writers and specific literary works; yet what they offer is not simply an interpretative strategy or methodology, but a rethinking of the

7

relationship between language, literature, thought, desire, action, social institutions, and material reality.

I have decided, therefore, to sketch a history of Deleuze and Guattari's activities both as critics and as philosophers, and to devote each chapter to the analysis of one or two key works. In Part One, 'Deleuze before Guattari', I outline Deleuze's Nietzschean philosophy of difference, as it is first introduced in *Nietzsche and Philosophy* (Chapter 1) and later developed in *Difference and Repetition* and *The Logic of Meaning* (Chapter 3). Within this general philosophy of difference, I try to situate Deleuze's literary studies of Proust and Sacher-Masoch (Chapter 2). In Part Two, 'Deleuze and Guattari', I trace the contours of Deleuze and Guattari's 'schizoanalytic' thought, considering their literary analysis of Kafka (Chapter 5) between examinations of the two volumes of their massive *Capitalism and Schizophrenia* – *Anti-Oedipus* (Chapter 4) and *Thousand Plateaus* (Chapter 6).

My decision to concentrate on the development of the arguments in individual books, rather than on recurrent themes or topics in the Deleuze–Guattari corpus, has been motivated primarily by a desire to correct a certain imbalance that has been prevalent in discussions of Deleuze and of Guattari. Commentators have generally emphasized the playful and extravagant side of their productions and said little about the systematic coherence of individual works or the fundamental continuity of their thought. Only a detailed explication of specific texts, I believe, can suggest the seriousness and logical rigour with which Deleuze and Guattari pursue their separate or collective ends, even if those ends include the subversions of conventional logic and traditional norms of intellectual decorum. Also, it is hoped that the close investigation of individual works may make this book useful to a wider range of readers than otherwise might be the case – to those who are simply curious about two unknown authors, but also to those who have delved into the often daunting body of Deleuzoguattariana and wish to consider other ways in which these texts may be interpreted.

Despite its advantages, such a focus brings with it certain necessary constraints. I have had to limit my discussion to a few central works, and to refer only occasionally to Deleuze's early studies of individual philosophers (save Nietzsche), to Guattari's non-collaborative publications, and to Deleuze's writings since *Thousand Plateaus*. I believe, however, that the texts examined do indicate adequately the fundamental orientation of the thought of

Deleuze and of Guattari, particularly in regard to language and literature. An extended analysis of their position within larger philosophical movements has also been precluded, although I have tried to situate them in relation to Derrida, Lacan, Foucault, and post-structuralism in general. The significance of their thought for psychoanalytical and political theory, easily the subject of an entire book, has necessarily been treated in a less than exhaustive manner. Finally, the fidelity to arguments as complex wholes has necessitated the introduction of some rather abstruse questions, before which a few readers may balk; the excision of such issues, however, would have removed that which is most vital in Deleuze and Guattari's thought.

In a real sense, the common denominator and unifying force of this study is Deleuze, yet it would be misleading simply to say that it is a book 'about Deleuze'. Guattari's position is scarcely that of apprentice to master Deleuze (hence my insistence on the somewhat awkward, but intellectually necessary, neologism 'Deleuzoguattarian' to refer to their collaboratively developed ideas). Many of the central concepts in *Anti-Oedipus* and *Thousand Plateaus* are Guattari's, as was the impetus for the initial critique of psychoanalysis and the project for a counter, 'schizoanalytic' theory. Guattari's position outside the academic philosophical tradition has clearly contributed significantly to the incorporation of more immediately political, social, and historical concerns in Deleuze's work since their collaboration. And Guattari's years of practical experience – in psychiatric hospitals working with psychotics; in the psychoanalytic milieu as an analysand and later as an analyst; and in the myriad political groups and research associations that he helped to form and sustain – provide an indispensable grounding for the heady flights of theoretical invention on which he and Deleuze so often embark (a point which should be considered well by those who accuse Deleuze and Guattari of political and psychoanalytic naïvety). As Guattari's several independently written works reveal, his is an incisive and engaging intellect that merits serious attention in its own right.

But most of all we should not presume the existence of such a thing as an unchanging, autonomous 'Deleuze'. Throughout his work, Deleuze shows a remarkable adaptability in his responsiveness to a wide variety of philosophers, made possible in large part by his abiding sense of the vital force proper to ideas themselves. 'A philosophical theory', says Deleuze in his early study of Hume,

9

is a developed question, and nothing else: by itself, in itself, it involves, not the resolution of a problem, but the development *to the fullest extent* of the necessary implications of a formulated question . . . .. To put things in question means to subordinate and submit things to the question in such a way that, in this forced and constrained submission, things reveal to us an essence, a nature.[9]

Yet combined with this gift for assimilation is an equal talent for transforming others' thought, an ability Deleuze displayed even as a *lycéen*, according to the novelist Michel Tournier, a contemporary and long-time friend of Deleuze:

> power of translation, of transposition: the whole of that wornout school philosophy, once it came in contact with him, became unrecognisable, imbued with an air of freshness, not yet assimilated, with a raw newness, completely disconcerting and forbidding for our weakness and laziness.[10]

That transformative power, ubiquitous in Deleuze's work, is an ability to reconfigure a body of thought by discovering its animating centre in an unexpected and unsettling locus, in a secondary correlate or subordinate doctrine. Philosophies are generally characterized in terms of first principles, remarks Deleuze, but

> the first principle is always a mask, a simple image, it doesn't exist; things only begin to move and come alive at the level of the second, third, fourth principle, and these aren't even principles any longer. Things only start to live in the middle. (D 68–9)

This power of assimilation and reconfiguration is not simply a capacity for appropriation. What one consistently finds in Deleuze is a subtle shift in orientation from one work to the next, as if each of his creative transformations of another's thought brought with it a parallel transformation of his own. In his collaboration with Guattari, Deleuze consciously seeks a mutual metamorphosis, a productive encounter in which each becomes other, but there is a sense in which every work of Deleuze's is an encounter, a collaboration that induces a decentring shift in the object of thought and in the thinker as well. The proper name of an author, says Deleuze, 'does not designate a subject, but something that happens, between at least two terms which are not subjects, but agents, elements' (D 65). It is for this reason that the ensuing 'history' of Deleuze and Guattari has been envisioned not as a genetic or evolutionary narrative, but as a map of a nomadic journey. Deleuze has said of Nietzsche that his is a nomadic thought, and the term applies equally well to Deleuze and Guattari. Nomadic tribes, in Deleuze and Guattari's account, impose no fixed and sedentary boundaries on a territory, but occupy a space to the extent of their capabilities and then move on. Each chapter of this book charts one or two nomadic encampments, each with its own configuration of tents, flocks, and tribesmen, structured in improvisatory conformity to topographical, meteorological, and internal tribal/social constraints. (The proper names of authors, says Deleuze, 'are not names of persons, but of peoples and tribes, of fauna and flora, of military operations or typhoons' (D 65).) At first the territories are clearly marked – Nietzsche, Proust, Sacher-Masoch – but gradually they become less recognizable, more sprawling, heterogeneous, and occasionally surreal. At a certain point the tribe of Deleuze is joined by the tribe of Guattari, and somewhat later they diverge, each tribe becoming more the other, yet each becoming more itself. At every encampment, weapons are seized, gifts received, local inhabitants adopted by the tribe; and as the journey continues, the adherents and converts become legion, the register of their tribal origins filling the footnotes of *Difference and Repetition* and *Thousand Plateaus*. Always the same tribe, never the same multiplicity, always the same process, never a stable state, always a single event, never a predictable outcome. A difference differentiating itself, like a theme of the Vinteuil sonata in Proust, which returns, 'but each time changed, in a different rhythm, with a different accompaniment, the same and yet other, as things return in life'.[11] Between each encampment, a drifting flux, a chance divagation. And always secret, parallel migrations, clandestine interactions between tribes whose exchanges form a complicit destiny – Deleuze, Foucault . . .

Part One
Deleuze before Guattari

1

Deleuze's Nietzsche:
Thought, will to power,
and the eternal return

Deleuze's *Nietzsche and Philosophy* (1962) marks a significant turning-point in French philosophy. Before Deleuze, Nietzsche had received little consideration in France as a serious thinker; by the late 1960s and 1970s, Nietzsche had become a major presence in French thought. Although it would be excessive to attribute this develop-ment exclusively to Deleuze, his study of Nietzsche was the first in France to treat him as a systematically coherent philosopher, and Deleuze's reading of Nietzsche opened up questions that became central in subsequent Nietzschean studies and in French post-structuralism in general.[1]

Nietzsche and Philosophy also marks an important stage in Deleuze's career, for here many of the central themes and concerns of his later work find their first enunciation. For Deleuze, Nietzsche is not a mere rhapsodic aphorist, but an intellectually consistent philosopher with a profound understanding of the history of philosophy, whose responses to Plato, Hegel, and Kant delineate the fundamental problems of modern thought. In Deleuze's view, Nietzsche's major goals are to overturn Platonism and develop a philosophy of becoming based on a physics of force; to replace Hegel's 'negation of negation' with a philosophy of affirmation; and to complete Kant's project for a critical philosophy by directing it against the traditional principles of Western rationality. These, too, are the ends that Deleuze himself pursues in much of his own work.

Central to Nietzsche's mature thought, in Deleuze's judgement, are the concepts of the 'will to power' and the 'eternal return'.[2] Although the two phrases occur frequently in Nietzsche's later works, particularly in the unpublished fragments collected in *The Will to Power*, commentators before Deleuze generally treat them

15

with no particular care, regarding them as loose expressions of vague and inconsistent notions.[3] Deleuze, however, sees 'all the rigour' of Nietzsche's philosophy in his terminology, arguing that Nietzsche 'uses precise new terms for very precise new concepts' (NP 52, *59*). In this chapter, I should like to trace the outlines of Deleuze's reading of Nietzsche, and to focus particularly on Deleuze's innovative interpretation of the will to power and the eternal return – two precise new terms for precise, if somewhat elusive, new concepts. Such an analysis, besides suggesting something of Deleuze's talent for transforming others' thought, will provide the necessary groundwork for a consideration of Deleuze's thought as a whole.

Evaluation, interpretation and the image of thought

Deleuze, in situating Nietzsche within the history of philosophy, is particularly careful to establish his relationship to Kant. Deleuze argues that in Nietzsche there is not only 'a Kantian heritage, but a half-avowed, half-hidden rivalry' (NP 52, *59*). Nietzsche's thought is an effort to complete the task of a *critical* philosophy only imperfectly begun by Kant. Where Kant fails, according to Nietzsche, is in his exclusion of *values* from critical analysis. Kant assumes the value of Truth, Goodness and Beauty, and his critique is wholly subservient to these unexamined values. Nietzsche therefore proposes to introduce the question of value into thought and to make the critique of value the centre of a new, genealogical philosophy.

Nietzsche seeks to evaluate values by tracing their lineage to their origin. Values stem from 'ways of being, modes of existence of those who judge and evaluate' (NP, 1, *1–2*), and all ways of being are either high or low, noble or base. The noble mode of existence is essentially active and affirmative, whereas the base mode of existence is reactive and negative. Values are created through ways of being, and their origin is always marked by a difference between high and low, noble and base. 'Genealogy signifies the differential element of values from which their value itself derives. Genealogy thus means origin of birth, but also difference or distance in the origin' (NP 2, *2*).

At the origin of values is difference, but there are two distinct ways of making differences, one affirmative and one negative. The affirmative and noble way is that of the master. The master affirms himself and labels himself good; he then recognizes the baseness of the slave and affirms his difference from the slave in calling the slave bad. The slave, by contrast, resents the master and calls him bad. The slave's initial act is a reaction, a negative evaluation of the master, and his declaration of himself as good is simply a second reaction, a second negation. The master says, 'I am good, therefore he is bad.' The slave says, 'He is bad [i.e. not good], therefore I am good [i.e. not not-good].'⁴ The slave 'needs to conceive of a non-ego, then to oppose himself to this non-ego in order finally to posit himself as self. This is the strange syllogism of the slave: he needs two negations in order to produce an appearance of affirmation' (NP 121, *139*). The slave is a covert Hegelian whose thought, like Hegel's, proceeds via contradiction and negation, and only arrives at affirmation through a 'negation of the negation'. The slave, like Hegel, cannot understand mastery, for he assumes that the master desires power and that he seeks recognition in the slave, a representation of his power in his opposite. But this, insists Nietzsche, is nothing but a slave's conception of mastery. Only the impotent desire power; only the reactive need confirmation of their power in someone else. The master does not seek recognition or the representation of his power, simply the affirmation of his power in its exercise and a subsequent affirmation of his difference from the slave, an 'affirmation of affirmation'. The master affirms his difference, the slave denies that which differs. One makes distinctions through difference and affirmation, the other through contradiction and negation.

An evaluation of values must start with the differential origin of values, with a determination of the way of life that creates those values. Such an evaluation necessarily involves interpretation as well, for the values of a way of life permeate all things and give them their meaning. The master's good and bad, for example, have nothing to do with the slave's good and bad, and only a discerning interpretation of those words reveals their divergent meanings. The meaning or sense (*sens*) of something is a function of 'the force which appropriates the thing, which exploits it, which takes possession of it or is expressed in it'. A phenomenon is 'a sign, a symptom which finds its meaning in an existing force. The whole of philosophy is a symptomatology, and a semeiology' (NP 3, *3*). Interpretation entails what Deleuze calls a 'method of *dramatisation*' (NP 78, *89*) in Nietzsche. The question Nietzsche asks is not 'what does it mean?' but 'who makes this meaning?' 'Good' and 'bad' have no intrinsic meaning, but are symptoms of the way of life of the speaker; only by 'dramatizing' the words, by putting them in the

17

mouth of a master or a slave, can one determine their sense.[5]

Interpretation and evaluation are the tools of Nietzsche's critical philosophy, but that critique itself, argues Deleuze, is in no way neutral or disinterested. Every evaluation expresses a way of life, and every interpretation is the symptom of a mode of existence. Nietzsche's ultimate goal is to enunciate an affirmative and active thought, one that will counteract the negative and reactive thought that has dominated Western philosophy from its inception. Active evaluation involves both the creation of values and the affirmative destruction of negative values. When the master evaluates, he affirms himself and thus creates values, and he affirms his difference from the slave and joyfully destroys that which is negative within himself. Nietzsche's critique, therefore, is not negative but affirmative, and it is inseparable from the creation of new values. Nietzsche's goal is to be an affirmative philosopher, one who is both an interpreter-physician who reads symptoms and prescribes cures, and an evaluator-artist who destroys negative values and creates new ones.

Deleuze argues that the ultimate result of Nietzsche's completion of the Kantian critique is the creation of a new image of thought. What Nietzsche finds missing in Kant's critique of reason is a genealogy of reason, an analysis of the 'genesis of reason itself', of 'the will which hides and expresses itself in reason' (NP 91, *104*). Such a genealogy is missing because 'Kant merely pushed a very old conception of critique to the limit, a conception which saw critique as a force which should be brought to bear on all claims to knowledge and truth, but not on knowledge and truth themselves' (NP 89, *102*). Nietzsche dramatizes the question of truth and asks, 'who is seeking truth? In other words: what does the one who seeks the truth want?' (NP 94, *108*). Nietzsche finds that the seeker of truth wants above all not to be fooled. The world is deceptive and misleading, a world of 'appearance', so the man of truth opposes it to another world, a world beyond, a true world. Beneath this speculative opposition is a moral opposition of good knowledge and false life, and this opposition is only a symptom of a will to correct life, to turn life against life and make life conform to knowledge. Ultimately, this will to correct life is a nihilistic will, for the man of truth wants life to become as reactive and vengeful as he is, to turn on itself and annihilate itself.

Beneath the seemingly innocent search for truth, then, Nietzsche uncovers a moral, ascetic and nihilistic will. He proposes to replace this will to truth with an affirmative will to falsehood, an artistic will that would turn a will to deception into a superior, creative will. A thought informed by such a will would not oppose knowledge to life, would not confine life within the narrow bounds of rational knowledge and then measure knowledge by the reduced standard of a reactive life. Rather, in such a thought life would become 'the active force of thought' and thought would become 'the affirmative power of life . . . Thinking would then mean *discovering, inventing, new possibilities of life*' (NP 101, *115*).

According to Deleuze, such a way of thinking entails a new conception of thought that is antithetical to the traditional, dogmatic image of thought in three ways. First, the element of such a thought is not truth but meaning and value, the categories of such a thought being 'not truth and falsity but the *noble* and the *base*, the *high* and the *low*' (NP 102, *119*). Second, the enemy of such a thought is not error, a force external to thought that diverts it from its natural course, but stupidity, a base way of thinking internal to thought: 'there are imbecile thoughts, imbecile discourses, that are made up entirely of truths; but these truths are base, they are those of a base, heavy and leaden soul' (NP 105, *120*). Finally, such a thought does not require method, which protects thought from error, but the violence of 'forces which take hold of thought'. Violence must be done to thought '*as* thought, a power, *the force of thinking*, must throw it into a becoming-active' (NP 108, *123*).

Thought is always interpretation and evaluation, and it is either noble or base, depending on the forces that seize hold of it. When thought becomes active, it results in a joyous destruction of all that is negative and a creation of new possibilities of life. Deleuze regards Nietzsche as an exemplar of the active philosopher, a physician who deciphers the symptoms of reaction and negativity, and an artist who creates a new image of thought and invents new forms for its articulation. Through the fragmentary aphorism Nietzsche interprets the meaning of a phenomenon, and through the poem he determines the hierarchical value of various meanings. 'But because values and sense are such complex notions, the poem itself must be evaluated, the aphorism interpreted. The poem and the aphorism are, themselves, objects of an interpretation, an evaluation' (NP 31, *36*). Interpretation and evaluation have two dimensions, 'the second also being the return of the first, the return of the aphorism or the cycle of the poem' (NP 31, *36*). In its affirmative guise, the return of interpretation and evaluation to which Deleuze refers is the eternal return, and that which interprets and evaluates is the will to power.

The will to power

The will to power is an elusive and easily misunderstood concept, and yet one that is central to Nietzsche's thought and, according to Deleuze, one that is integrally related to the concept of the eternal return. It is no easy matter to say what the will to power is, but one can easily state what it is *not*. It is not a 'will' in the common sense of the word, that is, a conscious agency of decision separable from the actions it motivates, for Nietzsche argues repeatedly that such an abstract notion is a fiction generated by the linguistic distinction between subject and verb, which encourages the development of the notion that the subject is an autonomous actor separate from its actions. Nor is the will to power a 'desire for power', since the will to power is for Nietzsche a source of affirmation, and the desire for power is a slavish, reactive and negative desire. 'The desire for power', says Deleuze, 'is the image which the impotent fashion of the will to power'.[6] The weak long for power in order to negate the power of the strong; the strong, by contrast, merely exercise power, never desire it.

Deleuze approaches the notion of the will to power by way of the concepts of force and the body. According to Nietzsche, ours is a world of becoming, of constant flux and change in which no entities preserve a stable identity. In such a world 'no things remain but only dynamic quanta, in a relation of tension to all other dynamic quanta'.[7] Nature, then, is an interrelated multiplicity of forces, and all forces are either dominant or dominated. A body is defined by 'this relation between dominant and dominated forces. Every relationship of forces constitutes a body – whether it is chemical, biological, social or political . . . . In a body the superior or dominant forces are known as *active* and the inferior or dominated forces are known as *reactive* (NP 40, *45*). We know little about force and the body because we generally form our knowledge on the evidence of consciousness, and consciousness is itself only a symptom of the presence of reactive forces. In Nietzsche, 'consciousness is never self-consciousness, but the consciousness of an ego in relation to a self which is not itself conscious. It is not the master's consciousness but the slave's consciousness in relation to a master who is not himself conscious' (NP 39, *44–5*). Consciousness inevitably views the body from its reactive perspective and misunderstands the nature of active forces, 'without which the reactions themselves would not be forces' (NP 41, *47*). A true science must be a science of activity, 'of what is necessarily unconscious' (NP 42, *48*). Such

20

a science will explore 'the power of transformation, the Dionysian power', which 'is the primary definition of activity' (NP 42, *48*). Deleuze finds the key to this science of activity in Nietzsche's philosophy of nature, which is ultimately a philosophy of dynamic relations of forces. Deleuze first distinguishes between dominant and dominated *quantities* of force and active and reactive *qualities* of force. He observes that Nietzsche at times treats qualities of force as mere functions of quantities, and at others resists reducing qualities to quantities. This is not evidence of confusion on Nietzsche's part, argues Deleuze, but of a concern that differences of quantity should not be treated in an abstract manner. The temptation in a quantification of forces is to establish equations of forces, mathematical equivalences of randomly combined forces, and to ignore the specific differences between forces. No two forces in a given relation are equal, and every force is in a relationship of difference with other forces. 'Difference in quantity is the essence of force and of the relation of force to force' (NP 43, *49*). Of two forces in a relation, one will be dominant and the other dominated, and each will have a specific quality, that of being active or reactive, which will be determined by that relationship.

Active and reactive qualities of force, however, must also be characterized in terms that are not strictly deducible from quantities of force. An active force commands, appropriates, and imposes forms on reactive forces (NP 42, *48*). It also 'goes to the limit [*jusqu'au bout*] of its power' (NP 59, *66*), whereas a reactive force limits itself and, 'even when it obeys, limits the active force' with which it is in relation (NP 56, *63*). A reactive force, then, tends to negate that which differs from it, whereas an active force affirms its difference from other forces. Finally, Deleuze asserts that 'the measure of forces and their qualification depend in no way on absolute quantity, but relative effectuation', and that 'the least strong is as strong as the strong if it goes to the limit [*jusqu'au bout*]' (NP 61, *69*). It would seem, then, that Deleuze's characterization of the relation of forces in terms of differences of quantity is limited to the relation of active to reactive forces and does not pertain to the relations of active to active, or of reactive to reactive, forces.

The characterization of quantities and qualities of force alone, however, is not sufficient to distinguish Nietzschean force from the mechanistic force of conventional physics. Therefore, says Nietzsche, the concept of force 'still needs to be completed: an inner will must be ascribed to it, which I designate as "will to power"'.[8] The will to power is internal to force, but not reducible to it, for, says Deleuze, 'force is what can, will to power is what wills (*La force est ce qui peut, la volonté de puissance est ce qui veut*)' (NP 50, *57*). Deleuze defines the will to power as

> the genealogical element of force, both differential and genetic. *The will to power is the element from which derive both the quantitative difference of related forces and the quality that devolves into each force in this relation.* The will to power here reveals its nature as the principle of the synthesis of forces. (NP 50, *56*)

Without the concept of the will to power, forces remain indeterminate. The will to power determines the relationship between forces, in terms both of quantity (as the differential element that determines the differences between quantities) and of quality (as the genetic element that determines the quality of each forces as either active or reactive). The will to power is a principle, but not in any abstract sense. It is a plastic principle which may be distinguished conceptually from force, but never removed from the specific forces it determines in any single instance. It is therefore neither a universal will (as in Schopenhauer) nor an individual, self-identical will (as in traditional psychology). 'The will to power is plastic, inseparable from each case in which it is determined; just as the eternal return is being, but being which is affirmed of becoming, the will to power is unitary, but unity which is affirmed of multiplicity' (NP 85–6, *97*).

Deleuze argues that the will to power has qualities which must be distinguished from the qualities of force: '*active* and *reactive* designate the original qualities of force but *affirmative* and *negative* designate the primordial qualities of the will to power' (NP 53–4, *60–1*). Although a basic affinity exists between active forces and the affirmative will to power, and between reactive forces and the negative will to power, the qualities of force and those of the will to power are quite distinct. Forces are mere instruments of the will to power, and they need the will to power 'as something which goes beyond them but is necessary for them to achieve their own ends' (NP 54, *61*). More importantly, 'affirmation and negation extend beyond action and reaction because they are the immediate qualities of becoming itself. Affirmation is not action but the power of becoming active, *becoming active* personified. Negation is not simple reaction but a *becoming reactive*' (NP 54, *61*). It seems that Deleuze here is positing the will to power as a kind of inner centre of force, a general orientation of becoming that only manifests itself in specific forces but goes beyond individual forces to link them in a line of development. 'It is as if affirmation and negation were both immanent and transcendent in relation to action and reaction; out of the web of forces they make up the chain of becoming' (NP 54, *61*). The will to power, one might say, is the power of becoming that plays through forces, differentiating them and linking them both spatially and temporally.

Deleuze further distinguishes between the will to power's determining activity as differential element and its *manifestation* as a power of affectivity. The will to power manifests itself as 'a capacity for being affected' (NP 62, *70*), a notion that Deleuze sees as closely paralleled by the Spinozist doctrine that a body's force is a function of the number of ways in which it can be affected, and that a body's capacity for being affected is an expression of its power.[9] Both in Spinoza and Nietzsche, the power of being affected 'does not necessarily signify passivity, but *affectivity*, sensibility, sensation' (NP 62, *70*). To simplify somewhat, the traditional notion of force needs to be supplemented not only with something like a will or inner centre that determines relations between forces, but also with 'senses', sensation-feelings that allow forces to 'perceive' each other and be affected by each other. The sensibility or affectivity of force is the manifestation of the will to power, and the more affirmative the will to power, the greater the power of being affected that is manifested in force. (One can see why Nietzsche attributes all utilitarian conceptions of the emotions to a negative will to power: to seek pleasure and avoid pain is to manifest a limited power of being affected.) Thus, the will to power involves a *feeling* of power, and all affectivity, sensation and emotion derive from it.

The will to power, then, is the genealogical element of force that establishes differential relations of quantities of force, from which issue the qualities of each force, whether active or reactive. The will to power is a kind of inner centre of force, a power of becoming active or reactive, whose quality is either affirmative or negative, and it is manifested as the affectivity of force, the power of being affected. In short, the will to power is that concept which makes possible a theory of nature as *relations* of forces – dynamic (becoming-active or -reactive), determined in quality (the genealogical element of force), and entailing the mutual effect of each force on the other (the affectivity of force).

Given this characterization of the will to power, one can understand why the will to power is also that which interprets and evaluates, that which seizes thought and determines whether it will be active or reactive, affirmative or negative. The problem of

23

interpretation is 'to estimate the quality of force that gives meaning to a given phenomenon, or event, and from that to measure the relation of the forces which are present' (NP 53, *60*). The problem of evaluation 'is to determine the will to power which gives value to a thing' (NP 54, *61*). Interpretation and evaluation, however, are not disinterested activities but themselves functions of the will to power. The will to power, as differential element of force, is that which determines the qualities of forces, and thus that which interprets. The will to power, as either force of affirmation or force of negation, is that which bestows value, and thus that which evaluates. The will to power is the source of meaning and value, and hence *'the will to power is essentially creative and giving*: it does not aspire, it does not seek, it does not desire, above all its does not desire power. It *gives'* (NP 85, *97*).

Becoming-reactive and the eternal return as cure

Deleuze's basic aim in his exposition of the will to power is to demonstrate that Nietzsche's philosophy of nature may be understood in terms of the interrelated concepts of dominant and dominated quantities of force, active and reactive qualities of force, and the affirmative and negative will to power. Such distinctions would seem superfluous, however, if dominant quantities and active qualities of force were associated only with the affirmative will to power, and if dominant quantities and active qualities of force were always triumphant. An initial complication of this model arises as soon as one turns from abstract forces to the actual configuration of force in bodies, which consist of complex combinations of active and reactive forces. Although the will to power can never be separated from the forces in which it is manifested, and although the will to power must not be thought of as a self-identical, individual will, one can speak of a single prevailing will to power in a body, and hence of an affirmative or a negative will to power controlling both active and reactive forces. But what most complicates the physical theory of forces is the fact that among human beings reactive forces, without ceasing to be dominated forces, are everywhere triumphant over active forces. Indeed, Nietzsche regards the history of the West as that of the triumph of reactive forces and the negative will to power, which he labels the triumph of nihilism. The crucial problem for Nietzsche is to determine how reactive forces conquer active forces and to discover the means whereby nihilism may be overcome and the affirmative will to power given expression. Only though the elaboration of a psychology of forces supplemental to a physics of forces can the problem be accurately stated and eventually solved.

One might assume that reactive forces triumph through sheer weight of numbers, and Nietzsche's frequent complaints against herd mentality and majority rule would seem to support such a conclusion. But Deleuze asserts that for Nietzsche 'even by getting together reactive forces do not form a greater force, one that would be active. They proceed in an entirely different way – they decompose; *they separate active force from what it can do*; they take away a part or almost all of its power' (NP 57, *64*). An active force 'goes to the limit of its power' (NP 59, *66*), and when it is prevented from reaching its limit, it becomes reactive. Thus, four different kinds of forces must be distinguished:

> 1) active force, power of acting or commanding; 2) reactive force, power of obeying or of being acted; 3) developed reactive force, power of splitting up, dividing and separating; 4) active force become reactive, power of being separated, of turning against itself. (NP 63, *71–2*)

Here Deleuze is moving from a physical to a psychological theory of forces. 'Developed reactive forces' and 'active forces become reactive' are secondary elements of original relations of active and reactive forces, new psychological forces that create new relations of power and a distorted image of actual quantities of force. Developed reactive forces appear to be strong and dominant, and active forces-become-reactive appear to be weak and dominated. A genealogical analysis of the origin of the forces shows, however, that the developed reactive forces are weak, and that they triumph through a new power, a kind of 'induced weakness' that causes the active forces to turn against themselves and put themselves under the sway of the reactive forces. (Deleuze does not specify how the power of the developed reactive forces should be conceived in terms of a physics of forces, nor does he differentiate between a physical and a psychological theory of forces. It would seem, however, that at a certain level of the organization of forces – the psychological – new relations of forces arise that are irreducible to those of less complex combinations of forces.)

In determining how the forces of nihilism triumph, one must first discover how an essentially reactive individual comes into existence. Human beings are made up of a multiplicity of forces, some active and others reactive. In a state of health, man's active forces precipitate action and command, and his reactive forces inhibit action and obey. Should a healthy man's reactive forces be impinged upon by an external force, his active forces control his reactive forces and convert an internal reaction into an externalized counter-action. In this sense, the healthy man 'acts his reactions' (NP 111, *127*), or, one might say, responds instead of reacting. Crucial to the maintenance of the active individual's health is a positive power of forgetting that renders the sensations and effects of the reactive forces unconscious at the same moment as the active forces form a counter-action to an external stimulus. In the reactive individual, the power of forgetting somehow atrophies, and the sensations and affects of the reactive forces become embedded in a painful and prodigious memory. The active forces are invaded by unending memory traces and deprived of the condition of their proper functioning, and thus are they '*separated from what they can do*' (NP 114, *130*). Once the reactive forces gain dominance in an individual, a spirit of revenge takes over, a permanent feeling of *ressentiment*, or resentment. Because the man of *ressentiment* is incapable of acting or ridding himself of his memory traces, every object that affects him causes pain, and he blames every object for that pain and seeks revenge against it. Eventually, that revenge is directed against active individuals.

In a brilliant reading of Nietzsche's *On the Genealogy of Morals*, which can only be summarized here in a cursory fashion, Deleuze details the complex stages whereby the reactive forces gain dominance over the active forces. The reactive forces, he shows, always conquer active forces through negative, imaginary fictions, the chief of which is 'the fiction of a super-sensible world in opposition to this world, the fiction of a God in contradiction to life' (NP 125, *143*). In a first stage, the fiction is created that a force can be separated from its effects, and active forces are blamed for exercising their power. (The lamb blames the bird of prey for not having the strength to control itself and be like the lamb.) In a second stage, active individuals restrain their active forces, and these forces then turn within to form bad conscience. Bad conscience causes pain, and the fiction of guilt makes of this pain an unpayable debt to society, church and God. In a final stage, bad conscience is made bearable through the projection of guilt onto the deity and the invention of an afterlife that redeems this world. This stage inaugurates the ascetic ideal, which expresses 'the affinity of reactive forces with nihilism' and exposes 'nihilism as the "motor" of reactive forces' (NP 145, *167*).

In nihilism, the negative will is revealed as a will to nothingness, and Deleuze distinguishes three different phases in its development. In *negative nihilism*, the fiction of a supersensible world is invented, and the will to nothingness is expressed in higher values that depreciate and devalue life. This is succeeded by *reactive nihilism*, in which the reactive forces, which have triumphed through the negative will, break their alliance with the negative will and rule alone. God is killed and pity, the love of 'the weak, sick, reactive life' (NP 149, *172*), becomes the reigning principle of value. The reactive man 'takes the place of God: adaptation, evolution, progress, happiness for all and the good of the community; the God-man, the moral man, the truthful man and the social man' (NP 151, *173–4*). The fiction of the higher world is no longer believable, but life none the less remains depreciated and devalued. The reactive forces cannot tolerate any will, any stimulus, and eventually reactive nihilism is supplanted by *passive nihilism*, life so exhausted that it 'prefers to not will, to fade away passively, rather than being animated by a will which goes beyond it' (NP 151, *174*).

Deleuze argues that for Nietzsche 'nihilism is not an event in history but the motor of the history of man as universal history' (NP 152, *174*). Man is essentially reactive, and human history is the universal becoming-reactive of force. The only way for man to attain true affirmation is to overcome himself, to become something other than human – to become the Overman. How is this to be done? Certainly not through the vapid affirmation of a universal 'yes'. The yea-sayers are the donkeys and camels of the world, those who shoulder the burden of the real and accept responsibility for all that reactive life has fashioned. True affirmation is light and irresponsible; it brings freedom from reactive forces, not acceptance of them. The only means to true affirmation, says Deleuze, is the eternal return, which, to be fully grasped, must be interpreted as a physical doctrine, an ethical doctrine, and a doctrine of selective ontology.

The eternal return

The idea of the eternal return came to Nietzsche as a sudden revelation. It was, he said in *Ecce Homo*, the 'highest formula of affirmation that is at all attainable' and the key concept of *Thus Spoke Zarathustra*.[10] And yet most commentators either ignore this idea or dismiss it as a cyclical theory of history. One must realize, Deleuze notes, 'that Nietzsche, in his published works, had only prepared the way for the revelation of the eternal return, but that he did not give, and did not have the time to give, that revelation itself'.[11] Nevertheless, one can immediately see that the eternal return is in no way a return of the same. 'It is not a cycle', says Deleuze.

> It does not presuppose the One, the Same, the Equal or equilibrium. It is not a return of the All. It is not a return of the Same, nor a return to the Same. It thus has nothing in common with so-called ancient thought, with the thought of a cycle which makes All come again, which passes through a state of equilibrium, which leads the All back to the One, and which comes back to the Same.[12]

Throughout his works Nietzsche criticizes the notions of the One, the Same, and the Whole, and, as Deleuze points out, in the period during which Nietzsche formulated the doctrine of the eternal return, he also explicitly criticized the cyclical hypothesis.[13]

What militates against any interpretation of the eternal return as a return of the Same is the fundamentally anti-Platonic nature of Nietzsche's thought. Sameness implies self-identity, essence, and being. For Nietzsche, the belief in things, substance, and being is the result of a grammatical prejudice created by languages that have as their fundamental elements nouns and verbs. We speak of actors as separate from actions, and as a result we conceive of things as stable entities and events as passing and separable phenomena. Everywhere reason

> sees a doer and doing; it believes in will as *the* cause; it believes in the ego, in the ego as being, in the ego as substance, and it projects this faith in the ego-substance upon all things – only thereby does it first *create* the concept of 'thing'. Everywhere 'being' is projected by thought, pushed underneath, as the cause; the concept of being follows, and is a derivative of, the concept of ego.[14]

Plato, of course, makes the unchanging and selfsame realm of being the object of true knowledge, and opposes it to our phenomenal world of flux, change, and becoming. Nietzsche regards this devotion to being as a veiled hatred of life, a means of finding our world guilty and deficient, and he proposes as the fundamental task of philosophy the reversal of Platonism through an affirmation of becoming.

If Nietzsche's philosophy is an affirmation of becoming, and if the eternal return is the 'highest affirmation', then, argues Deleuze, the eternal return must be a return, not of being and the same, but of becoming and difference. Deleuze finds the seeds of this reading of the eternal return in Nietzsche's early remarks on Heraclitus (in *Philosophy in the Tragic Age of the Greeks*). Heraclitus, says Nietzsche, conceived of the world as a realm of innocent becoming, of 'play as artists and children engage in it', exhibiting 'coming-to-be and passing away, structuring and destroying', as the 'game of the great world-child Zeus'.[15] Two moments may be distinguished in the child's play or the artist's creative efforts: a moment of absorption in the game or creative activity, and a moment of distanced contemplation of the game or creation. According to Deleuze, the thought of the eternal return may be understood in terms of these two moments. One first participates in becoming and thereby affirms it; then one recognizes that all moments of the world are moments of becoming, that the very being of the world is becoming, and one affirms the fact that every instant is the return or coming anew of becoming. Hence, argues Deleuze, 'return [*revenir*] is the being of becoming [*devenir*] itself, being which affirms itself in becoming' (NP 24, *28*).

The world of becoming is a world of flux and multiplicity, but also one of chance or chaos, and the affirmation of the eternal return bears on this aspect of becoming as well. To join in the play of the cosmos is, as Zarathustra says, to play 'dice with gods at the gods' table, the earth'.[16] The game of dice, like the play of the child and the creation of the artist, has two moments: the moment when the dice are thrown and the moment when they land and form a specific combination. The affirmation of becoming entails both an affirmation of all possible combinations in the throw of the dice and the affirmation of the specific result of the throw as a necessary outcome. Man, says Deleuze, is in general a bad player who counts on a large number of throws to get what he wants. 'In this way he makes use of causality and probability to produce a combination that he sees as desirable. He posits this combination itself as an end to be obtained, hidden behind causality' (NP 26–7, *31*). The good player, by contrast, affirms all chance in a single throw, accepting each result as the desired result. He affirms both chance and necessity, the chance of the throw and the necessity of the outcome. The traditional problem of chance and necessity is dissolved, for the problem only arises through the negative desires of controlling chance or escaping necessity. The affirmation of chance makes possible an *amor fati*, Nietzsche's 'formula for greatness in a human being',[17] an active love of fate that forces one to will whatever happens as the necessary manifestation of chance.

The will to power also has a specific relationship to the eternal return: 'the eternal return is the synthesis which has as its principle the will to power' (NP 50, *56*). What Deleuze means by 'synthesis' is revealed in his analysis of becoming and its implications for an understanding of time. One of the more troubling aspects of the concept of becoming is that it plays havoc with our common-sense notions of time. We usually distinguish past and future by their relationship to the present, but if the present moment is a moment of becoming, then in a strict sense that present moment is also the past-becoming-present and the present-becoming-future. Hence, 'the present must coexist with itself as past and yet to come' (NP 48, *54*). The coexistence of past and future within the present moment thus forms a synthesis of past, present, and future, and founds the relationship of the various moments of time to one another. If one considers the multiple entities of the cosmos at two contiguous moments, one must say that the diversity of the first moment and the reproduction of diversity in the second moment (or the difference of the first and its repetition in the second) are included or synthesized within the same moment of becoming. The concept of becoming thus forces us to think of every moment of becoming as simultaneously coextensive with the successive moment of becoming. It is the inclusion of the second moment within the first that forces us to an accurate understanding of becoming, and in a sense the second moment's 'coming again' or 'return' within the first is the revelation of the nature of becoming, of the being of becoming. Deleuze therefore says that the eternal return is 'a synthesis of time and its dimensions, a synthesis of diversity and its reproduction, a synthesis of becoming and the being which is affirmed in becoming, a synthesis of double affirmation' (NP 48, *55*).

The will to power is the principle of the synthesis of the eternal return, and the eternal return is 'the expression' of the principle, 'which serves as an explanation of diversity and its reproduction, of difference and its repetition' (NP 49, *55*). The will to power is the differential element which puts forces in relation, and the eternal return is the affirmation of difference in the guise of multiplicity, becoming, and chance: 'for multiplicity is the difference of one thing from another, becoming is difference from self, and chance is difference "between all" or distributive difference' (NP 189, *216*).

The will to power is also 'the power of becoming active, *becoming active* personified' or the power of becoming reactive, 'a *becoming reactive*' (NP 54, *61*), and the eternal return is the synthesis of becoming, which presupposes this principle of a ubiquitous becoming of forces.

This conception of the eternal return as the synthesis of forces which affirms becoming, multiplicity, and chance, Deleuze calls the physical doctrine of the eternal return. But Deleuze points out that the eternal return is also an ethical doctrine, which provides a preliminary means for man, the essentially reactive animal, to transform himself or herself and engender within himself or herself the affirmative will to power. The ethical doctrine of the eternal return may be formulated as the Nietzschean counterpart to the Kantian categorical imperative. As ethical doctrine, the eternal return functions as a selective principle that issues in a practical rule: '*whatever you will, will it in such a way that you also will its eternal return*' (NP 68, *77*). This, the *thought* of the eternal return, makes possible the elimination of all the half-desires and hesitant yearnings, the qualified excesses and provisional indulgences, of a cautious and calculating will.

The selective principle of the eternal return as ethical doctrine, however, cannot entirely eliminate the negative will. The will to nothingness can withstand this selection, for it can will the eternal return of its own negativity. A second selection, a selection of *being* rather than thought, is needed to usher in full affirmation, one that 'involves the most obscure parts of Nietzsche's philosophy and forms an almost esoteric element in the doctrine of the eternal return' (NP 69, *78*): the eternal return as selective ontology. If the eternal return entails the return of the negative as well as the affirmative will, then it is a disheartening doctrine that foretells the eternally repeated history of the becoming-reactive of man. However,

> the eternal return would become contradictory if it were the return of reactive forces. The eternal return teaches us that becoming-reactive has no being. Indeed, it also teaches us of the existence of a becoming-active. It necessarily produces becoming-active by reproducing becoming. (NP 72, *81*)

Deleuze somewhat clarifies this most obscure doctrine in *Difference and Repetition* by specifying the connection between active forces and becoming. Active forces, in going to the limit of their capabilities, transcend all constraints, including those of their own

31

identity. Active forces impose forms on other forces, but they also change form themselves; they are forces of metamorphosis and transformation which shape other forces and simultaneously 'become other' themselves. In this sense, active forces alone affirm becoming, and since the world is a world of becoming, active forces alone have true being. 'Only extreme forms return – those which . . . go to the end [*jusqu'au bout*] of their power, transforming themselves and passing one into the other. Only that which is extreme returns, that which is excessive, which passes into the other and becomes identical [with the other]' (DR 60). The reactive forces of self-preservation and conservation present the illusion of having being, but they too eventually become other and prove themselves to have no other being that that of becoming. The double affirmation of the eternal return gains a new sense in this second selection, for the eternal return, as physical doctrine, 'affirms the being of becoming', but 'as selective ontology, it affirms this being of becoming as the "self-affirming" of becoming-active' (NP 72, *81*).

Ultimately, then, the negative will passes away, and man, as the becoming reactive of forces, also passes away. The possibility of overcoming man and realizing true affirmation opens up in the second stage of nihilism, that of reactive nihilism. Here the negative will is separated from the reactive forces, and once separated, the negative will 'inspires in man a new inclination: for destroying himself, but destroying himself actively' (NP 174, *200*). The affirmation that announces the Overman entails a double negation: an active self-destruction of all that is human, which immediately precedes affirmation, and an active destruction of all known values, which immediately follows affirmation. This affirmation inaugurates the transvaluation of values – not simply the substitution of one set of values for another, but the establishment of a new, active way of life for the creation of values. This new way of life is that of the eternal return, the affirmation of the being of becoming, the unity of multiplicity, and the necessity of chance.

In describing Nietzsche's thought, Deleuze in large part characterizes his own. For Deleuze as well as for Nietzsche, the object of philosophy is the affirmation of difference as the chaotic multiplicity of the becoming of the world. For Deleuze too, thought must be directed against reason without ceasing to be thought; it must interpret and evaluate, but above all create new possibilities of life; it must find its origin in the violence of a force that seizes thought and compels it to think that which defies thought; and it must explore the body and the unconscious to discover the capabilities of the body, its powers of activity and affectivity. Like Nietzsche, Deleuze tries to combine critique and creation without surrendering to the rancorous, oppositional spirit of *ressentiment*. Finally, Deleuze follows Nietzsche in seeking new forms for the expression of thought, forms appropriate for a philosophy of difference.

It would be a mistake, however, to regard Deleuze simply as a disciple of Nietzsche. Deleuze's reading of Nietzsche is itself selective and creative, as much a development of certain possibilities in Nietzsche as an exposition of a philosophical system. Such is clearly the case, I believe, in Deleuze's formulation of the difference between affirmation and negation, between master and slave. The master affirms his difference, creates and gives values, and only as a consequence of his actions takes cognizance of the slave. The slave, by contrast, reacts to the master, opposes him, and tries to negate that which differs. 'Negation is *opposed* to affirmation but affirmation *differs* from negation' (NP 188, *216*). Vincent Descombes argues that Deleuze's notion of mastery is contradictory, in that the master's *evaluation* of values must entail a comparison of values, and hence opposition.[18] Descombes is correct in noting a contradiction in Deleuze's conception of mastery, but it is not in the notion of evaluation, which can be thought of as non-oppositional if evaluation is understood as the creative affirmation of a way of life from which values derive. The problem is at the more fundamental level of forces, whose relations are characterized by domination and hierarchy – concepts, I would argue, that are essentially oppositional and agonistic. The problem arises because Nietzsche's conception of mastery is much more conflictual than Deleuze allows. Deleuze finds a non-hierarchical model of difference in the eternal return (the difference between the numbers that come up in the various throws of the dice) and then tries to reconcile it with the hierarchical differences generated by the will to power.[19] Ultimately the reconciliation is incomplete since the Nietzschean theory of force is irreducibly conflictual, but the contradiction in Deleuze's conception of mastery as the affirmation of difference only arises because Deleuze exploits certain possibilities in Nietzsche's work (i.e., the eternal return) and attempts a creative reorientation of Nietzsche's thoughts in terms of those possibilities.

To anyone familiar with deconstruction, the repeated use of the concept of difference in Deleuze's reading of Nietzsche must be striking. One might be tempted to consider Deleuze as an early 'textualist' when he describes philosophy as a semiology and when he speaks of the innocent play of differences in the eternal return. It must be pointed out, however, that Deleuze's model of difference in his study of Nietzsche is based not on Saussurian linguistics, but on a theory of forces, a physics. Differences are not created through a system of relations of arbitrary entities (such as the phonemes of a language) but through the action of one force on another. The world is not a text in which signs only refer to other signs, but a network of forces in which signs are symptoms of forces (and philosophy is a semiology only in the older sense of the word – a symptomatology). The play of differences in the eternal return is innocent because the affirmative will refuses to find the world guilty, not because signs are arbitrary and have no necessary relation to reality.[20] Throughout Deleuze's work, force, bodies, and *physis* remain essentially irreducible to language. This is particularly the case in his study of Nietzsche.

Yet, despite the relative subordination of language to other concerns in *Nietzsche and Philosophy*, Deleuze's conclusions have important implications for the study of literature that in large part are consonant with those of other post-structuralists. Through his exposition of the concept of thought, Deleuze calls into question the distinction between philosophy and art, and secondarily between literary criticism and literature. Philosophy and art do not belong to separate domains of truth and fiction, or of objectivity and subjectivity, but inhabit a single realm of thought, whose fundamental goal is the creation of new possibilities of life. The interpretative and evaluative dimension of literary criticism, rather than being the unfortunate by-product of an unscientific and subjective approach to literature, is at the centre of thought and at one with the creative activity of the artist. It is no wonder, then, that when Deleuze returns from philosophical analysis to the analysis of literary texts, his approach in no way changes, for philosophers and writers are both, in his opinion, simply thinkers.

2

Two exemplary readings: Proust and Sacher-Masoch

If literary criticism is defined simply as the study of works of literature, then Deleuze's *Proust and Signs* (1964) and his *Presentation of Sacher-Masoch* (1967), an extended introduction to Leopold von Sacher-Masoch's novel *Venus in Furs*, would be classified as works of literary criticism. If, however, literary criticism is concerned primarily with the analysis of such things as plot, characterization, theme and style, then these studies must be assigned to another category. Although Deleuze touches on traditional literary questions in these works, his primary concern in each case is to delineate the system of thought that informs the corpus of each author's works. In his study of Proust, Deleuze shows that Proust's remarks on art and essences in the final volume of *A la recherche du temps perdu* provide the key to the interpretation of the *Recherche* as a whole, and reveal Proust to be a kind of anti-philosophical idealist for whom the central activity of thought is the interpretation of signs.[1] In his examination of Sacher-Masoch, Deleuze tries to revive the reputation of Sacher-Masoch, a celebrated and prolific novelist of the 1870s and 1880s now remembered only as the eponymous exemplar of masochism, by demonstrating that Sacher-Masoch is an astute psychologist and a profound thinker whose works, along with those of the Marquis de Sade, articulate a perverse idealism aimed at a subversion of the Kantian conception of law. Clearly Deleuze regards Proust and Sacher-Masoch as Nietzschean philosopher-artists who make of thought and creation the exploration of new possibilities of life. Deleuze's reading of Proust holds an important place in Proustian criticism, and his study of Sacher-Masoch and masochism is highly suggestive from both a psychoanalytic and a critical perspective.[2] But what is perhaps most significant about both analyses is Deleuze's demonstration of the way in which writers can reconfigure the relationship between literature and philosophy.

Proust

Proust's *A la recherche du temps perdu* is often regarded as a novel about the past – specifically, about the efforts of the narrator, Marcel, to recapture the past through the exploration of patterns of association within memory. English readers are no doubt particularly predisposed to such a reading of the novel, since the very title of the work in the standard translation betrays such an interpretation: *Remembrance of Things Past*, rather than the more literal *In Search of Lost Time*. Deleuze argues in *Proust and Signs*, however, that the *Recherche* is not about the past, but about the future, and that the famous Proustian 'involuntary memory' is of secondary importance in the novel and has nothing to do with a subjective association of ideas. The *Recherche*, claims Deleuze, is a novel of apprenticeship, in which Marcel finds his vocation as an artist and learns to decipher the signs of love, the social world, sensual experience and art. Eventually he discovers that art is the medium of truth and essences which illuminates the nature of signs and reveals time in its purest form, *le temps retrouvé*.

When Deleuze speaks of Marcel's apprenticeship, he refers both to Marcel's gradual training as an artist and to the educational process that leads Marcel to truth. To become an artist Marcel must learn to read signs, but he can only gain an understanding of signs through a search (*recherche*) for truth. (If the *Recherche* 'is called a search for lost time', says Deleuze, 'it is only to the degree that truth has an essential relation to time' (PS 15, *23*).) The signs Deleuze refers to are not vehicles of communication, but hieroglyphs, enigmas that must be deciphered, which Deleuze divides into four basic categories. The simplest are *worldly signs*, the fashions, manners and habits of thought that define a social world, its membership and its implicit hierarchy. Worldly signs are ultimately empty, for they simply stand in for action and for thought:

> nothing funny is said at the Verdurins, and Mme Verdurin does not laugh; but Cottard makes a sign that he is saying something funny, Mme Verdurin makes a sign that she is laughing, and her sign is so perfectly emitted that M. Verdurin, not to be outdone, seeks in his turn for an appropriate mimicry. (PS 6, *12*)

More complex are the *signs of love*, indications that the object of love

36

envelops multiple worlds which the lover must explore and unfold through loving. These worlds, however, inevitably exclude the lover, and their signs provoke pangs of jealousy and reveal themselves to the lover in the form of lies and deceptions. The *signs of sense experience* are those of involuntary memory, such as the complex signs of the madeleine that calls up Combray and the uneven cobblestones that evoke Venice. These signs offer a momentary glimpse of pure time and a realm of essences, but the epiphanies they instil can only be sustained for a few brief instants. The *signs of art*, by contrast, afford a full and stable revelation of essences and the pure form of time. They represent the culmination of the search for truth and provide a retrospective illumination of the true nature of the other three kinds of signs.

Two obstacles to the interpretation of signs confront the apprentice at each stage of his education: a belief that 'the "object" itself has the secret of the signs it emits' (PS 26, *37*), which Deleuze labels 'objectivism', and a belief that the truth of the sign is subjective. When the hero sees Mme de Guermantes, whose name so charms him, he tells himself 'that the inconceivable life this name signified was truly contained by this body'.[3] When in love, the hero believes that the uniqueness of the beloved belongs to her person. During an experience of involuntary memory, the hero initially conjectures that the madeleine must somehow hold the secret of Combray within it. And when searching for the art of Berma's performance, he first looks for the truth of that art within her. Such misleading assumptions are inevitable, for '*the intelligence tends toward objectivity, as perception toward the object*' (PS 28, *39*). Perception naturally refers signs to objects, and the intelligence naturally seeks explicit, objective significations: 'perception supposes that reality is to be *seen, observed*; but intelligence supposes that truth is to be *spoken, formulated*' (PS 28, *40*). It is the intelligence that 'impels us to *conversation*, in which we exchange and communicate ideas. It incites us to *friendship*, based on the community of ideas and sentiments. It invites us to *philosophy* – a voluntary and premeditated exercise of thought by which we may determine the order and content of objective significations' (PS 29, *40*). Conversation, friendship, voluntary memory and philosophy, however, cannot serve as guides to the interpretation of the signs of the world, love, sensations and art. Objectivism inevitably ends in disappointment, at which point a second temptation arises, that of finding a subjective compensation for a disappointment in the object. Perhaps, the hero reflects, the charm of Mme de Guermantes' name, the uniqueness of the beloved, the spell of the madeleine, the magic of Berma's art are all to be found in a subjective association of ideas. Perhaps, as Bergotte teaches the hero, Berma's Phaedra is great because 'a certain gesture of Berma's evokes that of an archaic statuette the actress could never have seen but which Racine himself had certainly never thought of either' (PS 34, *47*). Such subjective associations, however, betray the nature of signs, for they reduce all signs to a single network of arbitrarily and gratuitously interconnected experiences. The truth of the signs of art resides not in the equation of the madeleine and the Vinteuil sonata, but in 'alogical or supralogical' essences, 'beyond designated objects, beyond intelligible and formulated truths, but also beyond subjective chains of association' (PS 36, *50*).

The signs of art reveal the nature of essence, and essence reveals the nature of signs. To understand Deleuze's conception of Proustian essences and signs, we must turn briefly to an examination of the concept of *expression*, a concept implicit throughout Deleuze's reading of Proust, but only discussed in detail in his *Spinoza and the Problem of Expression*. Expression is a central concept in certain forms of Jewish and Christian neo-Platonism of the middle Ages and the Renaissance; according to Deleuze, it is also the controlling idea in the philosophies of Spinoza and Leibniz. In this neo-Platonic tradition, the verb *exprimere* is often closely linked with the verbs *involvere* (to wrap up or envelop) and *explicare* (to unfold, unroll or explain). A sign, object or being may be said to express something in two contrasting but complementary ways: either it envelops, implicates (*implicare*, to enfold or envelop) or implies (in French, *impliquer*) something; or it develops, unfolds, explicates, or explains something. In describing the relationship between the One and the multiple of the cosmos, for example, one might say that

> on the one hand, expression is an explication: development of that which is expressed, manifestation of the One in the multiple . . . . But on the other hand, the multiple expression envelops the One. The One remains enveloped in that which expresses it, imprinted in that which develops it, immanent to all that manifests it: in this sense, expression is an envelopment.[4]

The multiple is, as it were, rolled or folded up within the One, and the expression of the multiple is the unfolding or unrolling of that enveloped multiplicity. Each entity of the multiple, however, has enveloped within it the imprint of the One. The two dimensions of expression are not opposed but part of a single process whose synthetic principle is *complication*, which 'designates both the presence of the multiple in the One and of the One in the multiple'. According to some neo-Platonists, 'God is "complicative" Nature; and that nature explicates and implicates God, envelops and develops God. God "complicates" everything, but everything explicates and implicates Him'.[5]

According to Deleuze, the Proustian sign 'contains' its meaning, in that the meaning is implicated in the sign, rolled up within it. To interpret a sign is to unroll its implicated meaning, to explicate and develop it. In the work of art, sign and meaning are united, and essence is revealed as the complication of sign and meaning: 'essence complicates the sign and the meaning, it holds them *in complication*, it puts the one in the other' (PS 89, *110*). In a work of art, signs and meaning are adequate to one another in that the unfolding of the work is the unfolding of its signs, and the unfolded work is the explicated meaning of the work. The essence of a work of art, then, is like God, and the work of art is like Nature, implicating and explicating God, but being informed by the immanent principle of divine complication.

The essence revealed in a work of art is not limited to that work alone, but constitutes an entire world. 'Thanks to art', says Proust, 'instead of seeing a single world, our own, we see it multiply, and as many original artists as there are, so many worlds will we have at our disposal, more different from each other than those which circle in the void' (*Recherche* III, 895–6). One might be tempted to take this remark as an expression of the Romantic cult of genius, yet Deleuze argues that for Proust great artists reveal essences, but they do not create them. Essence is implicated within the individual as the ultimate quality of the individual. Essence is not subjective, but that 'which constitutes subjectivity. It is not the individuals who constitute the world, but the worlds enveloped, the essences, which constitute the individuals' (PS 43, *56*). In certain ways, says Deleuze, 'Proust is Leibnizian: the essences are veritable monads, each defined by the viewpoint from which it expresses the world, each viewpoint itself referring to an ultimate quality at the heart of the monad' (PS 41, *54*). In Leibniz, the One of the world is comprised of the multiplicity of monads, or indivisible atoms of substance, each of which envelops the One and expresses it from a specific point of view.[6] Leibniz often says that the various perspectives of the monads are like several views of the same city, each of which provides a different vision of the same entity. According to Deleuze, a Proustian essence likewise reveals a world, and the artist who discloses this world is subordinate to the essence, differentiated by the essence rather than giving it differentiation.

According to some neo-Platonists, *complication* is the name given to the original state of unity of the One and the multiple 'which precedes any development, any deployment, any "explication"' (PS 44, *58*). Since an essence is a complicated world, the unfolding of essence may be said to entail 'a beginning of the World in general' (PS 44, *57*) and of time itself. The time of essences is a complicated time, an original time, coiled, complicated within essence itself, embracing simultaneously all its series and dimensions' (PS 45, *59*). This is the *temps retrouvé*, or regained time, of essences, 'a primordial complication, a veritable eternity, an absolute original time' (PS 46, *60*). The explication of essence involves the inception of a world and of time, but the essence so explicated is also revealed in its originary complication. This revelation of the complicated state of essence is parallel to the theological revelation of God as the complicated state of Nature, the unity of the One, the multiple and all time.

The essences Deleuze finds in Proust, however, are distinguished from those of Leibniz and other traditional exponents of expression in one important way: essences for Proust are not principles of unity, but embodiments of difference. 'What is an essence, as revealed in the work of art? It is a difference, the absolute and ultimate Difference' (PS 41, *53*). As a result, the world revealed by each essence is radically different from the worlds revealed by other essences. For Proust, the cosmos is not a Leibnizian city which unifies all the perspectives of its various monadic points of view. The world we hold in common, the world of conversation, friendship and the exchange of ideas, is illusory and misleading. For Proust, 'there is no intersubjectivity except an artistic one' (PS 42, *55*), since only through art can we gain access to a different world of essence enveloped in another individual.

Yet in labelling essence 'the absolute and ultimate Difference', Deleuze does not mean simply that essences differ from one another, but also that each essence is 'absolute internal difference' (PS 42, *55*), which differentiates itself. Deleuze's model of essence is that of an originary chaos, a complication of spatial and temporal multiplicity, that incarnates itself in substance by unfolding itself, diversifying itself in ever-expanding entities. Each stage of diversification is an explication of the same difference, a repetition of that internal difference of essence. An embodied essence is like a phrase from the Vinteuil sonata, which returns, says Proust, 'but each

40

time changed, in a different rhythm, with a different accompaniment, the same and yet different [*autre*], as things return in life' (*Recherche* III, 259). Difference and repetition, says Deleuze, 'are the two inseparable and correlative powers of essence' (PS 48, *62*), of self-differentiating internal difference.

The signs of art are adequate to essences because they are immaterial signs, signs that transform the substances of art (words, paint, sounds) until they become so 'ductile, so kneaded and refined that they become entirely spiritual' (PS 46, *60*). An artistic essence is 'the quality of an original world' (PS 47, *61*), manifested as 'the unconscious themes, the involuntary archetypes' (PS 46, *60*) that are repeated throughout an artist's works. That which effects the transmutation of substance, and hence allows an artistic essence to be revealed, is style. Style 'is essentially metaphor' (PS 47, *61*) in that it extracts from two objects their common quality, that quality being the index of essence as 'quality of an original world'. But 'metaphor is essentially metamorphosis' (47, *61*) in that two objects linked by style 'exchange their determinations', as in Elstir's painting, 'where the sea becomes land, the land sea' (PS 47, *61*). Style 'reproduces the unstable opposition, the original complication, the struggle and exchange of the primordial elements which constitute essence itself' (PS 47, *62*). An essence is a birth of the world, and 'style is that continuous and refracted birth, that birth regained in substances adequate to essences, that birth which has become the metamorphosis of objects' (PS 48, *62*).

The signs of art are the highest signs because they transmute matter and express a meaning that is an essence. 'Identity of a sign, as style, and of a meaning as essence: such is the character of the work of art' (PS 49, *64*). Art is also 'the finality of the world, and the apprentice's unconscious destination' (PS 49, *64*), for through art the apprentice learns that all signs are incarnations of essence, although in differing guises. As the apprentice descends from the signs of art to those of sensation, love, and the world, he finds that essence is incarnated in increasingly intractable and contingent matter, that signs and meaning are in increasingly obscure relation to one another, and that essences are revealed in increasingly general forms. Nevertheless, all signs are transformed once they are viewed from the perspective of art, for their ultimate truth is seen to reside in essences.

The signs of sense experience – those of involuntary memory – are the closest to the signs of art since they offer a fleeting intimation of the existence of a realm of essences and pure time. Involuntary memory is more than a mere association of ideas, for the past and present experiences do not simply resemble one another, but share an identical quality which seems to coexist with itself in two different times. This identical quality, however, as index of 'the quality of an original world', or essence, only serves as a vehicle for the revelation of difference. When Marcel tastes the madeleine, its flavour is identical with that of a past madeleine eaten in Combray. But what is important is that the difference between the past madeleine and the past Combray as context of that madeleine, and the difference between the past madeleine-Combray experience and the present madeleine experience, are made internal to the present experience. Eventually, the madeleine falls away from consciousness and an essence of Combray arises, a Combray such as has never existed, a Combray as generative internal difference that incarnates itself in past and present madeleine experiences.

The experience of involuntary memory is important to an understanding of time because it reveals the existence of a pure past. It is here, in Proust's conception of the past, that Proust is Bergsonian, argues Deleuze, not in his sense of time as *durée* (as Proustian scholars so often claim). Bergson argues that memory generally treats the past as present moments that have ceased to be present. As a result, says Deleuze, 'memory does not apprehend the past directly: it recomposes it with different *presents*' (PS 56, *72*). According to Bergson, however, the past would never be constituted if the present did not 'pass' – that is, 'if the same moment did not coexist with itself as present *and* past' (PS 56–7, *73*). (Obviously this argument is a variation of the one Deleuze used in his study of Nietzsche to establish the eternal return as the synthesis of time.) If each present moment coexists with a past moment, and that past moment coexists with *its* past moment, the past as a whole must coexist with the present. In order for the present to pass, therefore, a single coexisting past must exist, a pure past that never was present (except as coexisting with a present moment). Such a pure past is real, but it is, in Bergson's terms, 'virtual' rather than 'actual'. In Deleuze's opinion, this pure Bergsonian past is the time that is revealed in the experience of involuntary memory, a time in which signs are, as Proust says, 'real without being present, ideal without being abstract' (*Recherche* III, 873).[7]

The signs of involuntary memory reveal the existence of individual essences and a pure time, but they are fleeting since they are linked to contingent and intransigent matter. The signs of love are even more material, and they embody essence only in a general and obscure way. Essence is revealed in love as the abstract 'theme' that makes of the lover's various love relationships a series conforming to the laws of a basic repetition. Marcel's love of Albertine is a repetition of his love of Gilberte, which in turn is a repetition of his love of his mother. The psychoanalytic reader is mistaken, however, in assuming that Marcel simply suffers from excessive attachment to the mother, for his mother is not the origin of the series of his love, but merely the first incarnation of the essence that informs the series. This theme or essence, this internal difference or complicated chaos, also extends the series of love to both a sub-individual and a supra-individual level. There are, for example, a plurality of Albertines, always the same but different, and Marcel's love of Albertine itself forms a series of repeated loves, each corresponding to the various refractions of his beloved. The series of Marcel's loves also includes within it Swann's love of Odette, Swann's jealousy being a repetition of Marcel's childhood anguish at separation from his mother. 'Thus the personal series of our loves refers both to a vaster, transpersonal series and to more restricted series constituted by each love in particular' (PS 70, *89*).

The signs of love are inherently deceptive, and every series of loves inevitably tends towards a series of disappointments and betrayals. To love is to unfold and develop the multiple worlds enveloped within the beloved. Some of those worlds, however, necessarily exclude the lover or suggest that someone else is loved, despite the beloved's protestations to the contrary. For the heterosexual male, all the deceptive signs of love ultimately 'converge upon the same secret world: the world of Gomorrah' (PS 9, *16*), the lesbian world of Mlle Vinteuil which constitutes 'an original female reality' (PS 10, *17*) from which the lover is forever barred. For the heterosexual female lover, the same is true of the homosexual Sodom of M. de Charlus. The worlds of Sodom and Gomorrah, however, reveal a truth more profound than that of the lover's exclusion from the enveloped worlds of the beloved; they point toward the truth of the 'isolation of the sexes' (PS 77, *98*). Every individual is a hermaphrodite, within whom 'the separated, partitioned sexes coexist' (PS 77, *98*). All loves are finally ruled by this hermaphroditic separation of the sexes, even heterosexual loves, in which the male plays the woman for the female, and the female plays the man for the male. Thus, beneath the serial repetitions of a theme, beneath the general series of deceptions and disappointments, lie the separate series of Sodom and Gomorrah, generated by the internal difference of an original hermaphroditism that repeats itself throughout human sexuality.

Worldly signs also embody essences, 'but at a last level of contingency and generality. They are immediately incarnated in societies, their generality is no more than a group generality: *the last degree of essence*' (PS 79, *100*). These vacuous signs attest to 'mechanical laws, in which Forgetting prevails' (PS 80, *101*). The prejudices of polite society change from the era of the Dreyfus affair to the era of the First World War, but this change is in reality only a repetition of a single essence of baseness and stupidity.

In large part, the originality of Deleuze's reading of Proust lies in his interpretation of Proustian essences as absolute internal differences. This characterization of essences allows Deleuze to rescue Proustian essences from a realm of murky mysticism and to make them the centre of the *Recherche* as a whole. It also affords Deleuze a means of effecting a rapprochement of Nietzschean and Proustian themes, for in the eternal return, as in Proustian essences, the controlling concepts are those of difference and repetition. A Proustian essence is an originary, complicated chaos which is manifested in implicated differences (signs) that unfold as diversified repetitions of those differences. From the perspective of the eternal return, the cosmos is seen as a chaos of differential multiplicity which is repeated at every moment. A Proustian essence is simply the eternal return *sub specie aeternitatis* and from a specific perspective, the multiplicity of essences being merely a version of Nietzschean perspectivism. The complicated time of essences is a time in which past, present, and future coexist. The pure past of involuntary memory is a limited portion of this complicated time, in which the present coexists with all the past. As we have seen, the synthesis of the eternal return requires that one think of the past, present, and future as coexisting, and the argument for the coexistence of these temporal dimensions is the same as that for the existence of a pure past. One may conclude, therefore, that Proustian essence is simply the idea of the eternal return.

Deleuze brings Proust closest to Nietzsche, however, in his analysis of Proust's relation to philosophy. According to Deleuze, Proust, like Nietzsche, is an enemy of philosophy's traditional image of thought as the voluntary exercise of a natural faculty that automatically seeks objective and universal truth. The *Recherche* is a search for truth, but for the truth of essences, a truth that cannot be gained through the good will of the thinker and cannot be communicated through the discourse of conversation and friendship. In Proust, thought always begins with a force that impinges on the hero – a troubling remark of M. de Charlus, a glance of Albertine's that fills him with jealousy, the taste of a madeleine, a theme from the Vinteuil sonata. The truths of traditional philosophy are arbitrary and abstract, the products of method and the free will of the thinker. Proustian truths are the products, not of method, but of constraint and chance, the fortuitous encounter with a sign that forces the subject to think. Such truths are necessary and particular, not arbitrary and abstract, those of a singular encounter in which the subject is, as it were, 'elected', chosen and compelled to the explication of a specific essence. And that which forces thought to think is the sign. The only true thought is interpretation, and the only true creation is the act of thinking. 'To think is always to interpret – to explicate, to develop, to decipher, to translate a sign. Translating, deciphering, developing are the form of pure creation' (PS 162, *119*). Proustian interpretation and creation parallel Nietzschean interpretation and evaluation (evaluation being described at times by Deleuze as the creative imposition of form), just as the force of the sign that compels the subject to think parallels the active will to power that seizes thought.

Sacher-Masoch

In Deleuze's study of the works of Sacher-Masoch, as in his examination of Proust's *Recherche*, the point of departure is a commonly held misconception. In the case of Masoch, the misapprehension is that sadism and masochism are complementary elements of a single illness – sado-masochism – and hence, that Masoch and masochism can easily be understood by simply reversing the terms of an analysis of Sade and sadism. As Deleuze notes, Sade has received serious attention as an artist, philosopher and psychologist by such eminent writers as Georges Bataille, Pierre Klossowski and Maurice Blanchot, but Masoch has remained largely ignored since his death in 1895.[8] Through a detailed comparison of the writings of Sade and Masoch, Deleuze tries to establish the importance of Masoch and to demonstrate that masochism is a perversion in many ways parallel to, but entirely distinct from, that of sadism.

Medicine has two sides, says Deleuze: aetiology, 'which is the scientific or experimental side of medicine', and symptomatology, 'which is its literary, artistic aspect' (M 115, *114*). Sade and

Masoch are great symptomatologists, argues Deleuze, not mere bearers of symptoms. They extract from the heterogeneous sphere of bodily and mental signs those symptoms that comprise a single and specific perversion. Moreover, they are 'great anthropologists, of the type whose work succeeds in embracing a whole conception of man, culture and nature; they are also great artists in that they discover new forms of expression, new ways of thinking and feeling and an entirely original language' (M 16, *16*). The domain of their investigation is, of course, that of sex and violence. As anthropologists, they seek to describe 'a sort of double of the world capable of containing its violence and excesses' (M 33, *33*). Since 'that which is excessive in a stimulus is, in a sense, eroticised' (M 33, *33*), eroticism serves as a suitable mirror of such violence and excess. As writers, they face the specific problem of articulating that which defies language – violence, which does not speak, and sexuality, which is little spoken about. They are not authors of pornography, which, says Deleuze, consists of 'a few imperatives (do this, do that) followed by obscene descriptions' (M 17, *17*), but of 'pornology', a literature in which language confronts its own limits (violence and eroticism), and in which the personal, pornographic language of imperatives and descriptions finds a higher, impersonal function, 'a pure demonstrative, instituting function' in the case of Sade, and 'a dialectical, mythical and persuasive function' in the case of Masoch (M 22, *22*).

In Sade, descriptions of bodies tend to resemble geometric diagrams, and imperatives seem to enunciate problems deriving from complex theorems. Everywhere the personal element of descriptions and imperatives remains subsidiary to the impersonal demonstration of an idea of pure reason – that of a natural world of pure negation. One must recognize in Sade the existence of two natures: a secondary nature, in which destruction and creation are two aspects of a single, unending process; and a primary nature of pure negation, 'a primal delirium, an original and timeless chaos solely composed of wild and lacerating molecules' (M 25, *25*). Our world is the world of secondary nature, and the sadist despairs when he sees that his destructive and negative actions have no permanence, but only serve as the occasion for further procreation and renewed life. He dreams of a primary nature of pure negation, but such a nature is never given in experience. It 'is necessarily the object of an Idea', and though pure negation is 'a delusion [*délire*]', it is 'a delusion of reason itself' (M 25, *25*). The Sadean libertine 'dreams of a universal, impersonal crime' (M 26, *26*) that will reproduce itself *ad infinitum* and serve as a demonstration (in the sense of a demonstration of a mathematical proof) of the efficacy of the idea. The repetitive scenes of torture in Sade express this desire to overcome secondary nature through an acceleration and multiplication of the instances of violence. Sade's supposed masochism is merely the side-effect of this pure negation, for the libertine wants to destroy all of secondary nature, including his own ego. Above all, the libertine is *apathetic*, eschewing all the personal enthusiasms and passions of secondary nature in order to enjoy the intense but impersonal pleasure of demonstrative reason.

Masoch also pursues a superior, ideal nature, but instead of trying to make the ideal real, he suspends the real and ascends via the sensual to a supra-sensual ideal. Masoch is Platonic, whereas Sade is Spinozist, and the impersonal function of language, through which Masoch transcends the personal function of pornographic imperatives and descriptions, is persuasive and dialectical. The Masochian hero persuades and educates his mistress, carefully working with her to train her for her role, unlike the Sadean hero, who demonstrates his reason and instructs his victim with no real consideration for the victim's approval or conviction. The Masochian hero's relationship with his mistress is dialectical, not only because it entails an ascent to the ideal via a process of inter-action, but also because dialectic 'implies transpositions and displacements', which result in 'a scene being enacted simultaneously on several levels with reversals and reduplications in the allocation of roles and discourse' (M 21, *22*). Just as Plato showed that Socrates appeared to be the lover but was funda-mentally the loved one, so

> the masochistic hero appears to be educated and fashioned by the authoritarian woman whereas basically it is he who forms her, dresses her for the part and prompts the harsh words she addresses to him. It is the victim who speaks through the mouth of his torturer, without sparing himself. (M 21, *22*)

The key concept in Deleuze's reading of Masoch and in his analysis of masochism is the Freudian notion of *disavowal* (*Verleugnung*), a concept particularly important in Freud's discus-sions of fetishism.[9] Disavowal is the refusal to recognize the reality of a traumatic perception. In the case of fetishism, the fetishist refuses to recognize the absence of the woman's penis and takes as his fetish the last object seen before becoming aware of the missing penis. Deleuze argues that what is essential about disavowal is that it radically contests the validity of reality. Through disavowal the fetishist denies that the woman lacks a penis, preserves his knowledge of the absence of the penis in a kind of neutralized, suspended form, and makes of the fetish a protest of the ideal against the real.

Masoch's art, Deleuze shows, is an art of disavowal and suspension. The Masochian hero neither destroys the real nor idealizes the real, but instead disavows the real and introduces the ideal within fantasy, an intermediary realm midway between the real and the ideal. In fantasy, sexual pleasure itself is ultimately disavowed, the scene of torture tending toward a frozen stasis, a pure waiting comprised of 'an indefinite awaiting of pleasure and an intense expectation of pain' (M 63, *63*). Frequently Masoch's heroes are literally suspended (hanged, crucified, and so on), and the gestures and poses of the female torturer are often arrested, the torturer identified with a statue, painting, or photograph. Erotic scenes are frequently repeated in Masoch, not in the mechanical, cumulative fashion of Sade, which accelerates movement, but 'in a sort of frozen progression [*cascade*]' (M31, *31*) that creates a type of static reiteration. Unlike Sade's descriptions, those of Masoch tend to avoid obscenity and specificity, serving instead to create 'a strange and oppressive atmosphere, like a sickly perfume' in which 'the only things that emerge are suspended gestures and suspended suffering' (M31, *32*).

The ideal Nature of Masoch is represented by the female torturer in furs. She, like Nature, is 'cold, maternal and severe' (M 45, *45*). Deleuze distinguishes between this woman and two other prominent female figures in Masoch's fiction: the sensual Grecian woman, lover of sexual pleasure and generator of disorder; and the sadistic woman, whose actions are usually prompted by a sadistic man. Readers often mistake the sensual woman or the sadistic woman for the Masochian ideal, but Deleuze argues that they represent the gross carnality and base violence of the real world, which the ideal woman in furs transcends. The sensuality of the sexual woman and the sadistic woman is replaced by the ideal woman's 'suprasensuous sentimentality, their warmth and their fire by her icy coldness, their confusion by her rigorous order' (M 45, *45*). Coldness is the pivotal characteristic of the ideal, 'the point of dialectical transmutation' (M 46, *46*), the element that suspends sensuality, that preserves a supra-sensual sentimentality 'buried under the ice and protected by fur', and that serves as a medium through which sentimentality radiates 'as the generative principle of new order, a specific wrath and a specific cruelty' (M 46, *47*). Unlike Sadean apathy, which signifies the negation of the emotions and feelings of secondary nature, Masochian coldness signifies the disavowal of sensuality and the ascent to the ideal, where, through a mystical transformation, the victim becomes what Masoch obliquely refers to as 'the new sexless man'.

Deleuze opposes the standard psychoanalytic reading of the masochistic fantasy, in which the female torturer is treated as a substitute for the father. Such a misinterpretation stems from a belief in the existence of a sadomasochistic complex and an assumption that the mother always represents nature and the father invariably stands for culture, law and authority. It is true, says Deleuze, that the father is the central figure in sadism, but masochism is not simply a reversed form of sadism in which the father lurks under the image of the mother. What Masoch teaches us is that in masochism the authority of the father is invested in the mother, and the father is tortured in the person of the victim. In the ultimate Sadean fantasy, the father and daughter form a perverse bond and then torture and murder the mother (symbol of the procreativity of secondary nature). In the Masochian fantasy, the son and the mother form an alliance for the humiliation and destruction of the father. Through the masochistic victim's torture, he is purged of the inner father and reborn via maternal parthenogenesis as 'the new sexless man'.

In Masoch, and in masochism generally, the mother is granted the authority of law, and one of the means of solidifying that authority is the contract. Many of Masoch's heroes, like Masoch himself in his personal life, draw up quasi-legal documents granting specific powers to the torturess for a certain length of time. Such contracts, however, tend to self-destruct, for eventually the torturess exceeds the limits of the agreement and the victim becomes an abject slave. Here Deleuze finds the essential humour of Masoch and masochism: a derisory mockery of the law through an exorbitant dedication to the letter of the law. Deleuze contrasts this humour with the irony of Sade, who mocks law by erecting a superior principle of absolute evil that institutes a kind of lawless super-law.

Deleuze sees Masoch and Sade both responding to the modern conception of law enunciated by Kant in the second critique.[10] Before Kant, law had been conceived along Platonic lines as subsidiary to a higher principle of the Good and to a consideration of the consequences of the application of the law (which Deleuze labels 'the Best'). Inherent in the Platonic notion of law is an ironic recognition of law's imperfection when viewed from the perspective of the Good, and a humorous attitude toward law's inadequacy when seen as flawed but necessary for the maintenance of societal order (as when Socrates, admidst the laughter of his disciples, decides that it is best to observe the law and drink the hemlock). In the *Critique of Practical Reason*, Kant articulates a new conception of the law as pure form, independent of the Good and the Best. The moral imperative in Kant cannot be grounded in considerations of the consequences of its observance, nor can its foundation rest in something external to itself. The law 'is no longer regarded as dependent on the Good, but on the contrary, the Good itself is made to depend on the law' (M 72, *72*). The law is an ultimate ground or principle, and as a result 'the object of the law is by definition unknowable and elusive' (M 73, *73*). Deleuze sees Kant as unwittingly elucidating the principles of Kafka's Law, as it is portrayed in *The Trial* and *In the Penal Colony*: an indeterminate law before which all are guilty and which only reveals itself through the execution of its sentences. Sade and Masoch respond to this law through irony and humour, but unlike Plato, they use irony and humour to subvert law. Sade replaces law with institutions which function as mechanisms of the perpetual implementation of an anarchic anti-law of pure negation. Masoch seems to obey the law, but his absurd contracts become parodies of legal documents. More importantly, the punishment he and his heroes undergo subverts the legal function of punishment, for the masochist's pain does not prevent forbidden pleasure but provokes and ensures it.

Clearly, if the superego is the psychic agency of law, Deleuze cannot support the orthodox psychoanalytical interpretation of masochism as a perversion caused by an overdeveloped superego. The torturess in furs is not the superego, but an idealized ego, which disavows the superego (rather than negating it), by humorously assuming the function of the superego as punitive authority while simultaneously punishing the superego in the person of the victim. The sadist, by contrast, does not lack a superego, as is commonly supposed, but identifies fully with an idealized superego, which destroys the ego.

By identifying sadism with the superego and masochism with the ego, Deleuze is able to specify the nature of the impersonal pleasures of Sade and Masoch. In *The Ego and the Id*, Freud speaks of two crucial stages in psychic development in which a desexualization of libido takes place: the formation of the narcissistic ego and the formation of the superego.[11] According to Freud, desexualization of libido can be succeeded either by neurosis (in which case resexualized libido takes the ego or the superego as its object) or by healthy sublimation (in which case the ego and superego can enter into a properly functional relationship). But Deleuze suggests that desexualization can also lead to perversion, in which case a desexualized element is itself resexualized while maintaining its desexualization in a different form. Deleuze notes that Freud identifies thought processes as fundamental instances of sublimation, in which desexualized libido is channelled into an acceptable activity.[12] Thought, according to Deleuze, is a form of sublimation that proceeds from the formation of the superego, and in sadism the desexualization attendant on the creation of an idealized superego is accompanied by a resexualization of thought itself. Thus, the impersonal, perverse pleasure of sadism is to be found in 'the sexualisation of thought and of the speculative process as such, in so far as these are the product of the superego' (M 109, *108*).

In the case of masochism, a similar desexualization accompanies the creation of the idealized ego, but resexualization here is directed toward the imagination, which is fundamentally allied to the narcissistic ego and the mechanism of disavowal. Disavowal, says Deleuze, is not 'just a form of imagination; it is nothing less than the foundation of imagination, which suspends reality and incarnates the ideal in the suspended world' (M 110, *109*). Disavowal is also central to the formation of the narcissistic ego, for the ego's internalized image of itself as jubilant and omnipotent (what some analysts call the 'ideal ego', as opposed to the paternal 'ego–ideal' associated with the superego) is created through an identification with the mother, and this identification can only be maintained so long as the mother's castration is disavowed.[13] The perverse pleasure of masochism, therefore, resides in a sexualization of the imagination and disavowal as such, under the auspices of a triumphant idealized ego.

Beneath the perverse sexualization of thought in Sade and imagination in Masoch, however, Deleuze finds a more fundamental force at work – that of repetition. He claims that the accelerated reiteration of scenes of violence in Sade and the frozen progression of torture tableaus in Masoch must be interpreted through the Freudian concepts of repetition, Eros and Thanatos, developed in *Beyond the Pleasure Principle* (1920). Deleuze argues that *Beyond the Pleasure Principle* is Freud's most philosophical work, for it is essentially a transcendental investigation (in the Kantian sense) of the ground upon which the pleasure principle is founded. Freud's purpose is not to isolate experiences in which the pleasure principle is contradicted, for there are none, but to discover that condition which makes the regularity of the pleasure principle possible. The ground or precondition of the regular, rule-governed discharge of excitation in conformity with the pleasure principle is the process of binding or linking (*Bindung*) of Eros, which forms the energetic links of excitations and the biological bond between cells. This ground (*fond*) of the pleasure principle, however, brings with it a ground-less element (*sans-fond*), the inanimate realm of Thanatos, from which life emerges and to which life returns, whose basic function is to unbind energy and dissolve the bonds of organic matter. Neither Eros nor Thanatos can be experienced directly; 'all that is given are combinations of both – the role of Eros being to bind the energy of Thanatos and subject these combinations to the pleasure-principle in the Id' (M 101, *100*).

Repetition is an elusive concept in *Beyond the Pleasure Principle*, but one that Deleuze says should be identified as 'a synthesis of time, a "transcendental" synthesis of time' (M 100, *99*). As we will recall, in his interpretation of Nietzsche Deleuze characterized the Eternal Return as the synthesis of time, arguing that time can only 'pass' or 'become' if past, present and future coexist simultaneously. Here Deleuze argues that the necessary precondition of the experience of time is a pure form of time in which past, present, and future are constituted simultaneously. As the transcendental synthesis of time, repetition 'is at once repetition of before, during and after' (M 100, *99*). Eros, as the linking of excitations or the binding of cells, is primarily the force of a temporal synthesis, that which contracts elements within a living present. If, for example, an excitation passes from point A to point B, that which contracts that passage within a single moment and makes of that moment a 'passing' of the excitation is a temporal synthesis of the present. Yet every synthesis of the present brings with it a preceding moment as well. The emergent moment of Eros at the origin of life, therefore, always includes within it the preceding moment of inanimate matter, of Thanatos. Likewise, it always brings with it the moment after life, of a returned Thanatos. Eros is an ever-repeating synthesis which constitutes the present, but Eros only emerges against the background of the larger field of the pure form of time. That field is the ground-less dimension of Thanatos, a dimension convulsed by an incessant repetition of a simultaneous past, present and future.[14]

The reiterated scenes of violence in Sade and Masoch function differently within the configuration of each author's perversion, but ultimately both authors find value in repetition itself. The pleasure principle rules the world of experience, and normally repetition is subservient to the pleasure principle (in that we try to repeat those experiences that are pleasurable). In sadism and masochism, however,

> repetition runs wild and becomes independent of all previous pleasure. It has become an idea or ideal. Pleasure is now a form of behaviour related to repetition, accompanying and following repetition, which has itself become an awesome, independent force. (M 104, *104*)

The pure repetition of Thanatos cannot manifest itself directly, for the pleasure principle always rules experience, and even the sadist or the masochist eventually finds his pleasure. But pain is not the source of sexual pleasure for the sadist or the masochist. It simply represents 'a desexualization which makes repetition autonomous and gives it instantaneous sway over the pleasures of resexualization. Eros is desexualised and humiliated for the sake of a resexualized Thanatos' (M 105, *104*). Pain is merely the effect of desexualization, just as pleasure is simply the consequence of the force of repetition.

Deleuze presents Sade and Masoch as idealists, but idealists of a very peculiar kind. Sade's ideal is a delusion of pure reason, a primary nature of absolute negation. He eroticizes thought itself, and dreams of institutions that will impose the ideal on the real, with all the force of a mathematical demonstration, in a perpetual proliferation of destruction. Masoch's ideal is a disavowal of the real, a nature that is cold, sentimental and cruel. He eroticizes the imagination and aspires to a mystical union with the ideal by suspending the real and bringing the ideal within an intermediate realm of fantasy. Both Sade and Masoch transcend the personal language of pornography through an impersonal, idealizing use of language, demonstrative on the one hand, dialectical and persuasive on the other. In psychological terms, they are also idealists, Sade fashioning an idealized, apathetic superego, Masoch an idealized, cold ego. The ideals they pursue, however, are antithetical to those of the idealist tradition, for they entail the subversion of law and the perversion of desire. Kant's moral imperative is ironically scorned in Sade's superior institutions of principled destruction, and it is humorously mocked in Masoch's excessive contracts that insure that the law's punishments will bestow the pleasures that the law prohibits. As masters of perversion, Sade and Masoch make of repetition itself an ideal, and by desexualizing Eros and resexualizing the repetition of Thanatos, they overcome the pleasure principle and turn pain and pleasure into the effects of repetition.

The Proust that Deleuze describes is also an idealist, and one who is much closer to Sade and Masoch than might at first be suspected. Proust's aesthetic idealism might seem more ethereal than Sade and Masoch's carnal, perverse idealism, but Deleuze insists that in Proust essences are always embodied, always implicated in matter, even in those works of art that somehow manage to transmute matter and emit immaterial signs. Proust's world is finally not one of two distinct entities, matter and mind, the physical and metaphysical, but of a single dimension in which

> everything is implicated, everything is complicated, everything is sign, meaning, essence . . . . Neither things nor minds exist, there are only bodies: astral bodies, vegetal bodies. The biologists would be right, if they knew that bodies in themselves are already a language. The linguists would be right if they knew that language is always the language of bodies. (PS 91, *112*)

Proust, Sade, and Masoch all explore a curious interworld, in which bodies and words, things and ideas interpenetrate and the traditional demarcations between the physical and the metaphysical become blurred. Proust sees the ideal as implicated in the real, Sade tries to saturate the real with a destructive ideal, and Masoch disavows the real and fantasises the ideal. In all three writers, the ideal represents, not a separate world beyond the sensible world, but a contestatory force of violent disequilibrium within the sensible world. In all three, the structure of the ideal, whether it be that of the complicated state of essences, or that of the pure form of time of Thanatos, is informed by the two fundamental principles of difference and repetition. As an investigation of Deleuze's *Difference and Repetition* (1968) and *The Logic of Meaning* (1969) will reveal, Deleuze is developing in his studies of Proust and Sacher-Masoch a highly unorthodox dualism of tumultuous, interfused bodies and *in*essential ideas, the latter constituting a realm of surface effects, simulacra, events, problems, meaning, and fantasy. It is only in these later, synthetic works that the full significance of Deleuze's interpretive strategies in *Proust and Signs* and *Presentation of Sacher-Masoch* becomes evident.

3

The grand synthesis: *Difference and Repetition* and *The Logic of Meaning*

During 1968 and 1969, in the space of less than a year, Deleuze published over a thousand pages of material: *Spinoza and the Problem of Expression* (1968), *Difference and Repetition* (1968) and *The Logic of Meaning* (1969). *Spinoza and the Problem of Expression* resembles Deleuze's earlier studies in its focus on the thought of a single individual and its use of a relatively traditional mode of exposition. *Difference and Repetition* and *The Logic of Meaning*, however, represent something new, for in these books Deleuze speaks 'on his own behalf'[1] and employs singular and challenging forms for the presentation of his thought. *Difference and Repetition* is an insistently abstract and demanding investigation of the concepts of difference-in-itself and repetition-for-itself, replete with discussions of most of the major (and many of the minor) philosophers of the West, presented in a seemingly conventional expository form, but actually constructed like a topological puzzle. As Deleuze suggests, it is part detective story and part science fiction (DR 3), the philosophical counterpart of abstract art in its exposition of aconceptual concepts and an imageless image of thought (DR 354), whose use of the history of philosophy parallels that of collage in painting (DR 4). *The Logic of Meaning* is an equally learned but much more openly playful study that combines an interpretation of Stoic incorporeals with an analysis of the works of Lewis Carroll. A 'logical and psychoanalytic novel' (LS 7) presented in thirty-four 'series', each devoted to the investigation of a specific paradox, *The Logic of Meaning* traverses much of the territory covered in *Difference and Repetition*, but introduces at every stage new and unexpected perspectives on earlier themes that defy ready assimilation.

Yet *Difference and Repetition* and *The Logic of Meaning*, although strikingly innovative in many ways, signal no major break in

Deleuze's thought, simply a broader, more synthetic approach to many of the themes investigated in his earlier studies. In this chapter, I should like to situate some of these themes within the basic framework of the 'transcendental empiricism' of *Difference and Repetition*, and then indicate in what ways Deleuze's philosophy of language, presented in *The Logic of Meaning*, may be made a part of that framework.

Simulacra and ideas: Overturning Plato and Kant

In *Nietzsche and Philosophy*, Deleuze presents Nietzsche as an anti-Platonic philosopher who tries to overturn Platonism by completing the Kantian project of a critical philosophy. In *Difference and Repetition*, Deleuze takes up this Nietzschean task himself. Deleuze's strategy in overcoming Platonism is not, as one might expect, simply to invert the hierarchy of essence and appearance, but to extract from Plato's texts a marginalized category that subverts both models and copies, both essence and appearance – that of the simulacrum. His tactic in transforming Kant is to propose a disjunctive use of the faculties, through which use the unconscious condition of each faculty is revealed, and to disclose a sensible realm of intensities and an ideal realm of problems. Behind Deleuze's appropriations of Plato and Kant is a single goal: to replace the philosophy of identity and representation with a philosophy of difference, both a physics and a metaphysics of the simulacrum.

Plato distinguishes between the idea and its physical embodiment, between the model and the copy, but he also occasionally discriminates between the good copy (*eikon*) and the bad copy (*phantasma*), or simulacrum (as in the *Sophist*, 234a–b, 264c). Deleuze argues that one of Plato's major concerns is to separate good and bad copies, true and false claimants to filiation with the ideal, by noting which copies have an inner resemblance to the ideal, and which bear merely an external and illusory semblance of the ideal. What Plato fears in illusory simulacra, claims Deleuze, are entities with no fixed identity, contradictory or disguised entities in which the dimension of an unlimited and illogical becoming is revealed, a dimension in which objects may be said to be simultaneously both hotter and colder, bigger and smaller, younger and older (*Philebus* 24a–d, *Parmenides* 154–5). Such objects escape the domination of the idea, and as a result threaten both models and copies. To overturn Platonism, then, one must simply make manifest what is latent in Plato: one must 'deny the primacy of an original over the copy, of a model over the image', and 'glorify the reign of simulacra and reflections' (DR 92).[2]

According to Socrates, the experiences that provoke thought are those of contradictory perceptions (*Republic* VII: 523). Such contradictions lead thought to essences, says Socrates, but according to Deleuze they are evidence of the existence of simulacra, which impinge on thought and force it into its proper activity. It is through such contradictory experiences that a critical examination of the mental faculties is made possible, one which Deleuze describes as a 'transcendental empiricism'. Kant's transcendental idealism, Deleuze argues, presumes the existence of *good sense* (whose function cannot be detailed here) and *common sense*, or a united and harmonious functioning of the faculties in common (*concordia facultatum*).[3] What allows an intuition (*Anschauung*) of the faculty of sensibility (*Sinnlichkeit*), for example, to pass during cognition through the schemata of the imagination (*Einbildungskraft*) and to be assimilated to a concept of the understanding (*Verstand*) without being confused with an idea of reason (*Vernunft*) is the common functioning of the faculties under the legislative control of a single faculty (in this case, the understanding). The common functioning of faculties in cognition makes possible the recognition of the object (the object sensed, imagined, remembered, conceived, etc. being recognized as the same object), and establishes the identity of the subject (as union of the faculties). The common sense of cognition, under the domination of the understanding and the concept, itself presumes a world subject to representation, whose four elements Deleuze describes as 'identity in the form of the *undetermined* concept, analogy in the relation between ultimately *determinable* concepts, opposition in the relation between *determinations* within the concept, resemblance in the *determined* object of the concept itself' (DR 44–5). Difference can only become an object of representation '*in relation to a conceived identity, a judged analogy, an imagined opposition, a perceived similitude*' (DR 180), never in itself, and it can only be apprehended through common sense in the form of a recognizable identity. In other words, difference in itself necessarily escapes the recognition of common sense and the representation of concepts. If, as Deleuze argues, being is difference, then being must be thought of through other means than recognition and representation.

What Deleuze proposes in his transcendental empiricism is a disjunctive use of the faculties, a determination of the limits of each faculty, by itself, under the general *dérèglement* of common sense. For each faculty there exists something that it alone can experience, something that cannot be experienced under the rule of common sense, and this something is revealed only in moments of disequilibrium, through contradictions and enigmas, in the form of signs (as developed in *Proust and Signs*). The reminiscence of Proust's involuntary memory, for example, is a *memorandum* of the memory, something that can only be experienced through memory when disjoined from common sense, a paradoxical entity that has never been present but exists only as past. The fantasy is an *imaginandum*, that which can only be imagined (hence the significance of Masoch's sexualization of the imagination within fantasy); the intensity, as we shall see, is that which can only be experienced by the senses – a *sentiendum*. The investigation of faculties is an experimental science, for the number and nature of faculties cannot be determined *a priori*. Perhaps, suggests Deleuze, there is a faculty of language whose transcendental object is meaning or sense (*sens*), a faculty of vitality whose transcendental object is the monster, a faculty of sociability whose transcendental object is anarchy. Deleuze's method is empirical because its object is experience (not the possible experience of Kant, which actually means 'capable of representation', but real experience, 'subrepresentative'). It is transcendental because empirical principles always 'leave outside themselves the elements of their own foundation' (DR 328) and hence require a transcendental analysis of their implicit condition or presupposition.

Deleuze's doctrine of multiple faculties might serve as an effective tool for the destruction of the Kantian mental map, but Deleuze's strategy in *Difference and Repetition* is to work within Kant's scheme of the mind and to 'overturn Kantianism' by characterizing thought in terms of ideas (which Kant labours to divorce from cognition) and the intensities of sense experience (whose existence Kant ignores because he conceives of sensibility, the faculty that apprehends sense experience, as a passive faculty shaped by the a priori forms of space and time, which, according to Deleuze, are merely the forms of *representable* experience). Deleuze's exposition of thought in terms of the ideal and the sensible might seem to bespeak a conventional dualism, but the ruling opposition here is between the virtual and the actual rather than the essential and the accidental, and underlying this opposition is a more fundamental distinction between subrepresentative, unconscious and aconceptual ideas/intensities and the conscious

58

conceptual representations of common sense.

Deleuze argues for the existence of ideas, not in the Platonic sense of simple essences, but in the Kantian sense of 'problems without solutions'.[4] Deleuze's main inspiration in his interpretation of ideas as problems, however, is not Kant, but the mathematician and philosopher Albert Lautman.[5] Problems are generally thought of as simply unsolved questions, but Lautman distinguishes between a level of problems and their conditions, and another level of specific equations and their solutions. Problems are immanent within, but irreducible to, their solutions. They establish the domain of possible solutions while remaining transcendent to those solutions. Lautman illustrates this distinction through an examination of singular points and the curves of differential equations. One can identify, in the curves of certain differential equations, singular points (foci, centres, nodes, and so on), which remain fixed within a domain during a transformation of all the points of that domain. Imagine, for example, a U-curve, symmetrically bisected along its vertical axis, which is rotated 360 degrees along that axis (hence generating a three-dimensional, hemispherical shape). All the points of that curve will move, except for the point at which the axis bisects the curve – the singular point of the curve. One cannot specify the value of that singular point without determining the values of all the other points of the curve. However, one can determine that such a point *exists* without specifying its value; in so doing, one delineates the general topology of the problem, the abstract domain of possible curves that can pass through that singular point. The problem, then, can be conceived of as a disembodied structure of relations of singular points, and the specific values of the solutions of various equations as the embodiment of that problem.

Problems are structures, but one must be careful not to confuse them with actual structures. First, they are virtual, not actual. Like Proustian reminiscences, idea/problems are, in Proust's words, 'real without being actual, ideal without being abstract'; hence, they occupy a paradoxical place between existence and non-existence. Deleuze describes the paradoxical nature of virtual ideas in various ways, saying at times that ideas subsist or insist rather than exist, that they have extra-being rather than being (as we shall see in our investigation of *The Logic of Meaning*), at others that they have a problematic being which may be expressed as '(non)-being' or '?-being' (DR 261).[6] Second, problems change their nature when they become embodied in actual structures. Just as the structure of genes bears no resemblance to the structure of an actual animal, so the structure of a virtual idea bears no resemblance to the structure of its actual embodiment. In the mathematical example above, each singular point of the problem is embodied in the regular points of the various curves generated by different equations and their solutions within a single problematic domain. Only after the regular points of the curve are determined may the singular point be specified – hence the temptation to consider the singular point as a mere residue of the solutions rather than an anterior element of the problem. Yet, despite the problematic status of ideas, they are not amorphous and undifferentiated masses, but distributions of singular points which are fully determined *as distributions*. These points, however, have no fixed identity, function or location, but only a differential relation with other singular points and a potential for various forms of embodiment. The domain of problems, then, may perhaps be imagined as a plane of scattered points, around each of which is a nebulous vortex delineating a domain of possible actualizations or embodiments of the problem.

A few examples may help to clarify Deleuze's understanding of ideas. First, one may consider the organism as a biological idea, each specific animal being an embodiment of the general problematic structure of the species (and of the larger problem of the structure of all organisms), the chromosomes of the animal expressing 'differential elements which characterise an organism in a global manner and which fulfil the role of singular points in a double process of reciprocal and complete determination' (DR 240). The chromosomes as a whole 'constitute a virtual, a potential; and this structure is incarnated in actual organisms' (DR 240). Second, one may regard the differential relations of production and property of Marxist thought as a social idea, a problematic that is embodied in various societies in diverse ways. Finally, one may view the Saussurian account of the phonological structure of language as a linguistic idea, phonemes constituting differential elements, the differential relations of distinctive traits determining the elements, and the phonemes functioning as singular points which organize pertinent oppositions. The elements and their relations are virtual and unconscious, both transcendent and immanent in the actually articulated sounds, and they undergo a double actualization in diverse languages and the various elements of a single language (DR 262–3). Deleuze cautions, however, that if Saussurian phonology is to be regarded as an idea, it must be rethought in terms of the active generation rather than the passive reception of sound, and it must be rephrased in terms of positive differences rather than the representational concepts of opposition and negativity.[7]

From the virtual to the actual:
Individuation and the intensity

That which effects the passage of the virtual into the actual is the *intensity* (or intensive quantity), whose essential activity is that of individuation. What Deleuze means by the intensity is best understood after a consideration of the concept of individuation, which Deleuze takes from Gilbert Simondon's *L'Individu et sa genèse physico-biologique*.[8] Simondon uses information theory to describe individuation in physical and biological systems, showing that traditional distinctions between form and matter, individual and milieu, animate and inanimate, and specification (the determination of species) and individuation must be reconceived in terms of information in order to take account of the reality of the *process* of individuation.

Simondon first considers the hylemorphic schema, or form–matter model, which has dominated Western thought about individuation from Aristotle to the twentieth century, offering as a simple example of the hylemorphic schema the manufacture of a brick using malleable clay and a wooden mould. Aristotle viewed the clay as the matter and the mould as the form, but this is an abstract interpretation of the facts. In actuality, Simondon argues, both the clay and the mould have form and matter, but the clay is in a metastable state, i.e. it possesses potential energy, or unevenly distributed energy, which is capable of effecting a transformation. The quality of the clay is the source of its form, and the mould merely puts a limit on the expanding form of the molecular organization of the clay as it fills the mould. The mould does not passively form the clay, but communicates a resonating action throughout the clay that alters the clay's molecular organization. Thus, the individuation of the brick, or the process whereby the clay assumes a specific stable form, should be described as follows: the malleable clay, initially in a pre-individual, metastable state, possessed of potential energy and capable of assuming any number of stable shapes, interacts with an external milieu (the mould), which sets up an internal resonance within the clay and allows the clay's uneven distribution of energy (potential energy) to assume an even distribution (the stable shape of the clay being possible only through the residual energy of the molecules that hold the clay together).

Another illuminating example of individuation offered by Simondon is the process of crystallization, which may be observed in the passage of a substance from a metastable, amorphous state, to a stable, crystalline state. Crystallization begins when a 'seed' crystal (or a different substance with an analogous structure) is introduced into a substance which is in an amorphous, metastable state, a state characterized by Simondon as an internal resonance of singularities. The seed crystal communicates its shape to a molecule of the substance, which then communicates the shape to another, and so on. (In some substances, several different kinds of crystals may be formed, the seed crystal determining which one will be actualized.) The process of individuation occurs *between* each crystal and the contiguous amorphous substance, always at the surface of the crystal, the individually formed crystals being the products of individuation and marking the cessation of the process of individuation. Individuation, therefore, precedes the individual. One can also see in crystals that the species and the individual are simultaneously determined, the seed dictating what kind of crystal will be formed (species) and the specific conditions of crystallization (perhaps the speed of formation, suggests Simondon), dictating the specific characteristics of the individual crystal.

Simondon argues that the simple model of crystallization may be used to understand the process of individuation throughout physical and biological systems. One can establish hierarchies of metastable states, each stable in relation to a higher metastable state, and one can distinguish between various levels of organization, from the microscopic to the macroscopic, but the process of individuation remains the same throughout. The difference between animate and inanimate matter is that animate matter manages to sustain certain metastable states that allow a perpetual individuation in the organism. (The completion of individuation, then, is not only the completed individual, but also the end of all change, process and becoming – in other words, death.)[9] We perceive distinctions between matter and form, organism and environment, species and individual, but these are merely manifestations of a single process of becoming, metastable and pre-individual, which constitutes the real.

In Deleuze's terms, a metastable substance is a difference in itself (e.g. sulphur capable of taking on several different crystalline forms), and individuation is a process in which difference differentiates itself. In the Spinozist language of expression, a metastable substance *implicates* (enfolds within itself) difference and *explicates* (unfolds) that difference through the process of individuation. At the most fundamental level, all processes of physical individuation may be thought of in terms of energy, and it is for this reason that Deleuze describes that which individuates itself as an intensity, or intensive quantity of energy that explicates itself as an extensive quantity and a physical quality (DR 287–8). The intensity, like the pre-individual metastable state, escapes our common-sense categories of understanding; nevertheless, the intensity can be experienced through a disjunctive use of the faculties, in moments of disequilibrium, vertigo, distortion of the senses, and so on. The most basic experience of intensities is that of an adimensional *profondeur* (depth or depths), which some psychologists of perception regard as implicit in the constitution of the dimensionality of space.[10] This experience of *profondeur* reveals the existence of a primal, groundless space (*spatium*) from which issues a dimensional and representable space (*extensio*) with identifiable coordinates of height, width and depth. The *spatium* is an implicate space which explicates itself in the *extensio*, and 'energy in general or the intensive quantity is the *spatium*' (DR 310). The space we perceive is that of the *extensio* because the faculties, under the regulation of common sense, perform a passive synthesis of the *spatium*, whose existence can only be revealed through a transcendental analysis of the ground – actually an *'Ungrund* or *sans fond'* (DR 296) – or condition of spatial perception.

The intensity is energy as difference in itself that explicates itself in qualities and quantities, manifesting itself in physical systems in general as the passage of metastable states into stable states, and in biological systems as the simultaneous process of specification (determination of species characteristics) and individuation (determination of parts). The intensity, however, is not a mere physical force, but a dimension of the idea, that which, within the idea, causes the virtual to pass into the actual.[11] The idea, then, has three dimensions: (1) singular points, which are embodied in quantities/parts; (2) the relations between singular points, which are embodied in qualities/species characteristics; and (3) intensities, which effect the spatio-temporal actualization of singular points and their relations. The intensity is that which the faculty of sensibility (the five senses) alone can experience, the *sentiendum* of sense experience, but the idea in general is not associated with any particular faculty. Rather, the idea is that which provokes each faculty into a disjunctive functioning, communicating its violence from faculty to faculty. The provocation of the idea, however, always begins with the intensity and sense experience, and then proceeds to the disturbance of other faculties. (Thus Marcel's experience of a pure past in the involuntary memory of a virtual Combray is that which memory alone can experience, but the virtual Combray only provokes the memory by passing through the sense experience of the madeleine, a sensible difference in itself, i.e. an intensity.)

Socrates says that thought begins with a contradictory experience, which Deleuze identifies as an encounter with the simulacrum. It is clear now that the simulacrum is the intensity, and one can understand why Deleuze says that 'the simulacrum is the true character or form of that which is – *"l'étant"*[Heidegger's *das Seiende*, or individual existing being, as opposed to being in general, *das Sein*]' (DR 92). The simulacrum possesses no identity, since it is a difference in itself, and it only appears by disguising itself. We perceive matter and form, individual and environment, species and individual, as distinct categories, but these are only the products of individuation, the masks in which pre-individual, metastable differences appear to us. Intensities necessarily explicate themselves in qualities and extensive quantities, but even when explicated they remain differences – except that once they are explicated, they become *disguised* differences. Thus the intensity, the potential energy of metastable states, the force of individuation, only reveals itself to the empirical experience of common sense as a masked difference, and reveals itself in the disjunctive use of the faculties as implicated difference, difference-in-itself, and difference-from-itself. In both cases, it discloses itself as a simulacrum.

The intensity, however, is only a part of the idea, and if the form of that which is, *das Seiende* or the individual being, is the intensity, the form of being, *das Sein*, is the idea as a whole, virtual and actual. The intensity is an implicate difference which explicates itself, but an implicate order exists within the idea itself, the singular points of the idea/problem being explications of the problem itself, which should be viewed as a 'perplication' (*perplicatio*) of singular points. Further, all problems communicate with one another and may be said to be explications of a single question. All idea/problems, therefore, coexist in a single virtual realm, an 'informal' (i.e. preceding all specific form), groundless (*sans fond*) unfounded (*éffondé*) Chaos (DR 94). The virtual is a chaos of chance which impinges upon us as an imperative (the violence of the idea as a provocation to thought) in the form of a question.[12] Ideas, the question and the imperative must all be thought of in terms of a game of dice: 'the singular points are on the die; the questions are the dice themselves; the imperative is the throw. The Ideas are the problematic combinations which result from the throws' (DR 255).

In *Nietzsche and Philosophy* Deleuze uses the image of the dice to describe the double affirmation of the eternal return, the affirmation of all throws in a single throw being the affirmation of the being of becoming (see Chapter 1). A new sense of this doctrine of double affirmation may now be discerned. The world of becoming is that of intensities, idea/problems in the process of individuation and explication. The being of this becoming is the virtual realm of coexisting and perplicated ideas as a whole. Deleuze indicates as well that the distinction between becoming and being may be characterized in Nietzschean terms as the distinction between the will to power and the eternal return: 'the will to power is the scintillating world of metamorphoses, of communicating intensities . . . a world of intensive intentionalities, a world of simulacra and "mysteries"', whereas 'the eternal return is the being of this world' (DR 313). To affirm the being of becoming is to answer the imperative of the intensity as provocation to thought and to ascend to an affirmation of the virtual dimension of coexisting ideas.

Since Deleuze identifies the virtual domain of ideas with the eternal return, it is no surprise that he also addresses the question of the relationship between repetition, the syntheses of time, and ideas. In *Nietzsche and Philosophy* Deleuze describes the eternal return as a synthesis of time, the coexistence of past, present, and future in a single moment that allows time to pass. In *Proust and Signs*, Deleuze delineates a pure, virtual past, in which all events coexist, and a complicated time of essences. In the *Présentation de Sacher-Masoch*, Deleuze identifies Freudian repetition as a synthesis of time, and finds the condition of the pleasure principle in the living present of Eros, below which he situates the groundless time of Thanatos. In *Difference and Repetition*, Deleuze combines and revises these accounts, and from them constructs a schema of what he calls the three passive syntheses of time. The first passive synthesis is that of a living present as a contraction of moments within a passing present (in Husserlian terms, the present as retention of the past and protention of the future). This synthesis of time resembles the synthesis of Eros described in *Sacher-Masoch*. The first synthesis is the founding (*fondation*) of time. The second synthesis, that of the Bergsonian/Proustian virtual past, is the foundation (*fondement*) of time. The third synthesis is that of Thanatos or the eternal return, a future-oriented synthesis which is the 'unfounding' (*éffondement*) of time, a complication of time (like the time of Proustian essences) which is time 'out of joint' (*hors de ses gonds*, literally 'off its hinges' (DR 119)).

Deleuze approaches the third synthesis through Kant's reflection on the formula *Cogito, ergo sum* in the *Critique of Pure Reason*.[13] Kant notes that Descartes' formula conceals the presence of two 'I's' and two kinds of existence, for the thinking I (*Cogito*) is self-present as the thought of itself, but the self that it knows, the object of its thought (*ego sum*), can only be known as an object within the form of time. Deleuze extracts this moment from Kant's critique and labels it the revelation of the fractured-I (*Je fêlé*) and the 'pure and empty form of time' (DR 117). Events do not unfold within the pure and empty form of time but time itself unfolds, and all identity of self, world, and God disintegrates. As the *spatium* is the groundless depth from which issues the dimensional space of the *extensio*, so the pure and empty form of time is the groundless form of time from which issues the foundation of time (the virtual past), the founding of time (the living present) and the empirical time of common sense. The pure and empty form of time, the time of the eternal return and Thanatos, is the time of ideas, the virtual time of coexisting, perplicated problems, of differences without origin (and hence independent of the logic of models and copies), which continually repeats itself in the dimension of actual intensities.

Deleuze overturns Platonism by inaugurating the reign of simulacra, replacing the opposition of appearance and essence with that of actual intensities and virtual problems. Kant provides Deleuze with the framework for a critical investigation of simulacra, but Deleuze's transcendental empiricism undermines the entire Kantian edifice. Sensibility no longer functions as the passive receptor of intuitions, but as the faculty capable of experiencing intensities. Far from presenting intuitions within the *a priori* form of space and time, sensibility encounters the groundless conditions of space and time as the depth of the *spatium* and the pure and empty form of time of the eternal return. The function of the schemata of the imagination as dynamic spatio-temporal determinations is fulfilled by the internal dynamism of intensities, which are related to ideas rather than concepts (DR 40, 281), whereas the imagination itself finds its transcendental object in the fantasy. Concepts prove to be illusory subjugations of difference to representation, and the understanding, far from legislating in cognition, virtually disappears as a faculty. Ideas gain pre-eminence, but only as problems partaking of a chaotic, perplicated domain of coexisting singular points. Reason, like understanding, is replaced by a faculty of thought, whose function is to think that which escapes common sense. In short, Deleuze constructs an anti-Kantian model of thought, aconceptual, non-representational, disjunctive, inchoate and unconscious, one that inaugurates the reign of simulacra and is itself a perverse simulacrum of Kant.

The Stoics and meaning

In *Difference and Repetition*, Deleuze identifies meaning as the *loquendum* of the faculty of speaking (DR 201), the contradictory simulacrum within language that jolts thought into a transcendental analysis of the ground or condition upon which language rests. In *The Logic of Meaning*, Deleuze conducts an exhaustive transcendental analysis of this *loquendum*, although in terms not of the virtual and actual, but of the Stoic dichotomy of incorporeals and bodies. Deleuze finds the Stoic schema attractive both because Stoic incorporeals share many of the characteristics of simulacra, and because the Stoic concept of the *lekton* or 'expressible' provides a useful tool for the exploration of the relationship between words and things.

According to the Stoics, all that exists is a body (including such things as the soul, qualities and virtues).[14] Each body, like a growing plant, is a dynamic entity which possesses an inner force that brings it to its completed form. Hence, for the Stoics each body is its own cause, and all causes are in harmony within the single body of the universe. Bodies constitute a realm of causes; effects, properly speaking, do not exist. None the less, the Stoics recognize the 'subsistence', or 'insistence' of certain effects, or 'incorporeals' (*asomata*), which haunt the surfaces of bodies, mere results of causes which have a minimum of being but no true existence. According to the Stoics, when a tree grows green, the 'greening' of the tree is a mere surface effect which partakes in no way of the being or the inner causal force of the tree. It is not an existing quality of the tree, but an ephemeral attribute, a passing surface effect or incorporeal. Such an attribute is an *event* rather than a state of things, a way of being rather than actual being, and the Stoics insist on expressing such events as verbs, reserving nouns and adjectives for the denotation of actual bodies and qualities.

The Stoics place time within the category of incorporeals, but in fact they recognize two forms of time: the variable present of bodies, or *chronos*, and the unlimited past and future of incorporeals, or *aion* (literally, eternity). Bodies have being and exist as causes in a perpetual present. Hence the time of *chronos* may be imagined as a series of Chinese boxes, each present contained by a larger present, the present of God containing all other presents. The time of *aion*, by contrast, is that of the past and future with no present. Like incorporeal attributes, past and future have no real existence, but insist or subsist; they form the continuum of time against the background of which the present emerges. A time of pure becoming, *aion* infinitely expands into an unlimited past and future and simultaneously contracts into smaller and smaller units of time, past and future being two of Zeno's arrows, ever nearing the target of the present but never arriving. *Aion* 'extends as a straight line, unlimited in both directions. Always already past and eternally still to come, Aion is the eternal truth of time: *the pure empty form of time*' (LS 194).

The Stoics, then, recognize two simultaneous and coextensive readings of the universe, one in terms of bodies, causes, and a perpetual present, the other in terms of incorporeals, surface effects, and a perpetually contracting and expanding past and future. This distinction between bodies and incorporeals cuts across the Platonic distinction between the sensible and the intelligible, for among bodies the Stoics include not only things, but also qualities, virtues, and ideas, and they regard incorporeals as simply the surface effects that haunt such bodies. The coherence of the Stoic system resides in the theological principle of the unity of causes, the doctrine of incorporeals arising only as the logical consequence of that principle. Deleuze's strategy is to remove the theological content of the system and then construct a new system (or anti-system) by equating incorporeals with problems, intensities, and simulacra, and by depriving the causality of bodies of any inner direction or systematic unity. Once unanchored, the Stoic system becomes a powerful tool for exploring the relationship between surfaces and depths, problems and bodies. But most important, the concept of the incorporeal affords Deleuze a point of entry into the investigation of language and meaning, for the Stoics regard both linguistics and logic as disciplines concerned exclusively with incorporeals.

The Stoics divide incorporeals into four categories – time (*aion*), place, the void, and the *lekton*, or 'expressible' – but only the *lekton* and *aion* are of major significance.[15] What I have called an 'incorporeal surface effect' or 'event' is a *lekton*, but the word is also used to designate what might be called 'meaning'. For the Stoics, words are bodies, in that they are sonic entities that possess real being. A word as sonic body, however, is the same entity for those who understand it as for those who do not (such as foreigners). That which makes a word understandable to one individual and not to another is its meaning, an incorporeal attribute which is added to the word and which in no way affects the word's being as a body. Both words and things, then, are bodies upon whose surfaces incorporeal *lekta* 'insist' or 'subsist', the surface effects of words being 'meaning', and those of things, 'events'.

Deleuze approaches 'events', or the surface effects of things, through the concepts of simulacra and problems. A problem, we will recall, is characterized in Deleuze's mathematical model by a singular point, which defines a domain of equations and solutions. That point may be specified only after the various equations of its domain are solved, and hence the singular point appears to be a mere result of the solutions, a residue of after-effect (simulacrum). In actuality, however, the singular point precedes all solutions and is immanent within them, for it defines a virtual field of possible equations within which various specific equations and solutions may be actualized. The problem, then, must be viewed in two ways: in terms of its manifestation as a secondary effect, and in terms of its immanent but virtual presence as a transcendental ground of possible actualizations. The same is true of the event, which may be usefully considered through Deleuze's example of a military battle (LS 122–3). A battle may be viewed exclusively in terms of bodies – those of the combatants, of their weapons, their cries, their wounds – but there is also a sense in which 'the battle' itself is an incorporeal surface effect produced by the bodies, a kind of floating entity which is everywhere apparent and yet nowhere localizable. The battle, as incorporeal event, is indifferent to the individuals involved and to the outcome of the fight, an impassive, anonymous process with no clear beginning and no clear end, never present, always future or past, a pure simulacrum. Yet the battle, although mere effect in one sense, in another is a vital entity with a life of its own, an aggregate of metastable states, a structure of *loci* of potential energy, of possibilities of development. Further, the 'event as such', *eventum tantum*, when grasped in terms of its transcendental condition, is a virtual entity, a problem or idea –

not a thing, but a verbal infinitive capable of various actualizations, not 'the battle', but 'to battle'. The *eventum tantum* is real without being present, ideal without being abstract, an idea that differs from Platonic ideas in that it is not fully individuated and it does not exist in any separate, transcendent realm. It is at once mere surface-effect and vital potential energy of individuation, 'insisting' or 'subsisting' in the past and future of *aion*, *'the pure and empty form of time'* (which, as we know, is also the time of the eternal return, Thanatos, or the third passive synthesis of time).

The incorporeal surface of words is that of meaning (*sens*), an entity every bit as elusive as the incorporeal event. It is everywhere present in language, and yet difficult to grasp. One may express meaning in a sentence, but one cannot simultaneously designate that meaning, i.e. make it the object about which one speaks. To designate the meaning of a sentence requires a second sentence ('What I mean is . . .'), but the meaning of the second sentence must be designated by a third sentence, and so on in an infinite regress. Meaning, too, seems to be something that is produced through language, a mere linguistic result or after-effect, yet at the same time, something that is presupposed by every statement as its antecedent condition. This is particularly evident if one approaches meaning through an examination of the relations of the logical proposition. Deleuze notes that three relations are commonly recognized in the logical proposition: designation (relation of the proposition to a state of things), manifestation (relation of the proposition to the speaker), and signification (relation of words to general concepts, and of syntactic links to the implications and consequent assertions of concepts). As Deleuze shows in some detail (LS 22–35), designation, manifestation, and signification presuppose one another, but all three presuppose that a person be 'situated "all at once" within meaning. Meaning is the sphere in which I must already be settled in order to perform various possible designations, and even to think their conditions' (LS 41). Deleuze therefore proposes the addition of a fourth relation to the proposition: that of expression, whose element is meaning. Meaning, he claims, is the 'ideal matter or "medium"' (LS 30) from which the other three relations emerge, but also the condition of truth – this despite the fact that signification is generally so designated. Signification, as the relation of implication and assertion, concerns the form of the proposition, a well-formed proposition guaranteeing truth if its contents are actually true. In this sense it functions as the condition of truth. Signification, however, cannot found truth, i.e. serve as truth's transcendental condition, for it presumes that which needs to be founded – the good sense of implication and assertion, the 'good form' of truth.

To determine the nature of this 'ideal matter' of the proposition, one must proceed by indirection, describing what it is *not* in order to grasp what it *is*. Since meaning precedes designation, manifestation, and signification, it must be independent of all the determinations of these relations (LS 44–9). It must be indifferent to questions of truth or falsehood, existence or non-existence (designation); it must have no fixed and stable objects or subjects (designation and manifestation); and it must be devoid of any irreversible relations of implication, including relations of cause and effect, before and after, bigger and smaller, etc. (signification). As Deleuze shows throughout *The Logic of Meaning*, the nonsense works of Lewis Carroll provide numerous examples of this pre-logical meaning, of shifting identities and reversible relations of causality and temporality, of contradictory realms in which real and imaginary, material and conceptual, possible and impossible objects coexist and interact. Carroll's works are usually characterized as nonsense works, but they are not devoid of meaning; they have a sense, simply not good sense, and hence they delineate an extended meaning that embraces both the logical and the illogical.

Yet Carroll's works ultimately do not present the 'ideal matter' of meaning as it is in itself, but as it insists or subsists within propositions, as it forces its way into language through paradoxes that transgress the logical relations of the proposition. The pre-logical, acategorical and pre-individual meaning which serves as the ground of the proposition, if it is to be grasped in itself, must be thought of as a dimension of action without actors, of process without objects or subjects, without temporal markers or univocal sequences, of verbs without nouns or tenses – in short, as a collection of infinitives existing in the reversible time of *aion*, the '*pure empty form of time*' (LS 194). This 'ideal matter' of meaning, as one can see, has the same features as the incorporeal event.

What, then, is the relationship between the incorporeal surface of meaning and the incorporeal surface of events, and why do the Stoics refer to them both as *lekta*? There is considerable debate about what the Stoics meant by the word *lekton*, but according to Emile Bréhier, whose analysis Deleuze follows, *lekta* are at once physical appearances, logical attributes, and concepts capable of expression (hence 'expressibles'). 'Today', says Bréhier, we would call them 'facts and events: a bastard concept which is neither that of a being, nor that of one of its properties, but that which is said or affirmed of being'.[16] The *lekton*, in other words, is both word and thing – or better still, between words and things. The sense of this characterization may perhaps be clarified through a consideration of a concept that resembles the *lekton* in important ways: the 'objective' (*Objektiv*) of the nineteenth-century philosopher Meinong. Meinong, like his contemporary Frege, notes that the same object may be spoken of in several different ways, and hence argues that one should distinguish between what one speaks of and how one speaks of it, between designation and expression, or reference (*Bedeutung*) and meaning (*Sinn*). In Frege's famous example, 'morning star' and 'evening star' designate the same object but express it in different ways; hence the two phrases have the same reference but different meanings. Unlike Frege, however, Meinong argues that the object of the expression ('morning star' or 'evening star') is not simply a way of presenting an object, but is itself an object, which Meinong calls an 'objective' (*Objektiv*). When I judge that the sky is blue, the 'being-blue-of-the-sky' (the objective) is a distinct 'something' separate from the sky and its physical properties in themselves. The being-blue-of-the-sky is a 'something' that may be judged and assumed, and may perhaps be the case, but is not the same thing as the sky itself (the object of reference). It only comes into existence within language, and it is inseparable from its linguistic expression, yet it is irreducible to language or mental entities. Such an objective exists, argues Meinong, but it does not have being in the same way as the sky itself; it has, in Meinong's terminology, not 'being', but 'extra-being' (*Außersein*).[17]

Meinong's 'objective', like the Stoic *lekton*, is a bastard concept, neither subjective idea nor empirical object; the object of expression yet irreducible to expression, it is the 'object-as-expressed', insisting and subsisting within language, possessed of extra-being but no true being. Meinong conceives of the object-as-expressed in terms of nouns and things, whereas the Stoics and Deleuze prefer to think of it in terms of verbs and events. But what is crucial about Meinong's presentation of the objective is that it makes clear the fundamental nature of the *logique du sens*, or logic of meaning: words express meaning, but that which is expressed is an attribute of things (i.e. an event). Meaning (the surface effects of words) and events (the surface effects of things), then, form a single surface with two sides, events only emerging within words, but that which emerges pertaining to things. This surface of meaning/events forms the surface between words and things and functions as 'the articulation of their difference' (LS 37).

One might suspect that Deleuze, in claiming that meaning and events form a single surface, is merely saying in a complicated way that we see the world through the spectacles of language, that, for example, we actually 'see' the-being-blue-of-the-sky, a simple linguistic creation, as a kind of phantom object superimposed on the real sky. But Deleuze is saying more than this. Meaning is a simulacrum, a paradoxical, contradictory entity that defies common sense. It is always expressed in language, but it can only be designated by initiating a process of infinite regression. It seems to inhere in language, but to appear in things. If one seeks it in words, it seems to be both a mere after-effect and something that is always already there. If one seeks it in things, it seems to be an event that is spatially and temporally 'there', yet always somewhere else, always already over and about to be. But there is a second sense in which meaning and events form a single surface. If one conducts a transcendental analysis of the condition of the proposition, one discovers that meaning is the 'ideal matter' of the proposition, an acategorical, pre-individual, alogical 'medium' which may be conceived of as a collection of virtual infinitives, each infinitive delineating a set of possible meanings, which may be actualized in language ('to love', for example, being actualized as 'I love you', 'I do not love you', 'you loved him before I loved you', and so on). If one examines the transcendental condition of physical occurrences as processes of becoming, one finds that events form a domain of singular points or *loci* of possibility, metastable states of potential energy which may be actualized in various ways, each singular point functioning as a kind of infinitive that may find a number of embodiments. The 'ideal matter' of words is not itself linguistic, and the singular points of things are not physical. They are simply centres of implicate, virtual difference as they exist before they are explicated or actualized in any specific form. Hence, meaning and events, as collections of implicate, virtual differences, form a single transcendental field or domain that may be referred to equally as a field of meaning or a field of events. That transcendental field is not just in our heads or off in a celestial empyrean, but on the surface of words and things, a 'metaphysical surface' (LS 150) that manifests itself to us through contradictory, paradoxical simulacra. It is useful to distinguish between meaning/events as a transcendental field and meaning/events as surface-effects or simulacra, but ultimately they form the same incorporeal, metaphysical surface.

Nonsense, structure, and the aleatory point

What is generally thought of as meaning or sense – the rational meaning of logical propositions – is simply common sense and good sense, according to Deleuze. What is often called nonsense – the paradoxical and contradictory world created by nonsense writers such as Lewis Carroll – is actually the full and unrestricted dimension of meaning or sense (or at least a linguistic approximation of that metaphysical surface of infinitive-like singular points). If sense is but good sense, and nonsense is sense, what, then, is true nonsense for Deleuze? Two answers are possible, one corporeal, the other incorporeal. Words as bodies, i.e. as physical sounds, are devoid of meaning and hence truly non-sense sounds; such sounds, despite their absence of meaning, have an important psychological function that Deleuze examines through the experience of schizophrenics. Incorporeal nonsense, by contrast, is the ever-elusive and paradoxical entity that traverses the metaphysical surface of meaning and establishes a structure of singular points.

Much of Deleuze's attention in *The Logic of Meaning* is directed toward the Stoic concept of incorporeals. Its complement, the concept of bodies, only becomes a central concern when he begins developing a psychological model of the origins of the metaphysical surface of meaning (LS 217–72). That psychological model is too complex to detail here; we may note simply that Deleuze posits a primal experience of a corporeal plenum of non-individuated bodies, 'bodies taken in their undifferentiated depths, in their unmeasured pulsation' (LS 149), from which emerge the essential psychic agencies of superego and ego, as well as an eroticized corporeal surface which is eventually doubled by a metaphysical surface of fantasy and thought. It is in this originary experience of undifferentiated bodies that Deleuze situates corporeal nonsense, the experience of words as bodies to which schizophrenics are particularly sensitive. As Freud often notes, schizophrenics treat words as things and things as words, and in this they resemble writers such as Lewis Carroll. Deleuze insists, however, that Carroll's humorous word-play involves the incorporeal surfaces of words and things (meaning and events), whereas the verbal constructions of schizophrenics are embedded in the corporeal depths of bodies without surfaces. Schizophrenics experience words as devouring, lacerating, or jubilant physical entities within a teeming plenum of matter. They have two fundamental intuitions of the body: as a collection of dissociated body parts, dismembered, interpenetrating and mutually devouring; and as a miraculously solidified 'body without organs', as the schizophrenic playwright and poet Antonin Artaud calls it (LS 108), a catatonic body 'without parts which does everything through insufflation, inspiration, evaporation, fluidic transmission' (LS 108). For schizophrenics, words either enter the dismembered body as exploded words, wounding, rending phonetic elements devoid of meaning, or issue forth from the body without organs as glorious unarticulated sonic blocks. Thus, two kinds of schizophrenic nonsense words correspond to the dismembered body and the body without organs: 'the passion-word which explodes into its wounding *phonetic* values, the action-word which welds together unarticulated *tonic* values' (LS 110).

Quite different is incorporeal nonsense, which functions as the structuring force of the transcendental field of singular points. For Deleuze, as for many post-structuralists, the search for a stable, intrinsic meaning within language is an endless and fruitless quest, a process of perpetual deferral as one word is defined by another, which is defined by still another, in an infinite and self-referential regress. Such a search is a hunt for the Snark, for a paradoxical element that is never where it is sought and always where it cannot be found. The Snark is like the word *mana*, the subject of well-known commentaries by the anthropologists Marcel Mauss and Lévi-Strauss, a term that is used by many tribes of Melanesia and Polynesia in widely varying contexts to refer to power, prestige, supernatural force and other intangible notions. *Mana*, as Lévi-Strauss argues, is a floating signifier, in itself devoid of meaning, and 'hence able to receive any symbolic meaning whatsoever'.[18] Like Jakobson's zero phoneme, which has no actual sound yet is opposed to the absence of a phoneme, *mana* and Snark function as zero signifiers, words with no set meaning yet opposed to the absence of meaning.

Snark and *mana* are instances of incorporeal non-sense. Such elements appear to be simple by-products of signification, violations of pre-existing norms, but in Deleuze's opinion they are linguistic manifestations of the transcendental force that imposes structures on singular points. Deleuze defines a minimal structure as two heterogeneous series of terms that are set in relation by, and converge in, a paradoxical element. The pursuit of the Snark produces a structure, in that it generates two series of terms and sets them in resonance:

They sought it with thimbles, they sought it with care;
They pursued it with forks and hope;
They threatened its life with a railway-share;
They charmed it with smiles and soap.

A series of bodies (thimbles, forks, soap) and a series of incorporeals (care, hope, life, railway-share, smiles), the two converging on a paradoxical element – such is the basic structure of meaning. Likewise, *mana* is the point of convergence of the series of signifiers and the series of signifieds in various Melanesian and Polynesian languages, a zero signifier that sets the structure of language in motion.

These structures, however, are mere embodiments of a transcendental structure, the two series in an empirical structure corresponding to 'two distributions of singular points' (LS 66) and the paradoxical element (Snark, *mana*) to an aleatory point. The aleatory point produces structures by effecting three syntheses: a connective synthesis that establishes a single series; a conjunctive synthesis that sets two series in resonance; and a disjunctive synthesis that causes series to branch out in divergent directions (LS 62). (In geometrical imagery, singular points are connected to form a line, two lines are conjoined in a set relationship, and those lines diverge toward other lines and delineate a plane or surface.) The connective synthesis establishes differences between terms within a series, the conjunctive synthesis creates differences between the differences of the two series, and the disjunctive synthesis affirms difference by differentiating itself into two divergent series. Ultimately, the paradoxical element sets all series in resonance and itself traverses all series, the Event of all events, the Action of all actions, and the Question of all problems:

> the *problem* is determined by *singular points* which correspond to series, but the *question*, by an *aleatory point* which corresponds to the empty slot or the mobile element . . .. The question is developed in problems, and problems are enveloped in a fundamental question. (LS 72)

The aleatory point creates structures, but those it establishes are far from stable. As it circulates among the singular points, the aleatory point establishes a '*nomadic distribution*' (LS 76) of singular points, the singular points taking on no set and prescribed configuration, but, like a flock of sheep in an open plain, occupying as much space as they can, forming structural relations, and then moving on without marking any territorial boundaries or sedentary domains.[19] Each singular point in turn delineates only a region of potential actualizations, for each is a metastable centre of individuation that can eventuate in any number of forms. One can see, then, that Deleuze's conception of structure is ultimately that of a structured chaos or chaos-structure: a nomadic distribution of singular points, each point undetermined within a range of possible actualizations, set in differential relations with other points through connective, conjunctive and disjunctive syntheses by an aleatory point that traverses all series and in the process envelops all problems within a single question.

Within language, the aleatory point manifests itself as nonsense, i.e., as a paradoxical element, like *mana*, which 'possesses no particular meaning, but is opposed to the absence of meaning' (LS 89). Thus, 'nonsense effects a *donation of meaning*' (LS 89) and has 'an original intrinsic relation' (LS 85) to meaning. Meaning may be said to be produced by nonsense or the aleatory point in three ways. First, the aleatory point produces the structure of the transcendental field of meaning/events. Second, it creates the meaning-effects which haunt the surface of words and things. Finally, it engenders the common-sense meaning enunciated through the linguistic relationship of signifiers to signifieds, for that which makes possible the fundamental relationship of propositions (signifiers) to things (signifieds) is their common articulation within a domain of singular points which, when manifested, insist or subsist within the proposition as the expressed meaning and float over things as surface events.

Perhaps the most counter-intuitive notion of *The Logic of Meaning* is that of the transcendental surface of meaning/events, a dimension that seems to mingle mental and physical phenomena without submitting them to the unifying force of either a divine Being or a transcendental form of consciousness. Advocates of traditional transcendental philosophy argue that either one must resort to essences and divine intervention to found the relation of empirical consciousness to its objects, or one must found that relation within an originary consciousness 'since the conditions of real objects of knowledge must be *the same as* the conditions of knowledge' (LS 128). Both metaphysical and transcendental philosophers assume, however, that one must posit either 'an abyss without differences and without properties – or a sovereignly individuated Being, a firmly personalized Form' (LS 129). Transcendental philosophy substitutes 'the finite synthetic form of the Person' for 'the infinite analytic being' of God (LS 129), but ultimately nothing important changes, for the forms of knowledge remain those of identity, recognition, and the Same. Deleuze accepts the necessity of a transcendental foundation of the relation of consciousness to its objects, but he refuses to model the ground on that which it founds. Instead, he treats consciousness and its objects as emissions from a dimension alien to God and the self, 'a world of impersonal and pre-individual singularities [singularities being used indifferently in *The Logic of Meaning* to refer to singular points and intensities], . . . of the will to power, free and unbound energy' (LS 130). Here the aleatory point, 'anonymous and nomadic', 'traverses men, plants and animals independently of the matter of their individuation and the forms of their personalities' (LS 131). Within the transcendental domain of problems itself, distinctions between logical, psychological, physical, aesthetic and linguistic reality simply do not pertain.

Language is ultimately allied to thought and things in *The Logic of Meaning*, but Deleuze, unlike Wittgenstein, Heidegger, Derrida, and other philosophers who have made the 'linguistic turn', does not posit an inextricable bond between thought and language. Thought begins with the jolt of a sign, a simulacrum that forces thought to investigate that which defies consciousness, recognition, and representation, whether it be the metaphysical surface of singular points or the pulsating *Ungrund* of the depths. Language, for Deleuze, is not the source of the forms of thought, but a product of the interaction of singular points/intensities (or 'singularities') and undifferentiated bodies that must be explored through the simulacra that haunt its surface and the sonic shards and blocks that resonate through the corporeal depths. Deleuze shares a good deal with Derrida and other exponents of deconstruction, particularly in his conception of difference. Yet one must conclude that Deleuze, unlike many deconstructionists, believes that there is something outside the text, and that thought need not be restricted to a critique of metaphysical oppositions embedded in language.

Indeed, Deleuze indicates that language, far from imposing a necessary constraint on thought, can serve a positive function in the creation of meaning and the exploration of problems. Meaning, we shall recall, can be expressed in a sentence, but that meaning can only be designated in a second sentence, whose meaning must be designated in a third, and so on. This paradox of indefinite regression attests to the weakness of the speaker, but 'the impotence of the empirical consciousness is here like the "nth" power of language, and its transcendental repetition, the infinite power of language to speak of words themselves' (DR 201). Similarly, language has in its abundant vocabulary, a 'most positive syntactic and semantic power' (DR 159) that allows a word to function as an aleatory point and create divergent and proliferating series of terms. Novelists like Joyce, Robbe-Grillet, Klossowski, Roussel, and Gombrowicz use this linguistic power to explicate worlds of difference via paradoxical elements which traverse multiple linguistic series (for example, the eraser, string, or spot of Robbe-Grillet, *billard/pillard* in Roussel, the name Roberte in Klossowski). These writers engage in no sterile formalism, but answer the imperative of an intensity within language and trace the unfolding of divergent series which are set in resonance by an aleatory point. Their fictions are examples of thought, both as experimentation (in that they explore contradictory experiences and the antecedent, unconscious singularities from which they issue) and as creation (in that the aleatory point, in traversing networks of singularities, produces truth). The generative force in these works, however, is not language itself, but the realm of singular points which plays through thought and art.

Kant splits the aesthetic into a theory of the sensible and a theory of the beautiful, but in Deleuze's transcendental empiricism 'the two senses of the aesthetic merge, at which point the being of the sensible reveals itself in the work of art, and the work of art simultaneously appears as experimentation' (DR 94). 'To think is to create' (DR 192), and only thought and art can fully affirm difference, the cosmic play of chance of the eternal return. 'And if one tries to play this game in any way other than in thought, nothing takes place, and if one tries to produce anything other than a work of art, nothing is produced' (LS 76). Deleuze's own books, then, must be conceived of as works of art, and his thought as a nomadic distribution of singular points. My emphasis has been on the continuity of his thought, but it is clear that Deleuze is not a systematic philosopher (unless by that one means a builder of multiple system-worlds, like Borges). Although *Difference and Repetition* and *The Logic of Meaning* bring together many of the themes introduced in Deleuze's studies of individual writers, the various syntheses of these themes represent a creative and ongoing production of interconnections, not the revelation of a prevenient whole. And despite the multiple parallels between *Difference and Repetition* and *The Logic of Meaning*, the books are not simply two versions of the same content. Each work is an experiment, a means of exploring, extending, modifying, and transforming ideas by setting them in resonance within a conceptual scheme (in the one case Kantian, in the other Stoic). In each work of Deleuze, then, the structure of a problem unfolds; in each subsequent work a metamorphosis of earlier materials within a new problematic takes place; and across all the works plays the aleatory point of a single question.

That aleatory point is the force of the unconscious, i.e. that which escapes consciousness and reveals itself as active, positive force. In *Nietzsche and Philosophy*, this force is the will to power, conceived of primarily in terms of a physics of becoming. In *Proust and Signs*, and later in *Difference and Repetition* and *The Logic of Meaning*, Deleuze gradually situates this force within a metaphysical surface of singular points, which he differentiates from the unformed depths of bodies. That force remains material, however, existing, as Foucault says, 'in what Deleuze would perhaps not allow us to call its "incorporeal materiality"'.[20] In the process of individuation, the surface and the depths are inseparable (DR 197), and though one may distinguish between bodies and incorporeals, both belong to the same realm of the unconscious. As we shall see, Deleuze, in his works with Guattari, abandons the distinction between surfaces and depths, but aspects of both domains persist within the single dimension of desiring-production.

Part Two

Deleuze and Guattari

4

Anti-Oedipus:
Nietzschean desiring-production
and the history of representation

Anti-Oedipus is by far the best known work by Deleuze or Guattari.
A *succès de scandale* in 1972, the book generated heated disputes and
violent polemics in France that have since reverberated, with varying degrees of intensity, across Germany, Italy, England, Australia,
and the United States. The modern counterpart of *The Antichrist* of
Nietzsche, *The Anti-Oedipus* (a more literal translation of its title) is
a frontal assault on the contemporary form of piety known as the
Oedipus complex. Although directed specifically against
psychoanalysis, a pervasive force in French social and intellectual
life in the late 1960s and early 1970s, *Anti-Oedipus* ultimately
challenges every psychological theory that elevates family relationships and the unified self to positions of pre-eminence. Deleuze and
Guattari argue that all desire is social rather than familial, and that
the best guide to social desire is the schizophrenic id rather than the
neurotic ego. They propose to replace psychoanalysis with a
'schizo-analysis', which focuses on sub-individual body parts and
their supra-individual, social interconnections, and which treats the
Freudian and Marxist theoretical domains as a single realm of
desiring-production. No mere Marxo-Freudian synthesis, *Anti-
Oedipus* subsumes Marx and Freud within a Nietzschean
framework, which serves as the basis, not only for a critique of
psychoanalysis and traditional Marxism, but also for the development of a history and a politics of social-libidinal activity.[1]

To readers acquainted only with Deleuze's early work, *Anti-
Oedipus* must seem at once both familiar and strange. Many of the
terms, concepts and themes of *Difference and Repetition* and *The Logic
of Meaning* appear in *Anti-Oedipus*, but redefined, reconfigured, and
resituated within analyses of a much more immediately political
import. Deleuze's genius for integrating heterogeneous elements

within a coherent structure is everywhere apparent, but his dry tone – which, reports Clement Rosset, a reader of Deleuze once likened to a cracker without butter[2] – yields to a much more impassioned and varied voice, one that is by turns irreverent, rhapsodic, witty, colloquial, gnomic and profuse. Deleuze's interdisciplinary argumentation continues in *Anti-Oedipus*, but references to academic philosophy tend to disappear and the authorities cited tend increasingly to be marginal (psychotics such as Artaud, Judge Schreber and Nijinsky), unfashionable (Wilhelm Reich and Henry Miller) or unconventionally applied (Nietzsche as anthropologist, Kafka as political theorist). To some extent, one can attribute these shifts in tone and mode of argumentation to the influence of Guattari, but for the most part it is the collaborative process itself that led to the creation of a work qualitatively different from anything Deleuze and Guattari had written before. In a 1972 interview, Deleuze recalls how he and Guattari set about writing *Anti-Oedipus*:

> So Félix and I decided to work together. At first it was done through letters. And then from time to time, meetings in which each listened to the other. We'd be very entertained. We'd be very bored. Always one of us talked too much. It would happen often that one would propose a notion that would say nothing to the other, and the other would only use it months later in another context. And then we read a lot, not entire books, but pieces . . .. And then we wrote a lot. Félix treats writing as a schizo flux that carries all sorts of things along with it. What interests me is that a page flee on all sides, and yet that it be very much closed in on itself like an egg. And then that there be retentions, resonances, precipitations, and lots of larvae in a book. Thus, we truly wrote as two, we had no problems in that regard.[3]

Deleuze and Guattari together developed not only a collaborative style and form for their work, but also collaborative concepts, arguments, and theoretical structures. Their joint venture was an instance of what Deleuze had described in *Difference and Repetition* and *The Logic of Meaning* as nomadic thought, non-personal, multiple, and unfixed. As Deleuze and Guattari have remarked, 'it is not enough to say "Long live the multiple", even though this cry is difficult to utter. No typographic, lexical or even syntactic device will suffice to make it audible. *One must do and make* the multiple [*Le multiple, il faut le faire*]' (MP 13).

84

It is perhaps at the level of the *production* of thought that Deleuze and Guattari's collaborative work is most original, but the *product* of that collaboration is itself hardly conventional or stereotypical. In what follows, I shall try to clarify some of the more unusual concepts of *Anti-Oedipus*, indicating briefly the nature of Guattari's contribution to the collaborative effort, and then sketching the rudimentary components of schizoanalysis. This outline will provide the foundation for a consideration of what I believe to be the most important element of *Anti-Oedipus*: Deleuze and Guattari's history of representation and social desiring-production. In this history, signs are treated as integral components of shifting social configurations of power and desire, configurations that radically alter the functioning of signs and the structure of representational systems from one mode of social organization to another. Deleuze and Guattari's history I see as fundamentally compatible with Foucault's influential histories of power and knowledge, in that they all insist on the existence of an immediately material and political dimension of the sign.

Guattari before *Anti-Oedipus*

It is easy to overestimate Deleuze's importance in the Deleuze–Guattari partnership, since at the inception of their venture Deleuze was already the author of several ambitious philosophical works, whereas Guattari had published relatively little. One can see that each contributed equally in their collective enterprise, however, if one looks at *Psychoanalysis and Transversality* (1972), a collection of Guattari's papers from 1955 to 1970 published about the same time as *Anti-Oedipus*. There one can trace the gradual development of a psychoanalytic and political theory of groups, which was generated through years of participation in a number of left-wing political organizations and in several associations devoted to the study and transformation of psychiatric institutions. Many of the themes and concepts of this theory play an important role in *Anti-Oedipus*.

Through his work at Jean Oury's Clinique de la Borde during the 1950s and 1960s, Guattari came to see the analysis of individuals as inextricably tied to the psychology of groups and institutions. Freud, he noted, had recognized that the unconscious is 'marked in an indelible way by the structural relations of social groups and by their diverse modes of communication', and it seemed to Guattari that one could extend analysis to the consideration of a group subjectivity 'with its own laws' (PT 93–4), its own forms of resistance, transference, fantasy, etc. Group subjectivity, he insisted, 'constitutes the *absolute preliminary* to the emergence of all individual subjectivity' (PT 90), and the individual's libidinal attachments, he argued, are immediately social: 'the very fabric of my most intimate existence is made up of the events of contemporary history, at least of those which have marked me in various ways' (PT 154). The psychotic, far from being out of touch with reality, is spread 'across the four corners of the historical universe; the delirious person starts talking in foreign languages, hallucinates history: class conflicts, wars become the instruments of self-expression' (PT 155).

Central to Guattari's theory of groups was his distinction between the subjected group (*groupe assujetti*) and the group-subject (*groupe-sujet*). The subjected group 'receives its determinations from other groups', whereas the group-subject 'proposes to rediscover its internal law, its project, its action in relation to other groups' (PT 156). The subjected group enforces traditional roles, concepts, hierarchies and modes of exclusion, engaging in 'a perpetual struggle against every possible inscription of non-sense', and refusing to face 'the ultimate signification of the enterprises' in which it is involved (PT 53). Such a group constructs a group fantasy around an 'institutional object' that is never called into question, thereby granting the individual a parasitic immortality (for example, the eternal Church and its God, the eternal Army and its corps of officers (PT 167–70)). The group-subject, by contrast, opens itself to its finitude, calls into question its goals, and attempts to articulate new significations and form new modes of interaction. The group-subject continues to produce fantasies, but these function as 'transitional fantasies' (PT 169) around which the group coalesces, but which the group eventually transcends through its self-directed actions (for example, the fantasy of 'going to the barricades' in the Student Revolt of May 1968). The group-subject reinforces neither vertical hierarchies of command nor conventional horizontal distributions of roles, but establishes unorthodox, transverse relations between various levels of a group or institution. The task of the group-subject is 'to modify the different coefficients of unconscious transversality at different levels of an institution' and to bring about 'a structural redefinition of the role of each person and a reorientation of the whole' (PT 80).[4]

As one can see, Guattari's psychological theory of groups has immediate political implications, and it was his concept of the group-subject that guided him in a prolonged critique of the Communist Party and its orthodoxies. A revolutionary party, he argued, should be a group-subject that structures the proletariat so that it may articulate its own desires, not a rigid, hierarchical 'representative' of the people that states in advance the workers' needs (PT 103, 126, 171). The Party misconstrues the nature of capitalism in believing that the seizure of State power is the object of revolution, for capitalistic power is decentralized in 'an infinitely complex network of relations of production' (PT 200), and even if a socialist state were to be established, it would be enmeshed in the international capitalist market system (PT 98–130). The Party, in concentrating on the acquisition of State power, also refuses to question the function of traditional institutions. Economic production is inseparable from 'the institution which supports this production', and the State is a 'machine of repression' which 'produces *antiproduction*, that is signifiers which are there to close off and forbid the emergence of every subjective group process' (PT 162). Such a repressive machine effects 'an imaginary territorialization, a fantasmatic corporalization of the group' in phenomena such as 'racism, regionalism, nationalism' (PT 164). Capitalism tends to undermine traditional customs and social relations, but to substitute for them other forms of repression: 'the more capitalism "decodes", "deterritorializes" according to its *tendency*, the more it tries to create or recreate artificial territorialities, residual codes, following a movement which contradicts its proper tendency' (PT 164). To perpetuate the structure of the State is to support an institution of repression and to leave untouched capitalism's complementary processes of deterritorialization and reterritorialization.

In his theoretical essays of the 1950s and 1960s, then, Guattari sought a realignment of Freud and Marx through an insistence on the libidinal nature of groups and the social nature of the unconscious. Capitalism he identified as a force of concomitant deterritorialization and reterritorialization; the State as a machine of anti-production (since it controls, and thereby limits, production); and revolutionary action as the formation of a group-subject, which breaks with established social codes and structures of domination. All of these themes became a part of *Anti-Oedipus* and provided the work with its basic political orientation.

Desire and production

For the most part, Guattari used Jacques Lacan's psychoanalytic terminology in the formulation of his group psychology, but in the essay 'Machine and Structure' (1969), he began to explore alternatives to the language of Lacanian orthodoxy. Here Guattari substituted for the problematic concept of 'subject', so easily confused with consciousness, the notion of the 'machine', calling the voice, for example, the 'machine of speech' which 'breaks and founds the structural order of language' (PT 243). The relationship between structure and the machine he characterized in terms of Deleuze's model of structure in *The Logic of Meaning*, labelling as structure the interrelationship of heterogeneous series and as machine the aleatory point which traverses those series. By the time Guattari and Deleuze met in 1969, Guattari had developed the notion of machines further, speaking to Deleuze of 'desiring machines' and 'a whole theoretical and practical conception of the unconscious-machine of the schizophrenic unconscious'.[5] Deleuze suggested that they develop these concepts, but that they do so in terms that owed nothing to traditional or Lacanian psychoanalysis (whose language Deleuze had himself used often in *Sacher-Masoch*, *Difference and Repetition* and *The Logic of Meaning*). No doubt this effort at terminological purification helped to lead Deleuze and Guattari to launch in *Anti-Oedipus* an attack on the entire psychoanalytic enterprise.

Deleuze and Guattari's thesis regarding psychoanalysis is relatively simple: the Oedipal family structure is one of the primary modes of restricting desire in capitalist societies, and psychoanalysis helps to enforce that restriction. Capitalism tends to reduce all social relations to commodity relations of universal equivalency. In the process, it 'deterritorializes' desire by subverting traditional codes that limit and control social relations and production, such as kinship systems, class structures, religious beliefs, folk traditions, customs, and so on. Yet it also simultaneously reterritorializes desire by channelling all production into the narrow confines of the equivalence-form. The Oedipus complex ensures that human desire is concentrated in the nuclear family, and hence individualized, and that only a residual and 'commodified' desire invests the larger social domain, which is regulated by the economic relations of capital. Capitalism, in its deterritorializing guise, then, sets adrift schizophrenic fluxes of bits and scraps of things, people, words, customs, and beliefs, which it then reterritorializes in the neurotic

Oedipal triangle of papa-mama-me. The schizophrenics who people psychiatric hospitals are those in whom Oedipalization has not 'taken', but who have found no positive means of acting on their desire and have ended up spinning in the void.

According to Deleuze and Guattari, the fundamental problem with psychoanalysis is its conception of desire. Plato construed desire in terms of a void in a subject that is filled by the acquisition of an object, and most philosophers in the West and all psycho-analysts have followed him in treating desire as lack.[6] Jacques Lacan accords *manque* (lack or need) a particularly important role in his psychoanalytic theory, defining desire as an unfillable lack which emerges between need and demand, which proliferates in language through endless substitutions in the chain of signifiers, and which is symbolized in the phallus, a *manque-à-être*, or lack which comes into being. In Nietzschean terms, such a negative definition of desire is symptomatic of a reactive, slave mentality. It is no wonder, then, that Deleuze and Guattari reject this notion of desire as 'an idealistic (dialectical, nihilistic) conception' (AO 25, *32*) and replace it with one in which desire is a primary force, rather than a secondary function of preliminary needs or goals (including pleasure).

Desire is production, or 'desiring-production', claim Deleuze and Guattari, not acquisition or lack. Desire is coextensive with natural and social activity, an unbound, free-floating energy which Freud called libido and which Nietzsche called will to power (D 109). Desire is essentially unconscious, and hence unrelated to negation (there is no 'no' in the unconscious), indifferent to personal identities or body images (central to Lacan's imaginary order) and independent of linguistic expression or interpretation (the core of Lacan's Symbolic order). Pure multiplicity, 'irreducible to any sort of unity' (AO 42, *50*), pre-personal and pre-individual, desire is 'not internal to a subject, any more than it tends toward an object: it is strictly immanent to a plane which it does not pre-exist, to a plane that must be constructed, in which particles are emitted, fluxes are conjoined' (D 108). Desire, in short, shares many of the characteristics of the nomadic and anonymous singularities of *The Logic of Meaning*, which traverse 'men, plants and animals independently of the matter of their individuation and the form of their personality' (LS 131).

The notion of desiring-production, of course, not only asserts the positive nature of desire, but also conjoins Freudian and Marxist terminology. Deleuze and Guattari extend Freud beyond the confines of the family, but they also libidinalize Marx, insisting that 'the social field is immediately invested by desire . . . and that libido has no need of any mediation or sublimation, any psychic operation, any transformation, in order to invade and invest the productive forces and the relations of production' (AO 29, *36*). This conception of libidinalized production does more than challenge the ascetic sobriety of party leaders, for it subverts the traditional Marxist distinction between production, distribution, exchange, and consumption, a distinction that is essential to the claim that the economy, in its narrow sense, determines social relations.[7] According to Deleuze and Guattari,

> everything is production: *production of productions*, or actions and of passions; *productions of recording processes* [a conflation of distribution and exchange], of distributions and of co-ordinates that serve as points of reference; *productions of consumptions* of sensual pleasures, of anxieties, and of pain. (AO 4, *10*)

The coupling of desire and production also problematizes the Marxist distinction between use-value and exchange value. If the exchange-value of an object is its relative value in relation to other commodities and its use-value is its value in relation to human needs, then the stable measure of value depends on the determination of a bedrock of pre-existing needs. Need, however, is another version of lack, and Deleuze and Guattari insist that

> lack is created, planned, and organized in and through social production . . .. The deliberate creation of lack as a function of market economy is the art of a dominant class. This involves deliberately organizing wants and needs amid an abundance of production; making all of desire teeter and fall victim to the great fear of not having one's needs satisfied. (AO 28, *35–6*)

Desiring-production concerns directly neither personal lack nor social need, and use-value and exchange-value are fluctuating functions of the forces of domination which counter-produce lack and need within desiring-production.[8]

Desiring-machines, the body without organs and the nomadic subject

Deleuze and Guattari present desiring-production in terms of a psychological model derived from the experiences of psychotics. Their object is not to romanticize mental illness, but to reveal the genuine questions of unconscious desire which all people face, but which psychotics confront in a particularly direct manner. Psychotics often experience various parts of their bodies as separate entities, and sometimes as invading, persecuting machines; schizophrenics enter catatonic states in which they seem to inhabit a body that has no organs; and some schizophrenics have shifting, multiple personalities and assume the identities of various historical personages (for example Napoleon, or Christ). These three psychotic experiences form the basis of the fundamental components of desiring-production: desiring-machines, the body without organs, and the nomadic subject. Each component is associated with a phase of the process of desiring-production – production proper with desiring-machines, recording (a combination of distribution and exchange, with echoes of the Freudian notion of unconscious inscription) with the body without organs, and consumption with the nomadic subject. The three syntheses that Deleuze introduces in *The Logic of Meaning* to characterize the structure of idea/problems are used in *Anti-Oedipus* to describe the functioning of the components of desiring-production, desiring-machines effecting connective syntheses, the body-without-organs disjunctive syntheses, and the nomadic-subject conjunctive syntheses.

The body is made up of various desiring-machines (often referred to simply as machines by Deleuze and Guattari), parts unrelated to any whole, which are connected to other desiring-machines, some within the body, some in the natural world, some in the social world. 'Everything is a machine' (AO 2, *8*), a part coupled to a second part, coupled to a third part, and so on, in a binary, connective synthesis, forming chains of machines through which pass flows or fluxes. Every machine 'is related to a continual material flow (*hyle* [Greek: *matter*]) that it cuts into', and 'each associative flow must be seen as ideal, an endless flux' (AO 36, *43–4*) or universal continuum of unceasing production. A flow of milk between a breast machine and a mouth machine, or a flow of words between a mouth machine and an ear machine, the fluxes that pass through machines may be actual flows of physical matter, flows of energy, or flows of information (in a very loosely cybernetic sense).

Deleuze and Guattari might appear to be simply reviving the eighteenth-century notion of *l'homme machine*, but actually theirs is not a mechanistic model of reality. They speak of machines to suggest that the unconscious is less a theatre than a factory, and to convey a positive, dynamic sense of the cosmos without falling into religious or anthropomorphic vitalism (since machines have no souls and no personalities). Deleuze and Guattari oppose both mechanism and vitalism, for mechanism extracts from machines '*a structural unity* in terms of which it explains the functioning of the organism', and vitalism 'invokes an *individual and specific unity* of the living being' (AO 284, *337*). Technical machines (machines in the usual sense of the word) differ from desiring-machines in that technical machines combine dependent parts into a whole which either functions efficiently or breaks down, whereas desiring-machines involve heterogeneous, independent parts and 'work only when they break down, and by continually breaking down' (AO 8, *14*; see also D 125–6). Interconnected desiring-machines are Rube Goldberg machines, machines like the one constructed by the narrator of Beckett's *Molloy*, consisting of sixteen 'sucking-stones' distributed in two greatcoat pockets and two trousers pockets, the stones passing from one pocket to another via the mouth that sucks the stones.[9] Deleuze and Guattari propose a 'functionalism' (AO 288, *342*), but one devoid of reference to goals, efficiency, or systematic unity, a cybernetics that recognizes equally differences that make a difference and those that do not.

Perhaps Deleuze and Guattari's most elusive concept is that of the body without organs, an entity produced by the desiring-machines and emergent in a second moment of desiring-production. Deleuze speaks of the body without organs (a phrase taken from Artaud) in *The Logic of Meaning*, identifying partial objects and the body without organs as the two elements of the schizophrenic depths, a savage realm which one is always in danger of falling into, but whose 'projection' onto the metaphysical surface of thought one can contemplate with safety. In Deleuze and Guattari's collaborative work, the opposition of depths and surfaces disappears, and with it the inherently threatening nature of the body without organs, but the central characteristics of the trans-cendental surface of idea/problems reappear as traits of the body without organs. In *Thousand Plateaus* Deleuze and Guattari describe the body without organs as '*the field of immanence* of desire, *the plane of consistency* proper to desire' (MP 191), on which flow 'pure intensities, free, prephysical and prevital singularities [i.e. singular points]' (MP 58). The body without organs produces and distributes intensities

in a *spatium* itself intensive, unextended. It is not space nor in space, but matter which will occupy space to this or that degree

– to the degree which corresponds to the produced intensities. It is intense and non-formed matter, non-stratified, the intensive matrix, intensity = 0. (MP 189)

During desiring-production, a moment comes when the desiring-machines congeal and form 'an enormous undifferentiated object. Everything stops dead for a moment, everything freezes in place' (AO 7, *13*). That undifferentiated object is the body without organs, the desiring-machines at a zero-degree of intensity, a moment of antiproduction constantly fed back into the process of production (hence Deleuze and Guattari's statement that desiring-machines only function by breaking down).

> The organs-partial objects [i.e. desiring-machines] and the body without organs are at bottom one and the same thing, one and the same multiplicity . . .. *Partial objects are the direct powers of the body without organs, and the body without organs, the raw material of the partial objects.* (AO 326, *390*)

The body without organs resembles Spinoza's immanent substance, and the desiring-machines its ultimate attributes (AO 327, *390*). The body without organs, however, is not the whole of which the desiring-machines are the parts, but an extra part produced alongside the desiring-machines. The whole is the organized system of production when taken from a totalizing perspective, the counterpart of the body as organism to which 'the body without organs and the organs-partial objects are opposed conjointly' (AO 326, *389*). The whole only exists at a molar, aggregate level of organization, whereas desiring-machines and the body without organs function at a molecular level.

Desiring-machines and the body without organs, then, are two states of the same 'things', a functioning multiplicity one moment, a pure, unextended, zero-intensity substance the next, in a constant oscillation such that the two states coexist as separate entities. A relationship of repulsion and attraction arises between the desiring-machines and the body without organs, forming first a paranoiac machine in which the body without organs repels the desiring-machines as so many persecuting objects, and then a 'miraculating' machine (a reference to the psychotic Judge Schreber, whose body was 'miraculated' by God's rays) in which the body without organs attracts the desiring-machines and the desiring-machines 'seem to emanate from it as a quasi-cause' (AO 10, *16*). The quasi-causality of the body without organs is best understood in relation to the larger social body without organs, which, in its reterritorialized form, Deleuze and Guattari call the *socius*. Every society produces a *socius*, which appears to be the natural or divine presupposition of production, the three fundamental types of *socius* being the body of the earth of primitive societies, the body of the despot of barbaric societies, and the body of capital of capitalistic societies. Primitive peoples fashion myths of the autochthonous origins of man, despotic regimes promulgate myths of the divine origin and absolute power of rulers, and, as Marx shows in the first chapter of *Capital*, capitalism fetishizes capital and mystically reverses the relationship between labour and capital, so that the social productive forces of labour appear to be produced by capital, rather than themselves producing capital. This mystical quasi-causality Deleuze and Guattari extend to all societies and attribute to the 'miraculating' relationship between desiring-machines and the body without organs.[10]

When the desiring-machines are 'miraculated', they 'attach themselves to the body without organs as so many points of disjunction between which an entire network of new syntheses is now woven, marking the surface off into co-ordinates, like a grid' (AO 12, *18*). Each binary chain of coupled desiring-machines is a line traversing the plane of the body without organs, a multiplicity of such lines crisscrossing that surface to form a grid, which inscribes or records the distribution of desiring-machines within the plane. A desiring-machine may function within several different binary chains (a mouth machine functioning as an eating machine, a breathing machine, a speaking machine, and so on) but not simultaneously. Such a desiring-machine, which stands at the intersection of various lines on the grid, serves as a point of disjunction, coupled now with this, now with that machine. The body without organs, however, performs a disjunctive *synthesis* whereby all the lines on the grid, all the chains of desiring-machines, are libidinally invested at once. In traditional logic, of course, a disjunctive synthesis is a contradiction in terms, since disjunction divides and synthesis unites. What Deleuze and Guattari posit is an 'affirmative, nonrestrictive, inclusive' form of disjunction, a 'disjunction that remains disjunctive, and that still affirms the disjoined terms, that affirms them throughout their entire distance, *without restricting one by the other or excluding the other from the one*' (AO 76, *90*) – in short, difference that differentiates itself and affirms its difference.

Social codes impose an exclusive, restrictive, and negative use of the disjunctive synthesis, and thereby channel desiring-production into prescribed pathways. But if those codes are scrambled, or deterritorialized, an inclusive investment of the body without organs becomes possible, and the nomadic subject, the third component of desiring-production, is produced. The nomadic subject is a point of pure intensity traversing the grid of the body without organs, a mobile locus of becoming commingling identities as it migrates from desiring-machine to desiring-machine. The nomadic subject traces a process of becoming other, becoming plant, animal, mineral, becoming 'races, cultures, and their gods' (AO 85, *101*), becoming all the names of history as it moves across the natural, social and historical body without organs of the world. At every point of intensity, the nomadic subject effects a conjunctive synthesis, exclaiming 'so *that's* what it was!', and 'so that's *me!*' (AO 20, *27*).

Following a suggestion of Deleuze and Guattari's (AO 19, *26*), we may envision the three agencies of unconscious desiring-production in terms of a giant egg covered with crisscrossing lines and a wandering point traversing the various pathways traced on the egg's surface. The body without organs is the world-egg, the cosmic embryo whose zones, gradients, intensities, and lines of potential cleavage correspond to the trace of the chains of desiring-machines inscribed on its surface. The lines represent the desiring-machines, and the wandering point, the nomadic subject. As one can see, this model is a modified version of the plane of singularities of *The Logic of Meaning*, the series of singular points corresponding to the desiring-machines, the plane of all singular points to the body without organs, and the aleatory point to the nomadic subject.

The universal history of representation

To call Deleuze and Guattari's schizoanalytic triad of desiring-machines, body without organs, and nomadic subject a psychological model is perhaps misleading, since there is little of the traditional psyche left intact in their account of desiring-production, the individual subject being a heterogeneous aggregate of parts that function as components of supra-individual social and natural machines. Theirs is rather an immediately physical and social model of desire, and in the longest section of *Anti-Oedipus* they offer a universal history of social desiring-production which focuses on the relationship between the *socius* and its related network of desiring-machines. They discuss, first, primitive societies and the exchangist model of structural anthropology; then despotic societies and theories of the state; and finally capitalist societies and Marxist economics. Within this tripartite schema, they integrate a Nietz-schean history of the origin, proliferation, and internationalization of debt, as well as a history of representation and the sign in oral, literate and electronic-information societies. This latter history of representation and recording within social desiring-production, surprisingly little discussed in critical treatments of *Anti-Oedipus*, is of particular interest and deserves especial attention in any account of Deleuze and Guattari's relationship to literary theory.

Deleuze and Guattari delineate three basic types of social machine – the primitive territorial machine, the barbarian despotic machine, and the civilized capitalist machine – which correspond roughly to three of Marx's modes of production, the primitive, Asiatic, and bourgeois.[11] Striking to any Marxist contemplating this scheme would be the absence of reference to the ancient, feudal, or socialist modes of production, and the centrality accorded the controversial Asiatic mode of production. Marx introduced the concept of the Asiatic mode of production to account for the stagna-tion of development in countries such as China, arguing that in such countries an imperial bureaucracy was superimposed on a primitive agrarian economy without altering that economy, the bureaucracy extracting income from primitive villages and enforc-ing on them a stasis in economic development. The concept of the Asiatic mode of production held no special place in Marx's thought, but it became the centre of heated debate when Karl Witt-fogel argued in *Oriental Despotism* (1957) that the modern capitalist and socialist states should be understood in terms of the Asiatic mode of production. Deleuze and Guattari accept Wittfogel's critique of modern bureaucracies, but argue that *all* forms of the state are versions of oriental despotism. Thus, they identify primitive societies as those which oppose the centralization of power, and hence all forms of state organization,[12] and they regard the capitalist state as a residual despotic archaism, which functions as a unit of antiproduction within the capitalist machine, but which has no intrinsic connection with capitalism itself. The three machines, therefore, may be roughly described as pre-state, state, and post-state machines.

The *socius* of the primitive machine is the body of the earth, the quasi-cause from which men, economic goods, and social relations appear to emanate. The primitive machine is 'the only territorial machine in the strict sense of the term' (AO 146, *171*) since the earth as immanent unity subdivides the people (the subdivision of the earth along property lines marking not an investment of the earth, but the imposition of a transcendent, despotic code on the earth that deterritorializes desire). Since in primitive societies most social relations are determined by kinship relations, Deleuze and Guattari identify the primary function of the territorial machine as that of '*declining alliance and filiation*, declining the lineages on the body of the earth' (AO 146, *171*). Kinship systems are grids which channel, restrict, and code the flow of goods, people, privileges, and prestige by organizing and co-ordinating blood relations (filiation) and marriage relations (alliance). Filiation is 'administrative and hierarchical', alliance 'political and economic', and 'filiation and alliance are like the two forms of a primitive capital: fixed capital or filiative stock, and circulating capital or mobile blocks of debt' (AO 146, *172*).

Deleuze and Guattari argue that debt is not an accidental by-product of a stable system of reciprocal exchange, as Lévi-Strauss and other exchangists claim, but a primary disequilibrium which sets in motion the circulation of gifts and counter-gifts (not the exchange of goods, which posits an abstract and idealistic system of reciprocal and total exchange, from which inequalities and privileges issue as secondary deformations of the system). Every gift-exchange presupposes an already established debt or obligation on the part of the giver and a certain prestige or privilege (a 'surplus value of code') on the part of the recipient. Each individual is assigned his or her place in the community network of gift-exchange, his or her debt in relation to the privileges of the elders, when he or she is initiated into the tribe. Hence, one may say that a unit of debt and a unit of 'surplus value of code' (privileges/ prestige) are produced through such ceremonies as initiation rituals, in which the bodies of the initiates, which are part of the earth, are inscribed – tattooed, scarred – with the signs of alliance and filiation.

This mode of inscription is the primitive form of representation. Deleuze and Guattari agree with Derrida (1967: 101–40) that primitives have writing: 'a dance on the earth, a drawing on a wall, a mark on the body are a graphic system, a geo-graphism, a geography' (AO 188, *222*). But this writing is not a proto-language of signifier and signified, for the graphic system 'is not aligned on the voice and not subordinate to it, but connected to it, co-ordinated "in an organisation that is radiating, as it were", and multidimensional' (AO 188, *222*). In an initiation ceremony involving ritual scarification, the voice 'is like a voice of alliance', the marks inscribed on the body like a graphics of 'extended filiation' (AO 188, *223*). The words pronounced and the signs marked on an initiate's body bear no resemblance to one another, but interact in a plurivocal manner. Each word and each mark have multiple connotations and an efficacious power, for primitive signs are 'embedded' in situations, not fully separated from bodies, specific places, rituals, gestures, stories, etc., yet not entirely fixed in their relationship to one another. The inscription, then, encodes the individual body via plurivocal signs, marks it with the kinship system, and assigns it a position within the general economy of debt and surplus value of code. But that economy of signs and gifts is also a libidinal economy of pain and pleasure. In *On the Genealogy of Morals*, Nietzsche asserts that the creditor–debtor relationship is fundamental in primitive societies, and that the common practice of compensating a creditor for an unpaid debt by allowing the creditor to inflict pain on the debtor only makes sense if the debtor's pain gives the creditor pleasure. Deleuze and Guattari argue that the equation of victims' pain and spectators' pleasure is operative in the initiation ceremony, that each unit of debt is also a unit of pain, each unit of surplus value of code a unit of pleasure. Such a system

> is indeed what must be called a debt system or territorial representation: a voice that speaks or intones, a sign marked in bare flesh, an eye that extracts enjoyment from the pain; these are the three sides of a savage triangle forming a territory of resonance and retention, a *theater of cruelty* that implies the triple independence of the articulated voice, the graphic hand, and the appreciative eye. (AO 189, *224*)

The advent of the state always befalls the primitive community as a catastrophe from without, never as an evolutionary development from within. Deleuze and Guattari follow Nietzsche in his account of the state in *On the Genealogy of Morals* as the creation of savage beasts of prey who with 'their hammer blows and artists' violence' impose an organization that appears 'as a fearful tyranny, as an oppressive and remorseless machine'.[13] This state 'megamachine' is 'a functional pyramid that has the despot at its apex, an immobile motor, with the bureaucratic apparatus as its lateral surface and its transmission gear, and the villagers at its base, serving as its working parts' (AO 194, *230*). The despot 'imposes a new alliance system and places himself in direct filiation with the deity' (AO 192, *228*), thereby overcoding all relations in terms of himself, depriving primitive alliances and filiations of their determining character, and establishing the barbaric *socius* as his own body. Primitive debt is rendered infinite through the invention of money, and that debt eventually becomes 'a *debt of existence*, a debt of the existence of the subjects themselves' (AO 197, *233*). The despot institutes law, but initially this law is Kafkaesque, one in which edicts are pronounced through punishments, in which punishment is no longer festive, as in the primitive machine, but vengeful (another Nietzschean theme). Finally, the despot invents writing: 'legislation, bureaucracy, accounting, the collection of taxes, the State monopoly, imperial justice, the functionaries' activity, historiography – everything is written in the despot's procession' (AO 202, *239*).

What separates oral from literate peoples is not the absence of a graphic system, but the absence of a fixed relationship between the speaking voice and the inscribing hand. Primitive representation is an 'order of connotation' since the spoken word is a plurivocal sign, and 'the thing designated is no less a [plurivocal] sign, because it is furrowed by a graphism that is connoted in conjunction with the voice' (AO 203, *241*). In despotic representation, by contrast, an order of subordination is instituted: the graphic sign is deterritorialized, deprived of its multiple connotations, and made a one-dimensional transcription of the voice; at the same time, the linguistic sound is associated with the meaningless, 'dead' letter of writing, and thereby rendered dead and arbitrary itself; finally the sound is given meaning, not by local networks of connotation, but by a transcendent authority that enforces a law of linguistic regularity, a fixed, one-to-one relationship between each sound and a corresponding concept. The graphic system, besides subordinating itself to the voice, extracts 'from the voice a deterritorialized abstract flux that it retains and makes reverberate in the linear code of writing'; simultaneously, it 'induces a mute voice from on high or from the beyond, a voice that begins to depend on graphism' (AO 202, *239–40*). The mute voice on high is the law of the despot-god, and the deterritorialized flux is the Saussurian signifier.

Saussurian linguistics, claim Deleuze and Guattari, is thoroughly grounded in despotic representation. In the Saussurian theory of the sign, as many have noted, the signifier effectively dominates the signified: signifier and signified are paired in the vertical relation of the sign, but the relative meaning (or 'value') of the signified is determined by the horizontal relations of difference between signifiers. According to many structuralists, meaning is produced by the systematic differences between arbitrary signifiers, but Deleuze and Guattari insist that the structural account of meaning presupposes two complementary forces – one that creates arbitrary signifiers (i.e. extracts a deterritorialized flux), and one that fixes the signifier–signified bond (i.e. imposes the transcendent law of language). It is no wonder, then, that Saussure and his followers associate the signifier with sovereign power and law, for the despot-function is implicit in their theory of the sign. The signifier is an arbitrary entity, but it is also the acoustic image within which echoes the mute voice from on high, 'a transcendence whence issues throughout the system the inarticulate material flux in which this transcendence operates, opposes, selects, and combines: *the* signifier' (AO 207, *245*).

If the despotic machine always comes from without, the capitalist machine always arises from within. What the primitive and despotic machines share is a 'dread of decoded flows – flows of production, but also mercantile flows of exchange and commerce that might escape the State monopoly, with its tight restrictions and its plugging of flows' (AO 197, *233*). The tendency of capitalism is to substitute for fixed and limiting relations between men and things an abstract unit of equivalence that allows the free exchange, and the aleatory substitution, of everything for everything. Not only are equivalences established between goods in an open market, but bodies, actions, ideas, knowledge, fantasies, images function as commodities which can be translated into other commodities, as deterritorialized schizophrenic flows that escape social coding. Capitalist exchange is the limit that haunts every pre-capitalist *socius*, that which the primitive machine codes and the despotic machine overcodes in an effort to conjure it away. Deleuze and Guattari's is a universal history because capital is the universal limit that eventually comes to triumph on a global level (though through no necessity, only through contingent, singular events).

The capitalist machine, however, does not simply decode flows, but constantly reterritorializes them through an axiomatic (i.e. a single system of interrelated mathematical axioms) 'of the social machine itself, which takes the place of the old codings and organizes all the decoded flows, including the flows of scientific and technical code, for the benefit of the capitalist system and in the service of its ends' (AO 233, *277*). The *socius* of the capitalist machine is the body of capital itself, all social relations emanating from capital as their quasi-cause. Put simply, the capitalist machine takes an abstract flow of labour (deterritorialized workers) and an abstract flow of capital (deterritorialized money) and conjoins the two flows in various relations (the set of abstract rules for the conjunction of the flows comprising an axiomatic). The particular qualities of human subjects in any concrete situation result from a specific conjunction of the abstract flows. The *socius* does not need to mark people, simply abstract quantities, since 'the person has become "private" in reality, insofar as he derives from abstract qualities and becomes concrete in the becoming-concrete of these same quantities' (AO 251, *298*). Worker and capitalist (and all variations thereof) are functions of capital, mere points of the becoming-concrete of abstract quantities. The alliance and filiation of primitive societies and the new, overcoded alliance and filiation of despotic societies are replaced by a 'new-new filiation' of industrial capital (money that begets money) and a 'new-new alliance' of commercial capital and financial capital (AO 228, *270*). In the absence of any direct marking of human bodies, the primitive age of cruelty and the despotic age of terror give way to the age of cynicism and piety, which

> taken together constitute humanism: cynicism is the physical immanence of the social field, and piety is the maintenance of a spiritualized Urstaat; cynicism is capital as the means of extorting surplus labor, but piety is the same capital as God-capital, whence all the forces of labor seem to emanate. (AO 225, *267*)

In this cynical piety one can distinguish the components of Nietzschean bad conscience, the holy State and God-capital functioning as an ersatz religious other-world, and the immanent debt which permeates economic (and hence social) relations creating in private individuals an infinite, internalized debt (AO 268, *320*).

The capitalist axiomatic differs from a social code in that a code establishes indirect, limited relationships between entities based on qualitative, non-economic differences, whereas an axiomatic establishes direct relationships between entities based on abstract qualities.[14] Further, an axiomatic possesses no inherent limit, since 'it is always capable of adding a new axiom to the previous ones' (AO 250, *298*). Capitalism, for example, 'was able to digest the Russian Revolution only by continually adding new axioms to the old ones: an axiom for the working class, for the unions, and so on' (AO 253, *301*). The capitalist machine has an ever-shifting limit, one that is perpetually established to ensure the machine's regular functioning and that is perpetually transgressed through its inherent deterritorializing activity. In capitalist representation, therefore, signs are not part of a stable code of clearly delineated and hierarchically organized signifiers and signifieds (the Saussurian, despotic sign), but 'non-signifying signs, point-signs [see chapter 6] having several dimensions, flows-breaks or schizzes that form images through their coming together in a whole, but that do not maintain any identity when they pass from one whole to another' (AO 241, *286*). One flow enters into a relationship with another flow, 'such that the first defines a content and the second, an expression' (AO 240-1, *286*), the units of content/expression comprising the non-signifying point-signs. Either flow may serve as content or as expression, and the units of each flow change configuration when the flows are conjoined with different flows. The capitalist sign, in other words, means nothing, but simply functions within the economic process as a medium for transcoding and co-ordinating various components of the circuit of production, exchange, distribution, and consumption. A flow of electricity, for example, can be conjoined with a flow of words, a flow of images, a flow of music, or a flow of digital commands controlling any number of technical machines; but the conjoined flows never mean anything, they simply channel flows in different directions, each sign resembling a cloverleaf junction into which and out of which stream various entities. Occasionally, however, these deterritorialized flows escape the rigid circuits of capitalist production, at which point redundant, regulated commodity-signs become schizophrenic flux-signs of desire.

The capitalist sign does not entirely displace the despotic, Saussurian sign, however, any more than the capitalist machine disposes of the despotic state. Despotic signs are simply absorbed by the capitalist machine, but given a new economic function, just as the despotic state is integrated into the capitalist machine as a bureaucratic agency of reterritorialization. The preservation of despotic signs and the despotic state within capitalist societies, in fact, is evidence of an exacerbated oscillation in such societies between the two fundamental poles of desire, paranoia and schizophrenia. Such societies

> are caught between the Urstaat that they would like to resuscitate as an overcoding and reterritorializing unity, and the unfettered flows that carry them toward an absolute threshold.

They recode with all their might, with world-wide dictatorship, local dictators, and an all-powerful police, while decoding – or allowing the decoding of – fluent quantities of their capital and their populations. They are torn in two directions: archaism and futurism, neoarchaism and ex-futurism, paranoia and schizophrenia. (AO 260, *309–10*)

In capitalism, the paranoiac and schizophrenic poles of desire are revealed in their most extreme, and hence most transparent, form: the intensified despotism of capitalism represents the paranoiac, fascisizing tendency of desire to assemble entities in molar aggregates and to impose on them a centralized, unified organization, whereas capitalism's accelerated deterritorialization of flows represents the schizophrenic, revolutionary tendency of desire to form molecular, nonsystematic associations of heterogeneous elements. (Molar and molecular, it should be stressed, refer not to the relative size of assemblages, but to their mode of organization.)

In a sense, Deleuze and Guattari's universal history is, as Paul Patton notes, remarkable for 'its abstraction and its anti-historicism'.[15] The social machines are general types rather than representations of any particular society, and their relationship to one another is non-evolutionary and allows for their mutual co-existence within a single social formation. Yet Deleuze and Guattari's presentation of the social machine does suggest the existence of an irreversible historical process of accretion whereby the primitive machine is appropriated by the despotic, and the despotic (and possibly residual aspects of the primitive) by the capitalist. Moreover, this history is informed by a general tendency, albeit a contingent one, toward a concomitant itensification of schizophrenic deterritorialization and paranoiac reterritorialization in social desiring-production. This history not only has a shape, but that shape reinforces the political conclusions that Deleuze and Guattari reach. One can see that for them, any return to the past is a return to domination, any effort to seize state control is an effort to perpetuate despotism, and any political programme for revolution is a blueprint for the molar, paranoiac investment of social desire. The only means of overcoming the paranoiac impulse is to intensify the schizophrenic tendency of capitalism to the point that the system shatters, and this can only be achieved through the creation of group-subjects that form transverse connections between deterritorialized flows that are no longer subject to the constraints of commodity exchange.

Most discussions of *Anti-Oedipus* have focused on Deleuze and Guattari's critique of psychoanalysis and their schizo-analytic politics, an unfortunate emphasis that has isolated, in the first instance, a specialized and somewhat overheated aspect of the work, and in the second, a relatively underdeveloped component of the argument. Deleuze and Guattari have certainly performed a useful service in posing several incisive questions of psychoanalysis – questions regarding the relationship between libido and lack, the social co-ordinates of extrafamilial desire, the historical position of psychoanalysis within Western civilization, and the relationship between psychic and economic life in capitalist societies. And however one might judge their aetiology of clinical schizophrenia (upon which the schizoanalytic enterprise does *not* depend), they have provided a sympathetic way of reading schizophrenic discourse that is far superior to Freud's. Yet their vociferations against the Oedipus complex, no doubt timely in France in 1972, and perhaps proportionate in vehemence to their opponent's strength, seem at times excessive and redundant, once removed from that context. One wonders, in fact, whether the dominance of French psychoanalysis did not lead Deleuze and Guattari to accord the Oedipus complex too important a role in the modern psyche, to treat it as a Freudian discovery rather than a Freudian invention.

As regards Deleuze and Guattari's politics of accelerated deterritorialization, many critics have complained, and with some reason, that Deleuze and Guattari seem to promote a simplistic, irrational anarchism in which all molar order is viewed as bad and all molecular disorder as good. In fact, their political position is neither this absolute nor this rigid. I concur with Foucault that it is 'a mistake to read *Anti-Oedipus* as *the* new theoretical reference', as 'that much-heralded theory that finally encompasses everything, that finally totalizes and reassures' (AO xii). The book, as Deleuze has suggested,[16] is a tool that readers may use if they find it useful, or abandon if they do not. For those who are engulfed by monolithic, hierarchical institutions and who wish to change them, *Anti-Oedipus* is an instrument that may point the way toward a micro-political intervention that effects a local transformation of the institution. For those who worry that the radical group they belong to is perpetuating the structures of domination of the institutions it is battling with, the book is a tool that might help in the dismantling of a micro-fascism and the initiation of some other mode of group interaction. The molecular is not intrinsically good, and deterritorialization is not a necessarily positive process, as is clear from Deleuze and Guattari's subsequent work on the dangers of molecularity and the suicidal or fascistic possibilities inherent in a body without organs (D 166-9, MP 185-204). Nor do all kinds of cognitive activity coincide with molar oppression. Positive deterritorialization in *Thousand Plateaus*, for example, is described in terms not of emotional excess but of philosophical, artistic, and scientific creation, in terms of 'abstract machines' and 'diagrams' that make possible new lines of thought. What Deleuze and Guattari are ultimately developing is a politics of creativity, a theory of revolution that is based neither on beginnings (the conquest of the old system) nor on ends (the implementation of a new system) but on middles – interregnums, intermezzos, the space in between, the unpredictable interstices of process, movement, and invention.

What is most important in *Anti-Oedipus*, I believe, is not its critique of psychoanalysis nor its conception of revolutionary politics, but its history of desiring-production, which may be regarded as a social history of the interrelationship of desire and power. To a limited extent, Deleuze and Guattari's history is a successor to Nietzsche's history of power in *On the Genealogy of Morals* and Bataille's history of a general, libidinal economy of excess in *La Part maudite* (1954).[17] But for the most part Deleuze and Guattari delineate in 'desiring-production' a new object of analysis, one which is similar to the object of Foucault's investigations in *Discipline and Punish* (1975).[18] Power for Foucault, like desire for Deleuze and Guattari, permeates all social relations, penetrates the body at a sub-individual level, and implements an immediately political investment of the body within larger circuits of action and production, which may or may not coincide with the structures of traditional institutions. From a Foucauldian point of view, the primitive, despotic, and capitalist machines of *Anti-Oedipus* are so many regimes of power, means for effecting, in Foucault's terms, 'the political investment of the body and the microphysics of power'.[19] Only in the case of the despotic machine does power emanate from the state apparatus, and even there the despotic machine's power may be traced in all monetary relations, in all punishment and law, and in all forms of writing and inscription. Likewise, Foucault's descriptions of the disciplinary technologies of the prison, the hospital, or school are, from Deleuze and Guattari's perspective, characterizations of circuits of desiring-production. Foucault's opposition of the *ancien régime*'s theatre of punishment, in which the sovereign displays his power through a brutal torture of the criminal's body, and the modern carceral machine of discipline, in which an anonymous and abstract system of surveillance trains the body's components and forms quantified individuals, may also be easily integrated into Deleuze and Guattari's descriptions of the despotic and capitalist machines. To explain the existence of structures of power, Foucault, Deleuze, and Guattari abandon any appeal to the stated desires, interests, needs, and rationalizations of those in power, and seek relations of power in heterogeneous arrangements of body parts, texts, machines, goods and institutions; such arrangements at once flatten elements from traditional, hierarchically differentiated codes into a single surface of components, and isolate specific elements of those codes within unconventional yet discrete units of analysis. The major difference between Foucault and Deleuze–Guattari is that Foucault sees power as primary, whereas Deleuze and Guattari regard desire as primary and power as a restricted reterritorialized form of desire. As a result, Deleuze and Guattari can recommend a politics of deterritorialization, whereas Foucault must advocate a politics of tactical constraint within inevitable relations of power. For all three, however, desire and power are not unrelated forces; the oppressed all too often desire their oppression, either because they code their desire within machines of domination, or because the machines of domination produce their desire.

5

One exemplary reading: Kafka's rhizomic writing machine

Kafka: for a Minor Literature (1975) is Deleuze and Guattari's most detailed and extended application of schizoanalysis to literature. In form and style, the book is somewhat more conventional than their other works, a brief repose between the synthetic mania of *Anti-Oedipus* and the explosive divagations of *Thousand Plateaus*. Their focus is that of the traditional *œuvre* of a single author, yet their treatment of this subject is far from conventional. The corpus of Kafka's writing, they argue, is 'a rhizome, a burrow' (K 7) – an uncentred and meandering growth like crab grass, a complex, aleatory network of pathways like a rabbit warren. A rhizome, as Deleuze and Guattari explain in *Rhizome: an Introduction* (1976), is the antithesis of a root-tree structure, or 'arborescence', the structural model which has dominated Western thought from Porphyrian trees, to Linnaean taxonomies, to Chomskyan sentence diagrams. Arborescences are hierarchical, stratified totalities which impose limited and regulated connections between their components. Rhizomes, by contrast, are non-hierarchical, horizontal multiplicities which cannot be subsumed within a unified structure, whose components form random, unregulated networks in which any element may be connected with any other element. The Kafka corpus, as a rhizome, therefore, has no privileged point of entry, no discrete *chef-d'œuvre*, no extra-literary texts and no intrinsic hierarchy of fragments and completed works. In *Kafka*, Deleuze and Guattari map the disseminating rhizome of Kafka's diaries, letters, short stories, and novels, asking not what that rhizome means or whether it is great or unified art, but how it functions and where it goes. When examining the corpus in terms of its active functioning, i.e. in terms of desiring-production, they treat it as Kafka's writing machine (hence a rhizomic machine – a typically

Deleuzoguattarian conjunction of the natural and the artificial), whose parts come equally and indifferently from art and life, and whose operation consists of a perpetual construction of 'machinic arrangements' (*agencements machiniques*), collections of heterogeneous elements that somehow function together.[1] That writing machine, as we shall see, is an anti-Oedipal machine, a revolutionary political machine, and an a-signifying linguistic machine.

Oedipal traps and lines of flight

Throughout *Anti-Oedipus* Deleuze and Guattari object to the psychoanalytic conception of the unconscious as a source of representations, and hence as an object of interpretation. The unconscious represents nothing, creates no symbols or signifiers, no veiled or distorted wishes that call for interpretation. The unconscious produces, and what it produces need only be described. Dreams indeed are filled with strange images, events, and words, people do make slips of the tongue or the pen, and neurotics do exhibit myriad and puzzling symptoms, but these oneiric elements, parapraxes and symptoms have no *unconscious* meaning. They simply *are*, and the only question is whether the heterogeneous connections produced by the unconscious open up new pathways or block the further proliferation of desire.

In *Kafka*, Deleuze and Guattari not only trace within the works of Kafka the multiple paths of desire, their openings, short-circuits, zigzags, blockages and metamorphoses, but also propose a critique of all readings of Kafka that are founded on a logic of representation and interpretation. They find grotesque the plethora of psychoanalytic readings of Kafka which treat Georg Bendemann, Gregor Samsa and Josef K. as so many surrogates for the Oedipally crippled author; the religious interpretations, which regard Kafka as a proponent of a negative theology; the expressive readings, which elevate Kafka as a tragic witness to the sufferings of the human soul.[2] They see in Kafka an author who is not tragic, but gay, who is not introspective and removed from the world, but eminently political. Kafka, like Nietzsche, may have suffered greatly as a man, but as a writer he practised the 'gay science' of affirmative laughter. No allegorist, symbolist, or absurdist, Kafka is an experimenter who tinkers with the wheels and gears of the social machine and sets them into a delirious overload. According to Max Brod, when Kafka read the opening chapter of *The Trial* to some friends, they fell into 'totally unrestrained laughter', and

Kafka himself 'laughed so much that at times he could not read any further'.[3] Those who do not read Kafka (or Nietzsche or Beckett) 'with a great deal of involuntary laughter and political shuddering', say Deleuze and Guattari, 'deform everything' (K 76).

Yet how, one might ask, can Deleuze and Guattari deny the importance of Oedipal themes in Kafka's work? Kafka's 'Letter to His Father', for example, is a text seemingly ready-made for an analyst, a virtual parody of Oedipal anxiety. There Kafka portrays his father as the ultimate paternal tyrant and blames him for virtually all of his problems. His father intimidates him, makes him feel physically weak, socially inadequate, and emotionally impotent. His father scorns his writing, yet, says Kafka, 'my writing was all about you; all I did there, after all, was to bemoan what I could not bemoan upon your breast'.[4] Even his inability to marry, says Kafka, is due to his father's influence:

> Marriage is certainly the pledge of the most acute form of self-liberation and independence. I should have a family, the highest thing that one can achieve, in my opinion, and so too the highest thing you have achieved; I should be your equal; all old and everlastingly new shame and tyranny would now be mere history . . ... But we being what we are, marrying is barred to me through the fact that it is precisely and peculiarly your most intimate domain. (DF 190–1)

Deleuze and Guattari do not deny the existence of such Oedipal motifs, merely the psychoanalytic interpretation of their significance. They claim, for instance, that the 'Letter to His Father' is less an anguished confession than an analysis and exorcism of the forces of Oedipalization. Here Kafka

> moves from a classical Oedipus of the neurotic type, in which the well-loved father is hated, accused, declared guilty, to a much more perverse Oedipus, who falls for the hypothesis of an innocence of the father, of a 'distress' common to father and son, but only to give way to an accusation to the nth degree, to a reproach so much stronger that it becomes unassignable and unlimited. (K 18)

Kafka's strategy is to inflate the father, to make him cover the world, to blow him up to absurd, and finally comic proportions. 'Sometimes', writes Kafka, 'I imagine the map of the world spread out flat and you stretched out diagonally across it. And what I feel then is that only those territories come into question for my life that either are not covered by you or are not within your reach' (DF 191). As the father's dimensions expand, other triangles emerge, other power structures (such as that of the father–employees–child in the family store), and the father dissolves within larger networks of social relations. When Kafka proposes the ultimate innocence of his father, noting that the father's case is typical of many rural Czech Jews who have come to the city, he makes the most serious accusation of his father – that of having submitted to an alien power and having betrayed his origins. 'The judges, commissioners, bureaucrats, etc., are not substitutes for the father; rather, it is the father who is the condensation of all these forces to which he submits himself and invites his son to submit' (K 21–2). Rather than bowing to the father's authority, Kafka pushes the paternal image to the limit until it explodes. Thus, Kafka does not represent his Oedipal anxiety in his letter to his father, but effects a progressive and parodic deformation of the structures of Oedipalization.

The problem in an Oedipalizing world is to find a way out, to find what Deleuze and Guattari call 'a line of flight' (*ligne de fuite*, an overdetermined expression which, besides bearing the sense of 'line of least resistance', 'point of leakage', and 'diverging line', is the term for the real or imaginary lines which converge on the vanishing-point in a perspective drawing). Kafka enunciates the theme most clearly in 'A Report to an Academy', in which an ape tells of his capture and his decision to become human. 'No', he says, 'freedom was not what I wanted. Only a way out; right or left, or in any direction; I made no other demand' (PC 177–8). He did not seek an absolute liberty or escape, simply a means of movement, a way of transforming the situation– in this case, by becoming human. The Oedipal son seeks reconciliation with the father or unconditional freedom from the father, in either case accepting the Oedipal structure of the situation; but the problem for Kafka is to find a way out, a means of changing the situation.

One story that shows the difficulty of such a solution is 'The Metamorphosis'. Gregor Samsa one morning starts becoming an insect. This is no metaphor, claim Deleuze and Guattari, and certainly no allegory. Gregor is engaged in a process of becoming-other, a process that is to be understood in terms neither of limitation nor of assimilation. Deleuze offers an illuminating explanation of becoming-other in *Dialogues*, using as an example of this process the evolutionary relationship between wasps and certain orchids, with wasp-like markings, that reproduce only through the mediation of pollen-bearing wasps:

> The orchid seems to form an image of the wasp, but in fact there
> is a becoming-wasp of the orchid, a becoming-orchid of the
> wasp, a double capture since 'that which' each becomes changes
> no less than 'the one which' is becoming. The wasp becomes
> part of the reproductive apparatus of the orchid, at the same
> time that the orchid becomes a sexual organ for the wasp. A
> single and same becoming, a single block of becoming, or, as
> Rémy Chauvin says, an 'a-parallel evolution of two beings
> which have absolutely nothing to do with one another'. In man,
> there exist instances of becoming-animal which do not consist of
> playing the dog or the cat, since the animal and the man only
> meet on the paths of a common, but dissymetrical, deter-
> ritorialization. (D 8–9; see also K 25–6)

Gregor, then, does not imitate insectness, nor does insectness
become assimilated to Gregor; rather, something passes between
Gregor and insects, a becoming which is a mutual deterritorialization. He does not turn into an insect, but remains a man-
becoming-insect, engaged in 'an *absolute deterritorialization* of the
human' (K 65) which leads him

> to cross a threshold, to reach a continuum of intensities which
> no longer have any value except for themselves, to find a world
> of pure intensities, in which all forms are undone, all significa-
> tions as well, signifiers and signifieds, in favor of a non-formed
> matter, of deterritorialized fluxes, or a-signifying signs. (K 24)

Gregor is caught in a familial trap, and through his becoming-
insect he seeks a line of flight, a means of transforming a situation,
just as the ape in 'A Report to an Academy' seeks a way out of his
cage by engaging in a becoming-human. Gregor's parents form a
typically Oedipal pair, but behind the father stands the chief clerk,
the boss, and finally the bureaucratic triangle of the three lodgers
who come to occupy the places 'where formerly Gregor and his
father and mother had eaten their meals' (PC 118). The Oedipal
triangle shows signs of unhinging and proliferating, and the sister
encourages Gregor's efforts to become-animal for a while, suggesting that Gregor's room be cleared of its furniture. (The circuit of
brother–sister desire is an instance of schizo-incest, according to
Deleuze and Guattari, an antifamilial and anticonjugal desire that
is not to be assimilated to Oedipal, mother–son incest.) But 'The
Metamorphosis' is 'the exemplary story of a re-Oedipalization'

(K 27), not of escape. Gregor's line of flight is blocked, his sister abandons him, and Gregor, good Oedipal son that he remains, dies for his family.

Oedipalization and blockage of the line of flight are the typical outcomes of the short stories, according to Deleuze and Guattari, and similar dangers haunt Kafka's letters, which, with the short stories, comprise two of the three components of the writing machine. (The novels function as the third component; Deleuze and Guattari do not include Kafka's diaries within the machine because they 'traverse everything: the diaries are the rhizome itself' (K 76), less an element of the machine than the element in which the machine functions.) The letters constitute 'an indispensable set of gears, a driving part of the literary machine such as Kafka conceives it, even if this machine is destined to disappear or explode, like the machine in the Penal Colony' (K 52). What Kafka attempts in his correspondence is 'a perverse, diabolical use of the letter' (K 52), one which, as Kafka says of his conduct during the hotel 'tribunal' over his broken engagement to Felice, is 'devilish in [its] innocence' (D2 65). Even in letters to his friends or to his father, there is always a woman on the horizon, the true addressee of his correspondence, who, however, is always kept at a distance. Kafka's practice is 'to substitute for love the letter of love(?). To deterritorialize love. To substitute, for the much feared *conjugal contract*, a *diabolic pact*' (K 53). A kind of Faust writing to his Gretchen, Kafka is also Dracula sucking the life-blood of his addressee through his letters, staying up nights writing while 'closing himself in his office-coffin during the day', fearing 'only two things, the cross of the family and the garlic of conjugality' (K 54). Kafka doubles himself as the speaking subject [*sujet d'énonciation* – the actual speaker] and the subject of speech [*sujet d'énoncé* – the pronoun 'I', for example, whereby Kafka refers to himself in his discourse], forever sending his double forth and forever avoiding a real meeting with his correspondent, inventing obstacles so that the letter machine can go on functioning. (Deleuze and Guattari insist that the many doubles in Kafka have nothing to do with narcissism, but are instead the elements of a particular form of bureaucratic desire.) The prevailing emotion of his letters is not the guilt so often attributed to him, but fear: the fear of being trapped in his own writing machine, a fear that finally becomes reality when he is submitted to the family trial for his reluctant courtship of Felice.

Desire and the law

The line of flight in the letters, as in the short stories, is eventually blocked. In the novels, however, it does not stop, but branches out and produces multiple series and rhizomic connections.[5] The novels are not so much unfinished works as open-ended machines which execute a perpetual deterritorialization by detailing the machinic arrangements of 'a bureaucratic, law-enforcing, judicial, economic or political Eros' (K 69). The writing machine, then, consists of 'the letters and the diabolic pact; the short stories and the process of becoming-animal; the novels and machinic arrangements' (K 72), and only one of the writing machine's components affords a continuing line of flight. In the short stories (for example, in 'The Metamorphosis') one encounters *machinic indexes*, working machine pieces, which indicate that a complex machine is functioning, but with no clear identification of what kind of machine it is and how it operates. One also finds in the short stores *abstract machines*, sharply isolated, intricate machines, which, however, are extracted from their context and hence rendered non-functional (for example the penal machine of 'In the Penal Colony'; abstract machines will be considered further in Chapter 6). But only in the novels does one discover *machinic arrangements*, complex, functioning machines whose operation is precisely delineated (K 86–9).

How such complex machines function may be illustrated through a brief consideration of *The Trial*. In this work, Kafka's purpose is 'to extract from social representations the arrangements of enunciation, and the machinic arrangements, and to dismantle these arrangements' (K 85). Kafka's aim is not a representation of an inner state or even the social world *per se*, but an experimentation, one that is critical, but not in the ordinary sense of the word: 'in the novels, the dismantling of arrangements makes the social representation flee, in a much more effective manner than a ''critique'', and effects a deterritorialization of the world that is itself political' (K 85). Such a method of active dismantling, say Deleuze and Guattari,

> does not move by way of a critique, which still belongs to representation. It consists rather of prolonging, of accelerating an entire movement that already traverses the social field: it operates in a virtual realm, already real without being actual (the diabolic powers of the future which, for the moment, are only knocking at the door). (K 88–9)

Among the diabolic powers of the future, according to Deleuze and Guattari, are the state machines of Nazi Germany, bureaucratic Russia, and capitalist, technocratic America (K 22). The prototype of these machines, extracted from the decaying Hapsburg empire, is set functioning and taken apart in *The Trial*.

The law seems to be an infinitely distant, mysterious and transcendent force in several of Kafka's works, and many critics read *The Trial* in this light, arguing that Kafka is the exponent of a negative theology or a theology of absence. But Deleuze and Guattari ask, not 'How does the Law describe itself?' but 'How does Justice function?', and they find that it functions not as law, but as desire. The law book in the court has obscene drawings in it; 'accused men are always the most attractive' (T 230), remarks K.'s lawyer; K.'s encounter with young women – Fraulein Bürstner, the woman at the court, Leni – all have a latent or overtly erotic content, as does K.'s meeting with the painter Titorelli. Titorelli's allegorical painting of blind justice wearing the sandals of winged Victory – which K. finds an inappropriate combination since a Justice that does not stand still cannot be fair – is the apt image of Justice as Chance, as ever-mobile polyvocal desire. Justice is never represented, is never directly confronted, but is always in the next room, the adjoining corridor or passage-way, an immanent force rather than a transcendent presence. Deleuze and Guattari note a proliferation of doubles, trios, and groups of figures in the novel, with the young women whom K. meets serving as connectors between series, offering new passages of movement, new lines of flight, combining the attributes of sisters, maids, and whores, all either antifamilial or anticonjugal types. Titorelli acts as 'the singular series of the artist, with manifest homosexuality and a force of continuity which exceeds all segments and puts all connections in motion' (K 126). The architecture of Justice is a rhizomic anti-structure, unlimited offices seemingly distant from one another, but connected by doors and passageways in unexpected and apparently impossible ways. Everyone belongs to the Court, the priest, the painter, even the little girls outside Titorelli's studio – everyone is part of the circuit of desire.

Justice functions as desire, but also as power:

> One would evidently be wrong here to take desire as a desire *of* power, a desire to oppress or even to be oppressed, a sadistic desire and a masochistic desire. That's not Kafka's point. There

is no desire of power, it is power which is desire. Not a desire-lack, but desire as plenitude, exercise and functioning. (K 102)[6]

There are two coexistent states of desire in the bureaucratic machine of *The Trial*, which correspond to the molar-paranoiac and molecular-schizophrenic poles of *Anti-Oedipus*:

> on the one hand, *the transcendent paranoiac Law* which never ceases to agitate a finite segment, to make it a complete object, to crystallize here or there; on the other, *the immanent schizo-law*, which functions as a justice, an anti-law, a 'procedure' which dismantles the paranoiac Law in all its arrangements. (K 109)

Those who find a negative theology of a transcendent Law in Kafka are not entirely wrong, for Kafka does speak of hierarchical powers infinitely removed which issue laws that are only enunciated through sentencing and punishment and that impute a universal guilt to their victims. In fact, Kafka has given the definitive descriptions of the power regimes from which such laws emanate in 'The Great Wall of China' and 'In the Penal Colony', and there is no doubt that Titorelli's description of the infinite hierarchy of judges points to the existence of such a structure in *The Trial*. But in addition to such a hierarchy, there is the bureaucratic rhizome, and Deleuze and Guattari argue that the hierarchy and the rhizome are two manifestations of the same structure. (In *The Castle* the same double aspect of power is evident, the Castle itself being an impossibly removed hierarchy which, however, contains a rhizomic sequence of offices and is surrounded by a similarly rhizomic village.) The two means of handling K.'s case outlined by Titorelli, ostensible acquittal and indefinite postponement (definite acquittal being an unfeasible option), represent the appropriate responses to each of these power configurations. Ostensible acquittal requires an affidavit of innocence, and if the measure is successful it brings a certain freedom, but with the threat that the case could at any moment begin again with another arrest. The case circulates within an endless hierarchy of judges, any one of whom may decide to arrest the accused again; hence, the accused is forever caught within an oscillating movement between innocence and guilt. In indefinite postponement, by contrast, the issue of innocence or guilt is not addressed. The accused must keep in constant contact with the Court, 'although only in the small circle to which [his case] has been artificially restricted' (T 201). Whereas in ostensible acquittal one seeks reconciliation with an infinite hierarchy and falls into an alternation between limited and discontinuous poles of innocence and guilt, of freedom and arrest, indefinite postponement entails continuous contact with a finite bureaucratic unit and an unlimited movement that perpetually escapes the Court's standards of judgement, a perverse usage of the law which sets it careening off its tracks.[7]

Minor literature and the deterritorialization of language

Such is the literary machine that Deleuze and Guattari find in Kafka, and they situate it within a general problematic of 'minor literature', a concept that they extract from an extended diary entry of Kafka's (25 December 1911) concerning Yiddish literature in Warsaw and Czech literature in Prague. A minor literature, in Kafka's analysis, serves as the focus of an ethnic group's collective life and, without solving social problems, provides a medium in which conflicts may be articulated. Such a literature has no great individual authors (such as Goethe in German literature or Shakespeare in English), but as a result it has no literary giants to intimidate later writers or induce in them a slavish emulation of canonical works. Most importantly, politics and literature are intimately related in a minor literature, and the maintenance of literary tradition is central to public life; in a nation with a minor literature, 'literature is less a concern of literary history than of the people' (D1 193). Although Kafka is ostensibly characterizing Yiddish and Czech literature in these remarks, he is clearly describing as well a utopian literary culture which he would like to be a part of.[8] Furthermore, argue Deleuze and Guattari, in his emphasis on the political nature of minor literature and the collective function of the individual writer, Kafka is characterizing his own literary practice.

Deleuze and Guattari extend Kafka's description of minor literature by defining it as literature that has an immediately social and political function; that fosters collective rather than individual utterances; and that uses a language 'with a strong coefficient of deterritorialization' (K 29). As we have seen, Deleuze and Guattari regard Kafka as a thoroughly political writer who does not express or represent his individual feelings or thoughts in his work, but manipulates social representations, such as those of the bureaucratic order of the Hapsburg empire, and thereby articulates them, 'not as they are imposed from without, but only as diabolical powers to come or revolutionary forces to be constructed' (K 33). Kafka's works, therefore, meet the first two criteria of minor literature. But in what sense does Kafka deterritorialize language, and in what way is such a practice typical of minor literature?

In a letter to Max Brod, of June 1921, Kafka says that Prague Jews writing in German have faced three impossibilities: 'the impossibility of not writing, the impossibility of writing German, the impossibility of writing differently'. Their efforts have resulted in 'a literature impossible in all respects, a gypsy literature which [has] stolen the German child out of its cradle' (LFF 289). Prague Jews found themselves between several languages and at home in none. The Czech of their rural origins (which Kafka learned to speak as a child) was being supplanted by the German of the cities, an artificial 'paper language' of commerce and government. The literary language of Goethe's German seemed admirable but remote, the religious language of Hebrew even more removed (Kafka studied Hebrew rather late in life), and Yiddish, as Kafka said, instilled in many 'a dread mingled with a certain fundamental distaste' (DF 382). This linguistic dispossession, claim Deleuze and Guattari, is not unique to Prague Jews in the early twentieth century, but is typical of those minorities and marginalized groups the world over who must express themselves in the language of an alien culture. Uzbek Jews speaking Russian, the Irish, American blacks, or American Indians speaking English, African blacks or Algerians speaking French, all operate as minorities within a major language, and in so doing they modify the major language to make it their own.

'Two conjoined tendencies have often been noted in so-called minor languages', remark Deleuze and Guattari, 'an impoverishment, a loss of syntactic or lexical forms; but at the same time a curious proliferation of changing effects, a taste for linguistic excess and paraphrase' (MP 131). These two tendencies are clearly present in Wagenbach's description of the Prague German of Kafka's day, the major characteristics of which are, in Deleuze and Guattari's summary,

> the incorrect use of prepositions [e.g. *darauf denken* instead of *daran denken*]; abuse of the pronominal [e.g. *sich spielen* instead of *spielen*]; the use of all-purpose verbs (such as *geben* for the series 'put, set, place, remove', which thereby becomes intensive); the multiplication and succession of adverbs; the use of words with pain-filled connotations; the importance of accent as an inner

tension in a word, and the distribution of consonants and vowels as internal discordances. (K 42)

Ultimately, major and minor languages are not 'two different sorts of languages, but two possible treatments of the same language', one of which extracts from linguistic variables 'constants and constant relationships', the other of which 'puts them in a state of continuous variation' (MP 131). Obviously, the expressive elaboration typical of a minor language tends to undermine the major language's constants and thereby deterritorialize the major language, but the lexical penury of a minor language also serves the same end. *Geben* in Prague German, for example, by usurping the function of the verbs *legen, setzen, stellen* and *abnehmen*, loses its semantic autonomy and becomes dependent for its meaning on less heavily coded elements, such as contextual clues, gestures, intonation, and stress, and in the process, the purely sonic, a-signifying aspect of the word gains emphasis. Thus it is that the linguistic impoverishment of a minor language encourages an 'a-signifying, *intensive usage* of language' (K 41).

Writers who work within a minor language often exploit the deterritorializing tendencies of that language, turning its processes of linguistic profusion or impoverishment into a source of creativity. Joyce and Beckett, for example, make use of the deterritorializing tendencies of Irish English, Joyce proceeding 'by exuberance and overdetermination', Beckett 'by dryness and sobriety, by willed poverty, pushing the process of deterritorialization until nothing remains but intensities' (K 35). For the most part, Kafka's contemporary Prague writers resemble Joyce in their effort 'to enrich [Prague] German artificially, to inflate it with all the resources of symbolism, oneirism, esoteric meaning, hidden signifiers' (K 34), whereas Kafka, according to Deleuze and Guattari, resembles Beckett, in that both writers discover an intensive usage of language through a voluntary linguistic asceticism.

Kafka found the inspiration for his creative deformation of German, Deleuze and Guattari believe, in his exposure to Yiddish and the Yiddish theatre from 1910 to 1912. Their primary evidence for this claim is a short speech on Yiddish which Kafka delivered in preface to a performance by the actor Yitzak Löwy in 1912. In this speech, Kafka offers a description of Yiddish that reads like a Deleuzoguattarian sketch of a minor language. The idiom of Yiddish 'is brief and rapid', says Kafka. 'No grammars of the language exist', for 'Yiddish remains a spoken language that is in continuous flux'. The language 'consists solely of foreign words; which 'are not firmly rooted in it', but 'retain the speed and liveliness with which they were adopted. Great migrations move through Yiddish, from one end to the other' (DF 382). Despite such constant variation, Yiddish can be understood – but only through 'forces and associations with forces' that enable one 'to understand Yiddish intuitively' (DF 385). Kafka did not write in Yiddish, nor did he imitate Yiddish diction, forms or techniques. What he learned from Yiddish, in Deleuze and Guattari's opinion, was how to deal with 'the impossibility of not writing, the impossibility of writing German, the impossibility of writing differently', by learning how 'to make German take off on a line of flight', how 'to wrest from Prague German all the points of underdevelopment which it wants to hide', how to 'make it cry with an extremely sober and rigorous cry', and how to fashion 'a syntax of that cry, which will fuse with the rigid syntax of that desiccated German' (K 48). What Kafka learned, in short, was the principle of a minor *usage* of a language, one that ultimately is not dependent on the existence of a polyglot culture or a social minority (although exposure to such a culture or minority may facilitate the discovery of a minor usage of language), but one whose secret is that of being 'like a foreigner *in* one's own language' (K 48).[9] In this minor usage of German, Kafka resembles not only Beckett in English (and French), but also Artaud and Céline in French, Artaud with his language of 'cries-whispers', and Céline with his intensive flux of the 'exclamatory taken to the extreme' (K 49).[10]

Representation and deformation

A minor usage of language entails linguistic deterritorialization and the liberation of a-signifying sounds, but not a reduction of language to the state of gibberish. Rather than obliterate the relationship between expression and content, a minor usage reverses the conventional relationship between dominant forms of content and dominated forms of expression. In a major literature, content precedes expression, the thought coming before the linguistic articulation of the thought. 'But a minor or revolutionary literature begins by speaking, and only sees or conceives afterward' (K 51–2). A minor literature uses deterritorialized sound to break apart conventional content, and then reassembles the fragments of that content in new ways: 'expression must shatter forms, mark new ruptures and functions. Once a form is shattered, the content, which will necessarily have broken with the order of things, must be reconstructed' (K 52). The minor writer engages 'a *machine of expression* capable of disorganizing its own forms, and of disorganizing the forms of content, in order to liberate pure contents which mingle with expression in a single intense matter' (K 51).

Exactly how this revolutionary practice works is not clearly delineated in *Kafka*, for Deleuze and Guattari offer no satisfactory examples of the process of transformation which leads from deterritorialized sound to a dissolution and reconstruction of content. Some clarification of this process may be gained, however, from a consideration of Deleuze's analysis of Francis Bacon's approach to painting in *Francis Bacon: The Logic of Sensation* (1981). Deleuze notes that for modern artists, the blank canvas is not a *tabula rasa*, but the space of unconscious visual preconceptions and received conventions of representation, which the artist brings to the canvas and which he struggles against and tries to vanquish, escape, or subvert. For Francis Bacon, the moment of subversion comes during the process of painting when a chance stroke of the brush introduces a small locus of chaos, a limited catastrophe that Bacon calls a 'diagram'. 'The diagram', says Deleuze, 'is indeed a chaos, a catastrophe, but also a seed of order or of rhythm' (FB 67). Bacon follows the suggested form, colour or line of this diagram and uses it as a generative device for constructing an intensive set of relations within the painting itself, which simultaneously deform the figure he started to paint and form a new figure of that deformed figure. Deleuze contrasts Bacon's practice with that of abstract formalists, such as Mondrian and Kandinsky, and abstract expressionists, such as Pollock. The danger of abstract formalism is that the constraints of representation may simply be replaced with those of an abstract code, in which case the diagrammatic possibilities of chaos or catastrophe are banished from the canvas. The danger of abstract expressionism is that the diagram may cover the whole canvas and result in nothing but an undifferentiated mess. Bacon's strategy is to paint portraits and studies of human figures, and hence to remain in a certain sense within the confines of representation, but to allow the diagram in each painting to deterritorialize the human subject, to introduce 'a zone of Sahara into the head', to split 'the head into two parts with an ocean' (FB 65), to make a leg melt into a puddle of purple or a body start to turn into a piece of meat. One finds resemblances between the configurations of paint and human figures, deserts, oceans, puddles, and rolled roasts, yet such resemblances are no longer productive, but simply produced. A resemblance may be said to be produced rather than productive 'when it appears suddenly as the result of entirely different relations than those which it is charged with representing: resemblance then surges forth as the brutal product of non-resembling means' (FB 75).

It would seem that the function of deterritorialized sounds in Kafka's writing is roughly analogous to that of diagrams in Bacon's paintings. An a-signifying, sonic disturbance emerges within language, a local catastrophe that sets expression and content in resonating disequilibrium. An intensive centre of metamorphosis opens up, a process of becoming-animal or becoming-other that functions as an active force of deformation and recombination within both the social representations of content and the linguistic forms of expression. An intrinsic logic of relations of sounds and representations suggests itself, and the composition takes form as the implications of these relations are developed and worked out. The finished composition may seem to represent institutions which resemble the Austro-Hungarian bureaucracy or a nightmare bureaucracy of a dystopian future (or a bank-prison, or a court-brothel, or any number of things), yet such resemblances are not productive but produced, the effects of an intensive force traversing social representations rather than causes of artistic representation. Within the functioning signifiers of expression, a libidinal, molecular cacophony pulsates and threatens at every moment to disintegrate the coded sounds into an unformed sonic matter.

What Deleuze and Guattari mean precisely by Kafka's intensive, a-signifying usage of language is difficult to determine from the evidence offered in *Kafka*. Although they cite passages from Kafka's works in which a-signifying sounds are described by the narrator, and a few diary entries in which Kafka speaks of sonic dissonance in his own writing, they offer no examples of Kafka's minor style *per se*. Such an absence of illustrations is perhaps unfortunate, but nevertheless understandable, for Deleuze and Guattari are much less interested in the problems of reading than in those of writing. Theirs is a Nietzschean aesthetic, in that they approach art from the perspective of artistic production rather than critical reception. Throughout *Kafka*, their emphasis falls on Kafka the writer and his strategies for dismantling social forms, exploiting a line of flight, perpetuating the operation of his writing machine, and extracting from language a libidinal scream or moan. One might wish that Deleuze and Guattari would isolate and identify the stylistic features produced through Kafka's minor usage of language, but their primary aim is to articulate an attitude toward language, a stylistic stance rather than a model or technique. If an awareness of this stylistic stance leads one to read Kafka differently, it does so by giving one new instructions for the *performance* of Kafka's texts ('try reading Kafka's work *this* way'), not for their critical dissection.

Doubtless Deleuze and Guattari's traversal of the Kafka rhizome will not convince all Kafka scholars of the judiciousness of their observations. Deleuze and Guattari often play fast and loose with Kafka's texts, particularly with certain passages from the diaries and letters, and their lack of concern for chronology occasionally reduces the plausibility of their arguments. Yet their reading of Kafka is not entirely at odds with the work of more conventional scholars. Many have noted the sober asceticism of Kafka's style. Increasingly, critics have come to recognize the influence of the Yiddish theatre and the political and social issues of Judaism on Kafka's writing. Several critics have remarked on Kafka's humour, usually focusing on its relationship to the grotesque and the absurd in his works. Deleuze and Guattari have simply taken these characteristics and pushed them to the extreme, ascribing to Kafka a postmodern attitude toward language, an avant-garde politics aimed at the creative subversion of social representations, and an impersonal Nietzschean laughter that transforms grotesque absurdity into affirmation through the productive activity of writing. Theirs is a deliberately polemical position, but one which, at the very least, challenges the image of Kafka as an introverted, guilt-ridden aesthete, and offers forceful and innovative readings of several works – especially, I would argue, of *The Trial* and *The Castle*.

Ultimately, however, *Kafka: for a Minor literature* is not so much a work of literary criticism as a manifesto and apologia for a literary/political avant-garde. In their basic approach to modern art and politics, Deleuze and Guattari are not especially eccentric or unorthodox. At least since Roland Barthes' *Writing Degree Zero* (1953), a number of critics and writers in France have been trying to reconcile formal experimentation and political activism in art, and many have argued that the deformation of naturalized, ideological codes of representation is an artistic strategy that is also a revolutionary practice. Robbe-Grillet, for example, explains that in his novels he takes as the raw material of his fiction the representations of myths and clichés of the modern world, but then disengages these myths from the machinery of conventional social discourse, breaks them apart, and recombines them in new ways which make the wheels and gears of ideology grind and whine.[11] Deleuze and Guattari, however, unlike most proponents of a literary/political avant-garde, situate literature within a general economy and history of desiring-production, link the artistic subversion of language to the group practices of actual linguistic minorities, and subordinate questions of signification to analyses of the relations between material forces and a-signifying fluxes. What precisely the relations between language, signs, and forces might be, is not developed fully in *Kafka*. In *Thousand Plateaus*, however, one may discern the contours of a schizoanalytic approach to linguistics and semiotics, the basic features of which will be the subject of the next chapter.

6

The grand proliferation:
Regimes of signs and abstract
machines in *Thousand Plateaus*

With *Thousand Plateaus* (1980), the schizoanalytic enterprise comes
to an end, at least in its collaborative guise. The second volume of
Capitalism and Schizophrenia, *Thousand Plateaus* takes up many of the
themes of *Anti-Oedipus* (volume one of *Capitalism and Schizophrenia*),
but in ways that do not so much complement as complicate the
elaborate schemata of the first work. In place of the opposition of
molar and molecular in *Anti-Oedipus*, one finds a triad of molar,
molecular and nomadic, to which correspond three 'lines': 'the
molar or hard segmentary line, the molecular or supple segmenta-
tion line, [and] the line of flight' (MP 249). Instead of a single body
without organs, one encounters three bodies without organs, or
rather the body without organs and its two doubles, the suicidal,
empty body and the cancerous, totalitarian and fascistic body (MP
204). The neat sequence of primitive, barbaric, and capitalist social
machines is disrupted by the addition of a nomadic machine and
a passionate-subjective machine (with indications that still other
machines could be isolated). The minor motif of becoming and the
nomadic subject, developed somewhat further in the concept of
becoming-animal in *Kafka*, occasions an extended section on
various 'becomings' – becoming-intense, becoming-woman,
becoming-animal, becoming-imperceptible (Plateau 10, 284–380).
Besides these thematic recapitulations and variations, *Thousand
Plateaus* also offers detailed elaborations of several new concepts,
including strata, regimes of signs, faceness (*visagéité*), the refrain (*la
ritournelle*), smooth and striated space, maps, diagrams and abstract
machines.

Apart from their remarks on Freud's analysis of the case of the
Wolf Man (Plateau 2), Deleuze and Guattari have little to say
about psychoanalysis in *Thousand Plateaus*, and a great deal to say

about virtually everything else. Each of the fifteen chapters of *Thousand Plateaus* is a 'plateau', a 'plane of consistency' or 'level of intensities' which traverses any number of traditional disciplinary domains and levels of analysis. Each plateau has its own themes and concepts, which are interrelated with those of other plateaus and which appear in other plateaus, but which finally are not reducible to any abstract system or 'plateau of plateaus'. Instead, the plateaus form a rhizome (the first plateau is itself titled 'Introduction: Rhizome'), a multiplicity that cannot be understood in terms of the traditional problems of the One and the Many, of origins and genesis, or of deep structures, in which any point can be connected with any other point, and any sequence of elements broken at any juncture. In *Anti-Oedipus*, the insistent alignment of elements in parallel triads perhaps encouraged the suspicion that schizoanalysis is simply a counter-system, with its own reductive terminology and its own strategies for premature closure. In *Thousand Plateaus*, however, that suspicion is quelled, for the various plateaus of this work clearly trace open trajectories rather than systematic boundaries, and the work's multiple concepts, although rigorously delineated and closely interrelated, form loose, resonating aggregates rather than finite structures, aggregates whose principle of formation is strictly additive and open-ended.

Even if *Thousand Plateaus* were not the massive tome that it is, its very mode of construction would obviously preclude any adequate summary of its contents. My purpose here is simply to outline some of the points that Deleuze and Guattari make about language and signs in *Thousand Plateaus* (especially in Plateaus 3, 4, and 5) and to situate those points in relation to their work in *Anti-Oedipus* and *Kafka*.[1] Such an exposition will help particularly to clarify some of Deleuze and Guattari's remarks about Kafka's writing and to indicate the close alliance between their work and that of Foucault.

Expression and content

Deleuze and Guattari reject any universal semiotics which seeks to explain all of reality in terms of signs. They find especially unacceptable the language-based Saussurian 'semiology' developed by Roland Barthes and others, and although they admire C.S. Peirce's non-linguistic semiotics and use many Peircean concepts in their work,[2] they finally conclude that the extension of the sign beyond the human domain is inadvisable. It is therefore with a certain irony in Plateau 3, '10,000 BC – The geology of morals (who does the earth think it is?)', that they undertake an analysis of the physico-chemical, organic and anthropomorphic 'strata' of reality in terms of the linguistic categories of content and expression. These linguistic terms, however, are used in such a broad way that they cease to function linguistically and become physical concepts, categories for understanding the articulation and organization of matter (especially since they are combined with the quasi-geological terminology of strata, epistrata, parastrata, and so on, which cannot be discussed here). The end result of Deleuze and Guattari's analysis of the content and expression of the strata of reality is not to convert the world into signs, but to situate material signs within a plenum of matter.

Deleuze and Guattari's use of the terms 'content' and 'expression' follows that of the linguist Louis Hjelmslev. Hjelmslev proposes to replace the Saussurian 'signifier' and 'signified' with the terms 'expression' and 'content', and to separate these concepts from those of form and substance. In the analysis of expression, as in the analysis of content, Hjelmslev distinguishes between an unformed material or *matter* (*Mening*, translated into English as 'purport', in French as both 'matter' and 'sense'), the *form* of individual elements shaped from that matter, and the *substance* of the elements, or the matter so shaped by the form. The matter, suggests Hjelmslev, may be conceived of as an undivided surface, upon which the shadow of a net or gridwork is cast. Each square of the grid delineates a form, and the matter within each square is a substance. Thus, in the analysis of language, Hjelmslev distinguishes between the raw sonic matter of expression, the expression-form imposed on this matter and the expression-substance created by this form (phonemes therefore having both a form and a substance). Likewise, the content presupposes an amorphous 'thought' matter from which a content-substance is created via the imposition of a content-form. The elements of expression and content comprise an expression plane and a content plane, but their designation as expression or as content, says Hjelmslev, is 'quite arbitrary. Their functional definition provides no justification for calling one, and not the other, of these entities *expression*, or one, and not the other, *content*'.[3]

Deleuze and Guattari find Hjelmslev's model attractive for a number of reasons, but above all because it subverts the traditional opposition of form and content, labels as arbitrary the designation of levels as either expression or content, and posits a material substrate which precedes the formation of the planes of expression and content. That substrate, or Hjelmslevian 'matter', they identify as 'the plane of consistency or the Body without Organs, that is, the non-formed, non-organized, non-stratified or destratified body' (MP 58). The level of content and the level of expression are formed from this plane of consistency, and 'between content and expression, there is no correspondence, no cause–effect relationship, no signified–signifier relationship: there is a real distinction, reciprocal presupposition, and only isomorphism' (MP 628).

Deleuze and Guattari formulate three basic models of the content–expression relationship, which correspond to the physico-chemical, organic, and anthropomorphic strata of reality. Within the great stratum or physico-chemical entities, content and expression may be construed primarily in terms of molecular and molar organization. Crystals, for example, are the macroscopic expression of a microscopic structure (content), that macroscopic expression emerging within a metastable chemical solution (matter, or plane of consistency). The distinction between content and expression in this stratum is real, in that the molecular and molar are not simply mental constructs; yet, although real, the distinction is merely formal, in that the molecular and molar are part of a single 'thing'. Within the organic stratum, by contrast, content and expression are independent of one another, the unit of expression being the linear sequence of nucleotides of DNA, and the unit of content the linear sequence of amino acids that corresponds to the DNA sequence. In this stratum, the distinction between molecular and molar is no longer decisive, for at this level expression, like content, is both molecular and molar. What assures the autonomy of expression is the linearity of the DNA sequence. In the organic stratum, 'expression ceases to be voluminous [as in the case of molecular structures that are combined to form molar volumes] or superficial [as in the case of crystals, which are always individuated along a surface] and becomes linear, undimensional' (MP 77).

In the anthropomorphic stratum, expression and content take on a new configuration:

> the form of content becomes 'alloplastic', and no longer 'homo-plastic', that is, it effects modifications in the external world. The form of expression becomes linguistic and no longer genetic, that is, it operates through symbols that are comprehensible, transmissible and modifiable from without. (MP 79)

The linearity of the genetic code yields to the 'superlinearity' of language, in that the spatially dependent sequence of DNA is replaced by the temporal sequence of words, a sequence which implies 'not only a succession, but a formal synthesis of succession in time' (MP 81). In the anthropomorphic stratum, the distinction between expression and content is not only real but '*essential* (as was said in the Middle Ages), as a distinction between attributes, types of being or irreducible categories: things and words' (MP 83). It is only at this level that a true translation [*traduction*] of signs occurs, the passage from the molecular to the molar being a mere *induction* of forms, and the conversion of nucleic acids into proteins a simple *transduction* of one sequence into another (MP 81). With the advent of language, 'there is not only an independence of expression in relation to content, but also an independence of the form of expression in relation to substances' (MP 81). As a result, language can 'represent' the various substances of reality and make possible a scientific conception of the world.

> The scientific world (*Welt* in opposition to the animal *Umwelt*) appears in effect as the translation of all fluxes, particles, codes and territorialities of the other strata into a system of signs sufficiently deterritorialized for the purpose, that is, into an overcoding proper to language. (MP 81)

In a sense, the anthropomorphic levels of content and expression correspond to those human properties which, according to André Leroi-Gourhan, are fundamental to the species: 'technology [*la technique*] and language, the tool and the symbol, the free hand and the supple larynx, "gesture and speech"' (MP 79).[4] Leroi-Gourhan argues that one can trace in human evolution a complementary modification of the function of the hand and the mouth that makes possible the development and use of both tools and language. When men assume an upright posture, their hands are set free from the task of locomotion (deterritorialization) and made available for fashioning the tools with which they shape the world (reterritorialization, or technological recoding). With hands and tools for seizing prey, men no longer need muzzle-shaped jaws and mouths suited for grabbing and tearing prey; hence, the mouth is set free from its primary hunting/eating function (deterritorialization) and made available for speech (reterritorialization and linguistic recoding). The recession of the muzzle jaw and the formation of the relatively flat human face are accompanied by modifications in the tongue, lips, and larynx which make them

suitable for speech; the flat face in turn makes possible a reconfigured skull with an expanded cranial cavity suitable for the
enlarged brain that language necessitates.[5] Thus, one can argue
that in the anthropomorphic stratum, content is linked 'to the
couple hand-tool' and expression 'to the couple face-language' (MP
79).

Deleuze and Guattari insist, however, that 'by content one must
not simply understand the hand and tools, but a social
technological machine which preexists them, and constitutes states
of force or formations of power [*puissance*]'. Likewise, 'by expression, one must not simply understand the face and language, or
languages, but a collective semiotic machine which preexists them,
and constitutes regimes of signs' (MP 82). A tool or invention
changes in function, and hence in nature, when it is transferred
from one social milieu to another. The stirrup, for example,
invented by central Asiatic nomads in the seventh century AD,
becomes a different device once it is introduced into Europe in the
eighth century, eventually forming an inseparable and central part
of the medieval feudal order.[6] The social machine, as Deleuze says
in *Dialogues*, is 'a collection of proximate elements [*un ensemble de
voisinage*] man–tool–animal–thing'; that collection

> is primary in relation to [the individual elements that comprise
> it] . . ... The history of technology shows that a tool is nothing
> outside the variable machinic arrangement which gives it a
> specific relation of proximity with man, animals and things . . ..
> The [social] machine makes the tool, and not the reverse. (D
> 126)

Similarly, words vary in function and meaning within different
social orders according to the specific organization of inextricably
related practices and signs which constitute a regime of signs (a
point which will be considered in detail later). In the anthropomorphic stratum, then, content and expression correspond to two
machines, a social technological machine (or technological
'machinic arrangement') and a collective semiotic machine (or
'collective arrangement of enunciation' or 'regime of signs'). Such
machines penetrate all strata and assemble men, women, animals,
plants, and minerals in heterogeneous, functioning circuits that link
man and nature, the organic and inorganic, the mechanical and
non-mechanical, in a single sphere of interaction. In this, the
extended realm of the anthropomorphic stratum, a new form of life
emerges, a machinic 'phylum' of non-organic life whose domain is

'the Mechanosphere, or rhizosphere' (MP 94). The Mechanosphere, however, includes within it not only the machinic arrangements of content and expression, but also 'abstract machines'; and the non-organic life of the Mechanosphere only exists in itself on planes of consistency composed by abstract machines.

Machinic arrangements and abstract machines

Perhaps the best illustration of the relation between machinic arrangements of content and expression and abstract machines in the anthropomorphic stratum is offered by Deleuze in his essay 'Ecrivain non: un nouveau cartographe',[8] an extended commentary on Foucault's *Discipline and Punish* (1975). (The principal arguments of the essay are summarized in MP 86, 175.) In *Discipline and Punish*, Foucault traces the origin and formation of the modern penal system, concentrating particularly on the emergence of the legal category of 'delinquence' in the nineteenth century, and on the rapid establishment of the prison in the late eighteenth and early nineteenth centuries as the dominant mode of punishment in Western countries. This dual history of delinquency and prisons is, in Deleuzoguattarian terms, a history of expression and content, of a segment of a regime of signs and an element in a social technological machine. The prison 'is a form, the "prison-form", which is linked with other forms of the same type (school, barrack, hospital, factory) and which is imposed at a given moment within the social field' (EN 1213). The form of expression aligned with the content-form 'prison' is not the word 'prison', but the expression-forms 'delinquent, delinquency', which 'express for their part a new way of stating, of classifying, of translating infractions, of determining and calculating penalties' (EN 1213). The expression-form, as Deleuze and Guattari make clear,

> is not reducible to words, but to a group of statements [*énoncés*] which arise in the social field considered as a stratum (this is what a regime of signs is). The content-form is not reducible to a thing, but to a complex state of things as formation of power [i.e. social-technological machine] (architecture, daily time schedule, etc.). (MP 86)

The prison does have its own statements, and delinquency its own contents, yet 'the two formations have each their own history, their own procedures, their distinct formalization, even though they meet and become tightly linked at a given moment' (EN 1214). The prison and delinquency are reciprocally determined, but their relationship is not one of structural homology, nor is it one of infrastructure to superstructure, signified to signifier, or thing to word.

If there is no resemblance or correspondence between the prison and delinquency, between content and expression, is there, Deleuze asks, 'something which functions as an immanent common cause?' (EN 1215). There is, he concludes, and that immanent cause is the mechanism of panopticism, which Deleuze calls an 'abstract machine'. Foucault treats Jeremy Bentham's 1791 'Plan of the Panopticon', a proposal for the design of an ideal prison, as an exemplary instance of a new social function, introduced in the nineteenth century, which eventually leads to the creation of our modern disciplinary society. Bentham's panopticon consists of a central surveillance tower and a surrounding ring of prison cells, constructed in a such a manner that the prisoners are always visible from the tower without the prisoners themselves being able to see those in the tower who watch them. Bentham's architectural model was adopted in the construction of several prisons in the nineteenth and twentieth centuries, but Foucault's point is not simply that a particular form of architecture became popular at a certain time, but that a generalized function, made particularly visible in the panopticon yet independent of any spatial configuration, came to permeate an entire society and serve as its organizing principle. According to Foucault, wherever power operates as an anonymous, immanent observation that individualizes and classifies subjects without their being aware of it, panopticism is at work. Its mechanisms are as varied as the prison, the standardized test, modes of physical education, or techniques for family counselling. Panopticism, says Deleuze, is an abstract machine, defined by 'a *pure function*, independent of sensible configurations and categorical forms in which it is embodied', and by 'a *pure matter*, independent of qualified substances into which this matter enters (a delinquent-, hospital-, school-, worker-, soldier-substance, etc.)' (EN 1216). Its function is 'to see without being seen', and its matter is 'any "human multiplicity" which is to be made countable and controllable' (EN 1216). This abstract machine is not an idea or model, but a 'diagram' of power, an immanent and generalized function. 'The diagram, the abstract machine coextensive with the social field, always plays the role of common, non-unifying immanent cause' (EN 1219).

The concept of the abstract machine figures prominently in

Thousand Plateaus as the necessary complement of the machinic arrangements of content and expression. Hjelmslev, we shall recall, distinguishes between unformed matter and the substances shaped by the forms of expression and content. Deleuze and Guattari, in a parallel fashion, posit an unformed plane of consistency (or body without organs) from which expression and content are extracted, each with its own form and corresponding substance. The plane of consistency 'is occupied, traced by the abstract machine' (MP 90): the machinic arrangements, or 'concrete machines' (in the anthropomorphic stratum, both the social technological machines of content and the regimes of signs of expression), '*put into effect* the abstract machine' (MP 91). Utilizing the Spinozist concepts of implication and explication, envelopment and development (see Chapter 2), Deleuze and Guattari explain that '*the abstract machine* now develops itself on the plane of consistency, whose continua, emissions and conjugations it constructs, now remains enveloped in a stratum whose unity of composition and force of attraction or prehension it defines' (MP 91). The plane of consistency is destratified, decoded, absolutely deterritorialized matter, which is not dualistically opposed to organized strata of content and expression but 'everywhere present, everywhere first and primary, always immanent' (MP 90). Indeed, the various strata 'are themselves animated and defined by speeds of relative deterritorialization'; they are 'fallen-back entities [*des retombées*], thickenings on a plane of consistency' (MP 90). The superlinear linguistic sequence of the anthropomorphic stratum is a relatively more deterritorialized form of expression than the linear sequence of DNA of the organic stratum, itself more deterritorialized than the molecular form of expression of the physico-chemical stratum. Within each stratum, expression is itself more deterritorialized than content: the molar has more options for development than the molecular, which is embedded in the molar; the DNA strand transduces an amino acid sequence, but also replicates itself; and language translates all contents into its own terms. But from the beginning, the absolutely deterritorialized plane of consistency is immanent within these forms of expression, which are characterized by the degree to which each form of expression restrains and slows the forces of deterritorialization. Thus, the relationship between the plane of consistency and a stratum of content and expression, between the abstract machine, which traces the plane of consistency and the machinic arrangements, which effect the abstract machine in a specific configuration of content and expression, may be regarded metaphorically in terms of two coexisting movements or directions of force: one passing from the abstract machine to the machinic arrangements (for example the path, traced by Foucault, of the abstract machine of panopticism, which permeates the various machinic arrangements of disciplinary technology), and one passing from the machinic arrangements to the abstract machine (the path of absolute deterritorialization always present within any stratum).

Deleuze and Guattari state that an abstract machine 'operates via *matter* and not substance; via *function* and not form' (MP 176). An abstract machine, then, may be characterized in part by its matter, i.e. by the configuration of its plane of consistency. A plane of consistency is destratified, decoded and deterritorialized, yet it is 'for all that neither a chaotic white night nor an undifferentiated black night' (MP 90–1). It has its own mode of organization, whose principles Deleuze and Guattari derive from Spinoza. In *Spinoza: Practical Philosophy* (1980), Deleuze explains that Spinoza defines a body in two ways:

> on the one hand, a body, no matter how small, always consists of an infinite number of particles: a body, the individuality of a body, is defined by relations of rest and movement, of swiftness and slowness among particles. On the other hand, a body affects other bodies, or is affected by other bodies: it is this power of affecting and being affected which also defines a body in its individuality.[9]

A body is not a form, but 'a complex relation between differential speeds, between a slowing and an acceleration of particles' (S 165), a relation that varies between bodies and within each body. Its affective powers may be limited or extensive. A tick, for example, is defined by three affects: 'the first, toward light (climbing to the top of a branch); the second, olfactory (letting itself fall on a mammal passing under the branch); the third, caloric (seeking the warmest region without hair)' (S 167). A human's affective powers, by contrast, are so numerous that it is only through an extended experimentation that we can come to know what a human body is capable of. A body and its milieu, the particles that affect it and those that it affects, are inseparable, interpenetrating, and always subsumable within larger bodies of particles, defined by different affects and relations of movement. Nature, then, when viewed from this Spinozist perspective, is made up solely of differential rhythms and affective intensities. The coordinates of any body are determined by what Deleuze terms the 'longitude' of its relations of rest and movement 'between *non-formed elements*' and the 'latitude' of 'the intensive states of an *anonymous force* (force of existence, power of being affected)' (S 171). 'The totality of longitudes and latitudes constitutes Nature, the plane of immanence or consistency, always variable, ceaselessly modified, composed, recomposed, by individuals and collectivities' (S 171). (As one can see, a body made up only of particles and affects is literally 'without organs', and Nature, as the sum total of particles and affects, may be described as the great Body without Organs.)

This Spinozist schema of longitude and latitude, of differential speeds between non-formed elements and intensive affects of anonymous forces, is used consistently in *Thousand Plateaus* to describe planes of consistency and their characteristic mode of individuation. (Deleuze and Guattari speak both of *the* plane of consistency of nature and of specific planes of consistency constructed by abstract machines which induce a co-functioning of certain particles.) One can speak of individuated entities within a plane of consistency, but they are not persons, subjects, things, or substances. Rather, they are what Deleuze and Guattari call 'hecceities' (a term borrowed from Duns Scotus, whose *haecceitas* may perhaps be translated as 'thisness').

A season, a winter, a summer, an hour, a date have a perfect individuality which lacks nothing, although it is not that of a thing or a subject. These are hecceities, in the sense that each is only a relation of movement and rest between molecules or particles, a power of affecting and being affected. (MP 318)

The 'body' of a hecceity may include any number of heterogeneous things or parts of things within it (since the plane of consistency is made up of non-formed particles, and hence contains no 'things', in the ordinary sense of the word), and its duration may be brief or extended.[10]

You are longitude and latitude, a collection of fast and slow speeds between non-formed particles, a collection of non-subjective affects. You have the individuation of a day, a season, a year, *a life* . . . of a climate, a wind, a fog, a swarm, a pack. (MP 320)

(It is on such a plane of consistency that Gregor engages in a becoming-insect in *The Metamorphosis*, in that a hecceity of speeds and intensities traverses him and an insect or insects. In fact, all 'becomings', becoming-woman, becoming-animal, becoming-imperceptible, occur on a plane of consistency.)

An abstract machine is characterized by its matter – its hecceities, or relations of speeds and affects – but also by its function. The abstract machine of panopticism, for example, consists of a 'pure matter', a human multiplicity, and a 'pure function', that of seeing without being seen. What is important to note is that this function is neither semiotic nor physical, neither expression nor content, but an abstract function that informs both the expression-form of the discourse on delinquency and the content-form of the prison. Such an abstract function, characteristic of every abstract machine, Deleuze and Guattari call a 'diagram'. Semioticians generally classify diagrams as simplified images, or icons, of things. But as Guattari points out,

> the image represents both more and less than a diagram; the image reproduces numerous aspects which a diagram does not retain in its representation, whereas the diagram brings together the functional articulations of a system with much greater exactitude and efficacy than the image.[11]

Visual graphs and charts are diagrams, but so are mathematical formulae, musical scores, and models in particle physics; and the more abstract the diagram is, the less it represents any particular thing, and the less it can be conceived of in terms of expression and content. Mathematical equations articulate a self-referential system of relations which may be embodied in diverse contexts. Musical scores, although heavily 'coded' in traditional music (specific designations of instruments, tempi, and so on), in much electronic music function as abstract diagrams of differential speeds and intensities which a synthesizer embodies in various sounds. Models in particle physics fuse mathematical theories and experimental particles (theories isolating particles and particles generating theories) to such an extent that one may speak no longer of particles or signs, but of 'particle-signs', units in a self-referential experimental-theoretical complex. The function of an abstract machine is a diagram of this sort, a function 'which has only "traits", of content and expression, whose connection it assumes: one can no longer even say whether a trait is a particle or a sign' (MP 176). Thus, in an abstract machine, content and expression yield to 'a content-matter which presents only degrees of intensity, resistance, conductibility, heatability, stretchability, speed or slowness; an expression-function which presents only "tensors", as in a mathematical or musical notation' (MP 176–7).

135

Regimes of signs

Language plays an important part in the constitution of the anthropomorphic stratum, but only as an element within a regime of signs.[12] In formulating the notion of a regime of signs, Deleuze and Guattari are interested above all in subordinating linguistics to pragmatics. Most linguists, they observe, posit the existence of linguistic constants or universals upon which they found their study. Their descriptions of a language system (*langue*) or its deep structure generally presuppose the existence of a standard, stable language which can be extracted from its various fluctuating instantiations (whether they be classified as *parole* or performance). This standard language functions as the norm against which are measured the linguistic deviations of groups (for example, dialects, argots, professional jargons) and of individuals (for example literary style, poetic language). But most importantly, such a standard language serves as a constant in relation to the changing circumstances of its utterance. Many linguists agree that the same words have different meanings in different contexts, but they regard the language as stable and relegate the study of contexts to a secondary field of pragmatics. Deleuze and Guattari, building on the work of Labov, Austin, Searle, Ducrot and Bakhtin, try to reverse this relationship and situate linguistics within a larger theory of action.

The primary function of language, contend Deleuze and Guattari, is not to transmit information or to allow communication, but to issue *mots d'ordre*, a phrase commonly translated as 'watchwords' or 'slogans', but used here with the literal sense of 'words of order', orders and commands which enforce an order – law and order. During the grammar-school language lesson, the teacher does not communicate information,

> but imposes on the child semiotic coordinates with all the basic dualisms of grammar (masculine–feminine, singular–plural, substantive–verb, subject of speech [*sujet d'énoncé*] – speaking subject [*sujet d'énonciation*], etc.). The elementary unit of language – the statement [*énoncé*] – is the *mot d'ordre*. (MP 95)

Language categorizes the world, and in learning a language one must to some extent accept the codes – codes of privilege, power, domination, exclusion, and so on – inherent in the language. But this is not the full extent of Deleuze and Guattari's point. Rather, it is that the basic function of language, its fundamental condition, is the transmission of others' discourse and the imposition of a collective order. Human language, rather than commencing with tropes or direct discourse, begins with indirect discourse, the reporting of someone else's words. Bees use tropes and engage in a direct discourse of sorts, but they have no language. After seeing a flower, a bee may return to the hive and signal to another bee the location of the flower, but the second bee cannot relay the message to a third. 'It is in this sense that language is the transmission of the word functioning as *mot d'ordre*, and not communication of a sign as information' (MP 97).

To a degree, Deleuze and Guattari are simply reiterating the findings of speech-act theorists who, since Austin, have called attention to the fact that saying something is often a means of doing something. When the pastor says, 'I thee wed', or the judge says, 'guilty', each, in so speaking, performs an action. And even when a specific formula is not involved, statements in certain situations constitute specific acts. When I make a promise, I may signal it by saying 'I'll take care of it', 'Okay', 'Don't worry', or 'Sure, I'll be there', but in every case the words will count as the act of promising. Speech-act theorists, however, tend to see such speech-acts as a discursive subcategory and to limit the import of speech-acts to the negotiation of uncontroversial social conventions. Deleuze and Guattari, by contrast, associate the *mot d'ordre* with no single category of statements and regard all language-acts as acts of power. *Mots d'ordre* 'are not simply related to commands, but to all acts which are linked to statements by a "social obligation". There is no statement that does not present this link, directly or indirectly' (MP 100).

Deleuze and Guattari explain the operation of *mots d'ordre* by relating them to the Stoic theory of incorporeals. The Stoics, it will be recalled (Chapter 3), divide the world into bodies and incorporeals. Words and things are bodies, but words and things also have an incorporeal dimension – words, that of sense/meaning, and things, that of attributes/events (as opposed to qualities, which are bodies). What links words and things is the inseparable relation between sense and attributes: sense is the expressive dimension of words, but that which is expressed is always an attribute of a thing. Language, therefore, may be seen as the vehicle through which an incorporeal attribute is assigned to a thing, as the vehicle of an incorporeal transformation. The function of the *mot d'ordre*, and the fundamental function of language, according to Deleuze and Guattari, is to effect such incorporeal transformations. In a criminal court case, for example, one can describe what happens before and after the verdict in terms of bodies (the bodies of the criminal, property, victim, prison, etc.), 'but the transformation of the accused into the guilty individual is a pure, instantaneous act or incorporeal attribute, which is the expressed element [*l'exprimé*] of the sentence of the judge' (MP 102). Love may also be described exclusively in terms of bodies, but the statement 'I love you' expresses an incorporeal attribute of those bodies. The transubstantiation of bread and wine, the awarding of a degree, the passage of a law, the arrival at one's majority – all are incorporeal transformations of bodies effected through language.

> In an airplane hijacking, the threat of the pirate who brandishes a revolver is obviously an action, as is the execution of hostages, if this should take place. But the transformation of passengers into hostages, and of the airplane-body into a prison-body, is an instantaneous incorporeal transformation, a *mass-media act*, in the sense that the English speak of a *speech-act*. (MP 103)

Although specific individuals may enunciate such transformations, the transformations themselves, the *mots d'ordre*, are social in origin. They are part of a 'collective arrangement of enunciation', or 'regime of signs', which may be defined as 'the set of *incorporeal transformations* which are in effect in a given society, and which *are attributed* to the bodies of that society' (MP 102). One can see, now, why Deleuze and Guattari do not analyse signs or language in terms of words and things, or signifiers and signifieds, but in terms of an expression-level of regimes of signs, or *acts* which produce incorporeal transformations through signs, and a content-level of social technological machines, which shape bodies. In their analysis of Foucault's *Discipline and Punish*, they identify as expression the collection of judgements, verdicts, evaluations and classifications which transform bodies through the discourse of delinquency; and as content, the prison-machine, a specific collection of functioning, heterogeneous entities. In their reading of Kafka, they similarly differentiate expression and content, identifying various regimes of signs, each 'with its incorporeal transformations, its acts, its death sentences and its verdicts, its trials, its "law"'; and various machines, such as 'the castle-machine' or 'the tribunal-machine', each 'with its pieces, its wheels and gears, its processes, its entangled, conjoined, disjoined bodies' (MP 112). *Mots d'ordre* are expressed in words, but they are not reducible to words. The same expression may put into effect different *mots d'ordre*, and various

138

expressions, even in different languages, may perform the same incorporeal transformation of things. Words, of course, as vehicles of incorporeal transformations, are clearly related to things; but they do not represent things so much as they intervene in them, 'in order to anticipate them, reverse them, slow them down or speed them up, detach them or reunite them, cut them up differently' (MP 110). An analysis of expression (regimes of signs) and content (social technological machines) therefore must consider actual discourse and the interrelationship between words and things, but without reducing incorporeal transformations to signifiers or social machines to semiotic constructs.

In Plateau 5, '587 B.C. – 70 A.D. – On a Few Regimes of Signs', Deleuze and Guattari offer an 'arbitrarily limited' (MP 149) classification of regimes of signs, isolating a *pre-signifying* regime, typical of primitive societies (roughly as described in *Anti-Oedipus*), a *counter-signifying* regime, characteristic of nomadic warrior tribes (portrayed more fully in Plateau 12), a *signifying* regime, found in despotic societies, and a *post-signifying* regime, exemplified in authoritarian, 'passionate' social formations. What is meant by a 'regime of signs' is perhaps best indicated through a brief consideration of the signifying and the post-signifying regimes of signs, the two regimes discussed in greatest detail in Plateau 5.

The signifying regime resembles in many ways the order of despotic representation presented in *Anti-Oedipus*. This regime of signs 'has a simple general formula: the sign refers to the sign, and refers only to the sign *ad infinitum*' (MP 141). Signs emanate from the despot, the master signifier, in a spiral of ever-widening circles (one for each class, sex, profession, sect, club, and so on), the spiral of infinite signification itself requiring a mechanism of continuous interpretation to ensure the interrelation of the various circles and their dependence on the despotic centre. A despot/god at the centre, a contiguous temple in which the priests reveal the despot's will, a network of priest-bureaucrats interpreting the holy pronouncements within the various circles, and a city or state wall which marks the limits of signification – such is the map of the signifying semiotic.

In *Anti-Oedipus*, Deleuze and Guattari state that the despotic sign, which may be thought of as a decoded or deterritorialized primitive sign, is reterritorialized in the body of the despot. In *Mille Plateaux*, they specify that the despot's body is above all a *face*, 'which is itself a complete body: it is like the body of the center of signification, on which are attached all the deterritorialized signs, and it marks the limit of their deterritorialization' (MP 144). Expression and content, in the great anthropomorphic stratum, are allied to the development of the opposition of face-language and hand-tool, and the more dominant the linguistic pole is in a given regime of signs, the more important the face becomes as a centre of codification. Much has been written about infant–mother communication via facial expressions, about facial cues in social interaction, and about the function of the standardized 'talking head' on television news programmes and documentaries. Deleuze and Guattari, however, do not agree with most analysts of facial signs that facial expressions constitute a universal semiotics; rather, they contend that the face functions differently in various regimes of signs. In despotic regimes, 'the signifier is always "face-ified" [*visagéifié*]' (MP 145), tied implicitly to the approving or disapproving face, the benignant smile or the hostile frown, of the centralized social authority and its *mots d'ordre*. Primitives, by contrast, do not relate all signs to the face, but to various body parts, to animals, to plants, places, or things. Among primitives, 'even masks assure the appurtenance of the head to the body rather than raising it to the level of a face' (MP 216).[13] The limit of despotic signification, therefore, is also the limit of despotic facial coding. Opposed to the face of the despot is the 'counter-body' (MP 145) of the scapegoat, in its double guise as faceless torture victim, executed at the limits of the city wall, and as animal wanderer, expelled from the community and driven into the desert waste. Both aspects of the scapegoat are found in Oedipus, who defiles the face in the name of the law and who then pursues the line of flight of nomadic exile.

The scapegoat's exile may trace a path of absolute deterritorialization, of a facial decoding, a becoming-animal and a pure nomadism. But it may also inaugurate another regime of signs, the post-signifying, authoritarian, 'passionate' [*passionnel*] regime, with its own form of 'faceness', one of subjectification [*subjectivation*] rather than signification. The Jews in their exodus from Egypt engaged such a regime of signs, embracing the interdicted line of flight from despotic Egypt and converting the negative path of the scapegoat into a positive course of divine destiny. In the post-signifying regime, signs become detached from the despotic centre and form bundles of migrant, drifting signs, the ark, for example, serving as 'a little packet of signs that the people carry along with themselves' (MP 153). In the relationship between God and the prophet one may discern the major traits of the post-signifying regime. The prophet is not a despotic priest who interprets God's word, but someone who is possessed and overwhelmed by God, whose relationship with God is 'passionate and authoritarian rather than despotic and signifying'. The prophet 'takes the vanguard and detects the powers of the future instead of applying the powers of the present and past' (MP 156). Between the prophet and God emerges a non-despotic faceness, one in which 'God turns away that face which no one may see' and the prophet 'turns away his own, stricken with a veritable fear of God'. Thus, 'the faces which turn aside and become profiles replace the radiating full-face visage' (MP 154) of the despot.[14] God and prophet also enter into a relationship of mutual betrayal, one that is inaugurated by Cain, who turns from God, and from whom God turns, but who is preserved from death by God's mark of permanent, but postponed condemnation. (Cain's relationship with the Law, therefore, is one of 'indefinite postponement', as described by Titorelli in *The Trial*.) Jonah continues this relationship, doing God's will by fleeing God,[15] and Jesus

> pushes this system of treason to the universal: betraying the God of the Jews, betraying the Jews, betrayed by God (why hast thou forsaken me?), betrayed by Judas, the true man. He takes the evil upon himself, but the Jews who kill him also take the evil upon themselves. (MP 155)

The principal traits of the post-signifying regime, then, are 'a double turning-away, betrayal [and] existence in a stay of execution [*en sursis*, the "indefinite postponement" of *The Trial*]' (MP 161). The map of this regime may be envisioned, not as a spiral emanating from a despotic centre and ending at a wall, but as a straight line divided into finite segments. The line commences with a 'point of subjectification', proceeds through a point indicating the position of the 'speaking subject' [*sujet d'énonciation* – the actual person speaking], and reaches the end of a segment with a point marking the 'subject of speech' [*sujet d'énoncé* – the pronoun 'I', for example, whereby a person refers to himself or herself within his or her discourse]. The point of subjectification may be 'anything whatever' (MP 161), God in the case of the Jews, food in the case of the anorexic, a shoe in the case of a fetishist, the beloved in the case of a lover. From the point of subjectification

> the speaking subject [*sujet d'énonciation*] is derived, as a function of a mental reality determined by this point. And from the speaking subject in turn is derived a subject of speech [*sujet*

141

d'énoncé], that is, a subject situated in statements that conform
to a dominant reality. (MP 162)

In the Jews' post-signifying regime, God corresponds to the point
of subjectification, the prophets to the speaking subject, and the
people to the subject of speech. When Moses ascends Mount Sinai,
for example, God serves as a point of subjectification, the principle
from which issues a specific mental reality and a corresponding
type and locus of subjectivity (Moses turning his face away from
the overwhelming but hidden face of God). Moses occupies the
position of the speaking subject, the voice through which God
speaks, and the people (who introduce the motif of betrayal) function as the subject of that discourse, the 'subject situated in
statements that conform to a dominant reality'.

What is crucial in the post-signifying regime is the doubling of
the subject, in the speaking subject and the subject of speech, and
the reduction of the one to the other. The speaking subject reveals
a mental reality, the subject of speech a dominant reality, and the
post-signifying regime ensures the conformity of mental and
dominant reality via an internal process of subjection. 'There is no
longer any need for a transcendent center of power, but instead for
an immanent power which merges with the "real", and which
proceeds via normalization' (MP 162). This internal process of
subjection is best illustrated, not through the Old Testament, but
through what Deleuze and Guattari refer to as 'Christian, or so-
called modern, philosophy' (MP 160), as inaugurated by Descartes
and developed by Kant. For Descartes, the point of subjectification
is 'the idea of the infinite'; the speaking subject is the *cogito*, 'which
is only conceived following a line of deterritorialization represented
by methodical doubt'; and the subject of speech is 'the union of
soul and body . . . which will be guaranteed in a complex fashion
by the cogito, and which will effect the necessary reterritorializa-
tions' (MP 160). The *cogito* initially is at one with a deterritorializing doubt, but it inevitably becomes identified with a specific
existence (*ergo sum*) and implicitly with a dominant reality (Cartesian philosophy always eventuating in the discovery of basically
orthodox truths). In this doubled subject of *cogito* and *sum* one finds
the rudiments of the 'paradox of the legislator-subject', so important in Kantian philosophy, the subject 'as *cause* of statements of
which it itself is a part in another of its forms' (MP 162). In
Descartes and Kant, the legislator-subject 'replaces the despotic
signifier: the more you obey the statements of dominant reality, the

more you command as speaking subject within mental reality, for finally you only obey yourself . . .. A new form of slavery has been invented, that of being a slave to oneself, or that of ''pure'' reason, the Cogito' (MP 162).

One can perhaps see now how the Old Testament regime of signs may be assimilated to that of Cartesian and Kantian philosophy. The prophet, as deterritorialized speaking subject in a delirious relation with God, enunciates the future of the subject of speech (the people), but always in conformity with a dominant reality. Moses is legislator, but legislator of himself as well as the people, and the law he pronounces reinforces a dominant order rather than disclosing new lines of flight. One can also see how psychoanalysis may be approached in terms of a post-signifying regime of signs. The psychoanalyst functions as the ideal point of subjectification, the patient both as speaking subject and as subject of speech. The patient freely analyses himself or herself, but perpetually institutes a normalizing alignment of the analysing subject and the analysed subject that ensures the analysand's subjection to a dominant reality. At each point that the speaking subject and the subject of speech become identified, a segment of the straight line of the post-signifying regime is terminated. The line, however, does not stop, for new segments continually succeed the old. The *cogito* is 'always to be recommenced as a trial [*procès*], with the possibility of betrayal which haunts it, God the deceiver or the evil Spirit' (MP 160). Each prophet is followed by another, the word of God always being subsumed within a dominant tradition. The analysand's cure proceeds by stages, but stages which are ultimately interminable. And within this delirious regime a new priesthood and a new bureaucracy take form, ones that induce a proper self-subjugation, for example by training the *cogito* to find itself in a dominant reality, by guiding the prophets in the enunciation of an orthodox tradition, or by helping the analysand to identify with a 'healthy ego'.

It should be evident that Deleuze and Guattari do not mean by 'regime of signs' simply a macro-political social organization, such as a state or a kinship system. The post-signifying regime of signs may be isolated in the history of Judaism, but also in the Protestant Reformation, psychoanalysis, Clérambault's 'passionate delirium', anorexia, fetishism, or medieval Courtly Love (for example in the story of Tristan and Iseult). Likewise, the signifying, despotic regime may be exemplified in a political organization, a family, or a particular form of paranoia. Deleuze and Guattari offer,

143

therefore, no history of regimes of signs, no analysis of their invention, development, or evolution, but instead 'maps of regimes of signs: we can turn them around, retain this or that coordinate, this or that dimension, and we will have a social formation, a pathological delirium, or a historical event . . . etc.' (MP 149–50). It should also be clear that there are no pure examples of a specific regime of signs, but only instances in which a given regime is more dominant than others. Psychoanalysis, particularly in its Lacanian formulation, partakes of a despotic regime of signs, but it manifests as well the presence of a post-signifying regime. The Old Testament history of the Hebrew people is a primary record of a post-signifying regime of signs, but it also testifies to the presence of a counter-signifying, nomadic regime (particularly in its military episodes) and a despotic regime (in the thematics of the quest for a king and a permanent temple).

Every social semiotic, then, is a mixture of regimes of signs. None the less, Deleuze and Guattari insist that the various regimes be carefully differentiated, since their basic modes of operation are incommensurable. The despotic, signifying regime and the post-signifying regime, for example, are intertwined throughout much of Judaeo-Christian history, but they function according to different principles. The despotic regime is characterized by a relative deterritorialization of signs (for example a decoding of primitive, territorial signs) and a reterritorialization of signs within ever-widening circles of signification and interpretation via a centralized, totalizing, transcendent power. The post-signifying regime, by contrast, commences with a point of subjectification, which absolutely deterritorializes all signs by serving as the focus of a passionate, delirious fixation (God for the prophet, the idea of the infinite for the *cogito*, food for the anorexic, the beloved for the lover); those signs, however, are reterritorialized through the immanent, self-subjugation of the speaking subject (mental reality) to the subject of speech (dominant reality). Unlike the despotic regime, which operates via a paranoiac assimilation of signs within a giant system, the post-signifying regime functions in discrete, finite segments, a confrontation with an external point of fixation occasioning a local self-subjugation, succeeded by another such confrontation, and so on. The despotic face is ever-visible, the ultimate embodiment of all codes, whereas the pair of post-signifying faces are hidden and yet all-absorbing, faces that turn away but also serve as black holes, abysses into which all signs gravitate. The turning-away constitutes a mutual betrayal, but a complicit betrayal that solidifies a relationship of perpetual trial-without-execution between the speaking subject and the point of subjectification (Cain and God, Descartes and the evil spirit/deceiving God, but also the anorexic who betrays food and who is betrayed by food, with its hidden worms and germs, or Tristan and Iseult, continual betrayers of one another, as well as of King Mark). The prophet, the *cogito*, the anorexic, and the lover, in sum, are overwhelmed and disoriented by God, the idea of the infinite, food, or the beloved; but rather than enter into a process of unlimited deterritorialization, each falls into the vortex of an obsession – divine, rational, alimentary or passionate – which reinforces a dominant reality, whether religio-social, philosophical, nutritive or erotic.

Language and the abstract machine

Deleuze and Guattari, as we have seen, find in Kafka's works an exemplary articulation of the functioning and interaction of two kinds of machinic arrangements, the expression-arrangements of regimes of signs and the content-arrangements of social-technological machines. They also discern in Kafka illuminating instances of the signifying and post-signifying regimes of signs, aligning Titorelli's 'ostensible acquittal' and 'indefinite postponement' in *The Trial*, for example, with a circular, despotic regime and a segmentary, passionate regime of signs (MP 154–5).[16] Yet they do not regard Kafka simply as a sociologist or historian who minutely describes the technological and semiotic machines around him, but as a writer who experiments with and creates through the real without representing it. To understand how such experimentation and creation are possible within language, one must relate language not only to the immanent pragmatics of regimes of signs, but also to the immanent yet virtual force of abstract machines.

Deleuze and Guattari contend that a language should not be characterized 'by its constants and its homogeneity, but instead by a variability which has the characteristics of being immanent, continuous, and regulated in a quite specific way' (MP 118–19). Consider, for example, various pronunciations of a given word. The 'standard' pronunciation of a word is not a constant against which regional, class, or occupational variations are measured, but itself a variable in a particular relation to other variables. 'Dog', 'dawg' and 'dag', for instance, may serve as rough approximations of three possible pronunciations of the word *dog*, three variables,

145

one of which is perhaps statistically more common and more prestigious than the others, but none of which is stable or fixed. Nor are the three versions of 'dog' simply instances of *parole* in relation to a stable *langue*, three mutable performances of an ideal phonemic unit. Rather, the three variables are internal to the language, whose structure should be described in terms of abstract 'lines of variation' rather than constants. In this particular case, the 'line of variation' passes through 'dog', 'dawg', 'dag' and every other pronunciation of the word in English. This line of variation 'is virtual, that is, real without being actual' (MP 119); all pronunciations of *dog*, in this sense, are virtually present within each individual pronunciation of the word. Further, the line of variation includes possible but as yet unrealized pronunciations of *dog*, future variables that may or may not come into existence. The line of variation, in this case, is a kind of continuum of possible *dogs*, 'do-aw-a-au-uag', a line of continuous variation along which are distributed the several standard, regional, deviant, and mutant pronunciations of the word. It is the sum of such lines of variation that comprises the 'abstract machine' of a given language, and it is the collection of 'concrete machines' of a regime of signs that determines which variables will be standard and which will not.

Abstract lines of continuous variation affect all aspects of a language, grammatical, syntactic, and semantic as well as phonological. The existence of a semantic line of variation is particularly important to note, for it necessitates the inclusion of contextual variables within semantics (just as the phonological line of variation necessitates the inclusion of performance variables within phonology). 'Take the single statement, "I swear!" It is not the same statement when spoken by a child before its father, by a lover before the beloved, or by a witness before the court' (MP 119). 'I swear!', in other words, is not a linguistic constant, a single semantic unit with a stable core of meaning that occurs in three different situations. Rather, each 'I swear' is a variable through which a virtual line of variation passes, the three enunciations of 'I swear!' gaining their apparent synonymity from the control and regulation of those variables by an intralinguistic power structure, i.e. by a regime of signs. One can see, then, that to speak of 'a language', such as English, as a single entity is itself misleading, for every language consists of a plurality of languages, a multiplicity of semantic worlds.

In a single day, an individual passes constantly from one language to another. By turns, he speaks as 'a father must speak', then as a boss; to his beloved, he speaks in a puerile language; while falling asleep he sinks into an oneiric discourse, and abruptly returns to a professional language when the telephone rings. (MP 119)

A statement has a certain stability from situation to situation, and a semantic field of parental, professional, or amorous discourse a certain coherence, yet not because of invariants, which anchor a language, but because of 'the line of continuous variation which traverses it' (MP 119).

A major usage of a language restricts linguistic variation, isolates certain variables, and assigns them the function of constants, whereas a minor usage of a language (as noted in Chapter 5) puts linguistic variables into continuous variation. One encounters a minor usage of a language in many marginal languages and minority dialects, but above all in the modern writers and artists whom Deleuze and Guattari admire – Kafka, Beckett, Godard and Gherasim Luca, among others. Such writers make an atypical use of language, not in order to deviate from a norm, but in order to engage the virtual line of variation, which is immanent within linguistic variables. When e.e. cummings writes 'they went their came', he does not simply combine the standard phrases 'they went as they came, they went their way, they came and went', etc., but rather sets the standard phrases in disequilibrium by availing himself, through the atypical phrase, of a line of variation.

> The atypical expression constitutes a point of deterritorialization of language; it plays the role of a *tensor*, that is, it makes the language tend toward a limit of its elements, forms or notions, toward a before or a beyond of language. (MP 126)

The conjunction 'and', for example, can serve as a tensor if used as a sort of zero-degree conjunction, in which case 'and' becomes 'less a conjunction than an atypical expression of all possible conjunctions which it puts into continuous variation' (MP 126). When Kafka introduces the motif of the anomalous trial in his works, he does not merely extrapolate an atypical content-form from a standard model, but finds the line of variation that passes through 'the trial of the father, in the family; the engagement trial, in the hotel; the trial before the tribunal' (MP 120). Out of the boy's implicit 'I swear!' before his father, the betrothed's 'I swear!'

to his fiancée, the defendant's 'I swear!' before the court, Kafka 'constructs the *continuum* of I swear!' (MP 119), a continuum of *mots d'ordre* and their various linguistic expressions, which play through a regime of signs.

When writers invent, they both experiment with something that is already 'there' and create something new, for they invent at the level of the abstract machine, which exists yet also must be constructed. 'The lines of change or creation' in a language 'are part of the abstract machine, fully and directly' (MP 125), and in one sense writers simply experiment with and extend the lines of variation already present within collective arrangements of enunciation. Those lines of variation, however, are virtual and potential rather than actual, and they dictate no single, determinate course of development, but many possible directions of metamorphosis. An abstract machine

> is not an infrastructure in the last instance, any more than it is a transcendent Idea in a supreme instance. Rather, it has a pilot role. An abstract or diagrammatic machine does not function in order to represent something, even something real, but it constructs a real to come, a new type of reality. It is thus not outside history, but rather always 'ahead' of history, at each moment that it constitutes points of creation or potentiality. (MP 177)

Paradoxically, writers must simultaneously 'follow' the lines of variation of the abstract machine, immanent within collective discourse, and 'produce' the abstract machine, actualizing a specific line of flight, a single 'real to come' (such as Kafka does when he discloses 'the diabolical powers of the future'). We must remember, however, that at the level of the abstract machine, it is imprecise to speak any longer of linguistic experimentation or invention, for the abstract machine is made up of the unformed matter and anonymous forces of a plane of consistency, hecceities of particles and diagrams of force. At this level,

> there is no longer any assignable distinction at all between content and expression; . . . the alimentary regimen of Nietzsche, of Proust or of Kafka is a writing, and they understand it as such; to eat–to speak, to write–to love, never do you seize one flux all by itself. (D 145)

First and last, then, is the plane of consistency, the plane of unformed matter and anonymous forces from which the various strata of expression and content are formed. In the physico-chemical stratum, expression and content correspond to the molar and molecular levels of organization; in the organic stratum, to the linear sequence of DNA and the corresponding sequence of amino acids; and in the anthropomorphic stratum, to rcgimes of signs and social-technological machines. Yet throughout these strata one finds an immanent plane of consistency, whether it be construed as the great plane of Nature or a specific, singular plane of invention and experimentation. Language has an important function within the anthropomorphic stratum, but only as a component of a semiotic machine, i.e. a collective arrangement of enunciation or regime of signs. Yet an abstract machine, which produces a plane of consistency, is also immanent within every regime of signs, and hence within language as well. The plane of consistency is a plane of absolute deterritorialization, the various strata defined by their degree of relative deterritorialization and reterritorialization. Language produces a high level of deterritorialization, even though it enforces a parallel reterritorialization within a regime of signs, linguistic and semiotic regularities instituting *mots d'ordre*, those incorporeal transformations of bodies that allocate subjects and signs their positions within an order of social obligation. *Mots d'ordre* intervene in bodies, and social-technological machines and regimes of signs assemble in complex alignments of power. None the less, immanent within every power structure, within every regime of signs and every language, are the lines of continuous variation of the abstract machine and the plane of consistency. It is on this plane that all invention, all experimentation, and all creation take place. An artisan works in wood, a writer in words, a philosopher in concepts, a scientist in atomic particles, an inventor in metal and plastic, but all follow and produce the lines of variation of the plane of consistency. Within the anthropomorphic stratum, the plane of consistency is revealed as a mechanosphere, an amalgam of the physical and the mental, the natural and the artificial. The unformed matter of this plane of consistency contains equally and indifferently fluxes of words, plants, ideas, minerals, dreams, and animals, shifting configurations of particles and alignments of force, and it is on this plane that a non-organic life emerges, the life of the abstract, immanent, virtual lines of variation of all experimentation, creation, and becoming.

Epilogue

In this study, I have endeavoured to outline two bodies of thought: Deleuze's philosophy of difference, and Deleuze–Guattari's schizoanalytic philosophy of desiring-production. Fundamental to both bodies of thought is a single, Nietzschean conception of the cosmos as the ceaseless becoming of a multiplicity of interconnected forces. That multiplicity admits of no stable entities but only of 'dynamic quanta', and hence must be understood in terms of difference rather than identity. In *Nietzsche and Philosophy* Deleuze isolates within this cosmos of forces a (primarily) spatial dimension of difference and the will to power, and a temporal dimension of becoming and the eternal return. The will to power, which determines the relations between forces, is the active difference between forces that affirms itself (in its positive guise) by transforming forces and transforming itself (and thus, as a power of metamorphosis, the will to power partakes of both the spatial and temporal dimensions). The eternal return is the temporal synthesis of becoming, which brings about a coexistence of past, present, and future (since without that synthesis the present would never be able to 'pass'). The will to power, as relational power of metamorphosis, is the principle that informs the synthesis of the eternal return.

In Deleuze's philosophy of difference, the will to power and the eternal return are in a sense 'extracted' from the world of forces and assigned to a separate and opposing realm of difference. In *The Logic of Meaning* this opposition of Nietzschean forces and the will to power/eternal return is formulated in terms of the Stoic dichotomy of bodies and incorporeals. Stoic bodies might not seem to correspond directly to Nietzschean forces, but by 'bodies' Deleuze means 'bodies without surfaces', i.e. undifferentiated bodies forming a single corporeal plenum – not unlike Nietzsche's multiplicity of interfused 'dynamic quanta'. If one recalls that in *Nietzsche and Philosophy* Deleuze defines a body as a particular configuration of forces with certain affective powers (power of affecting other forces and power of being affected), one can see that Stoic bodies, which form the domain of action (bodies affecting bodies) and passion (bodies affected by other bodies), may be thought of as combinations of Nietzschean forces. Incorporeals, by contrast, comprise a metaphysical surface, or transcendental field, of self-differentiating differences (will to power) which 'insist' or 'subsist' in the temporal dimension of *aion* (eternal return).

Deleuze's major concern in his philosophy of difference is to describe this metaphysical surface of incorporeals, which he maps in terms of structures. Each structure consists of a nomadic distribution of a minimum of two series of singular points. Each singular point delineates a virtual domain of possible actualizations of the structure. The singular point as locus of individuation is analogous to a metastable state of unequally distributed energy in a substance (such as molten metal before it conforms to the shape of a mould). That metastable state, however, must be thought of as virtual rather than actual, as a self-differentiating difference that 'explicates' itself in individualized forms and remains 'implicated' within particular entities as a disguised difference. The time of these singular points (the time of the virtual as opposed to the actual) is that of an unstable past and future with no present, ceaselessly expanding toward an infinite past and future and simultaneously contracting toward an elusive present. This is the time of the eternal return. In *Nietzsche and Philosophy* Deleuze describes the eternal return simply as the coexistence of past, present, and future, but in *Difference and Repetition* he specifies that the eternal return is the third of three passive syntheses of time, the first providing the *founding* of time (the present that 'passes' because of the coexistence of past, present and future), the second establishing the *foundation* of time (the virtual past which coexists with the present but only as a past that has never been present), and the third introducing the *unfounding* of time (the pure and empty form of time, in which time itself unfolds).

In Deleuze's philosophy of difference, then, Nietzschean forces become bodies, and the will to power and the eternal return become incorporeal singular points and the pure and empty form of time. Yet Deleuze does not entirely isolate forces from the will to power/eternal return, for incorporeals are immanent within bodies and the two dimensions are always manifested together in ordinary experience. Nor does the dualism of bodies and incorporeals correspond to a conventional distinction between the real and the ideal. Both bodies and incorporeals comprise alien, non-rational domains that defy common-sense understanding. What leads Deleuze to distinguish between bodies and incorporeals, between forces and the will to power/eternal return, is his desire to undermine what he often refers to as the three metaphysical certainties of God, the self (*le moi*) and the world (e.g. LS 11). He subverts idealism and the divine, not by denying the existence of the ideal, but by describing it as immanent rather than transcendent, impassive rather than active (or passive), a realm of effects rather than causes, of problematic differences rather than individuated forms. He overthrows the self by substituting for Kant's transcendental idealism (which preserves the certainties of God by grounding them in man) a transcendental empiricism, which posits 'an impersonal and pre-individual transcendental field' (LS 124) of singular points that 'traverse men, plants and animals independently of the matter of their individuation and the forms of their personalities' (LS 131). Finally, he disrupts the world by problematizing the notion of matter. Rather than countering idealism with a naïve materialism, Deleuze characterizes the world as the interaction of formless forces and incorporeal surfaces and thereby deprives thought of any foundation in an empirically certain *physis* (especially when one considers that this incorporeal surface, immanent within bodies, forms the surface of words as well as things).[1]

In Deleuze and Guattari's collaborative works, the Nietzschean model of the cosmos remains in effect, but with the emphasis on forces, and with no strict separation of forces and the will to power. (The temporal synthesis of the eternal return is not a major theme in their jointly authored writings.) In *Anti-Oedipus*, the world is described as a single 'process of production' embracing man and nature: '*productions of productions*, of actions and passions; *productions of recording processes*, of distributions and of co-ordinates that serve as points of reference; *productions of consumptions*, of sensual pleasures, of anxieties, and of pain' (AO 4, *10*). All is production and process – in other words, an active becoming of positive forces. This single process of production takes place on two levels, the molecular level of desiring-machines and the body without organs, and the molar level of social machines (desiring-machines fixed in a specific social formation) and the *socius*. In *Thousand Plateaus*, these two levels are described as opposing planes, the plane of consistency occupied by the abstract machine, and the plane of organization traced by machinic arrangements (regimes of signs and social-technological machines).

To a certain degree, one might think of the molecular level, or plane of consistency, as a fusion of Stoic bodies and incorporeals, a dimension of bodies/forces possessing many of the attributes of the metaphysical surface of singular points. In *Anti-Oedipus*, Deleuze and Guattari indicate that molecular desiring-production involves impersonal, pre-individual multiplicities that are interrelated through the same connective, conjunctive, and disjunctive syntheses that determine the structures of singular points. In *Thousand Plateaus*, Deleuze and Guattari associate the plane of consistency with the time of *aion* (MP 320) and an unextended, intensive *spatium* (MP 189; compare the transcendental *spatium* of DR 310). The plane of consistency, they state, is crisscrossed by lines of continuous variation, which resemble series of singular points. These lines of continuous variation are abstract lines of virtual possibilities that are actualized in various machinic arrangements. Each machinic arrangement is '*un ensemble de "voisinage"*' (D 125), a collection of heterogeneous terms held together in a topological relation of 'proximity' or 'vicinity', and it is 'the abstract line that traverses [the terms] and makes them function together' (D 126). The virtual, abstract line of continuous variation, in other words, is something like the will to power – a self-differentiating difference that establishes relations of 'proximity' (or difference) between terms. Yet the plane of consistency, besides sharing many of the characteristics of Stoic incorporeals, remains a plane of forces and bodies, each body defined by the longitude of its 'relations of movement and repose, speed and slowness' and the latitude of the 'intensive affects of which it is capable, according to its given power [*pouvoir*] or degree of force [*degré de puissance*]' (MP 318). As Deleuze specifies in *Spinoza*, the longitude of relations of movement and repose involves '*non-formed elements*', and the latitude of affective powers (power of affecting and being affected) involves 'the intensive states of an *anonymous force* [*une force anonyme*]' (S 171).

Thus, the plane of consistency or molecular level is in some ways an elaboration of a Nietzschean physics, which treats the cosmos as the becoming of a multiplicity of forces, differentiable in terms of dynamic quanta rather than stable objects. One might say that the plane of consistency is a sea of molecules, an oceanic fluid or gas (but a liquid or gaseous multiplicity, irreducible to any unity), in which one may discern the movements of non-formed elements and anonymous forces – fluxes, flows, differential speeds, vectors, becomings, and atmospheres.[2] This physical model is not entirely adequate, however, for the plane of consistency, as the dimension of unshaped matter and formless functions, does not admit of any distinction between semiotic and empirical entities, or between mental and material reality. (Thus the *hecceity*, for example may be defined as an 'atmosphere', in the sense both of a particular meteorological configuration and of a given ambience or affective milieu.) Furthermore, the plane of consistency is the *virtual* dimension of difference and the will to power, and as such it thoroughly defies representation within a physical model of actual and manifest forces (even though this virtual dimension remains a dimension of *forces*).

Central to the Deleuzian philosophy of difference and the Deleuzoguattarian philosophy of desiring-production, then, is an extended Nietzschean meditation on the problematic nature of *physis* – both as the becoming of a multiplicity of forces, and as the virtual domain of difference and the will to power/eternal return.[3] That meditation is itself informed by an essentially Nietzschean conception of thought as creation and experimentation, as an exploration of that which escapes common sense, rationality, and representation. In his philosophy of difference, Deleuze embraces Nietzschean perspectivism and aestheticism, arguing that all thought presupposes evaluation and interpretation, and that truth is created rather than discovered. Difference, he claims, necessarily eludes reason, since reason functions in terms of a logic of identity and the Same. The thought of difference, therefore, must begin with a paradoxical element (an intensity or singularity) that defies rational comprehension and throws the mental faculties into disequilibrium. Thereafter, thought must 'explicate' or unfold the world of difference 'implicated' within the paradoxical element, at once inventing a perspectival truth and exploring the virtual domain of difference through an experimentation of the real.

Deleuze and Guattari do not develop these Nietzschean themes at any length in their collaborative efforts (save in their remarks on the plane of consistency as the pre-existing, yet produced, dimension of creation), but from comments Deleuze has made in recent interviews it is evident that this Nietzschean conception of thought informs their work. When asked during a 1980 interview in what genre he would classify *Thousand Plateaus*, whether literature, ethnology, ethology, politics, music, and so on, Deleuze replied, philosophy, nothing but philosophy, in the traditional sense of the word. When one asks what painting is, the response is relatively simple. A painter is someone who creates in the domain of lines and colours (even though lines and colours exist in nature). Likewise a philosopher is someone who creates in the domain of concepts, someone who invents new concepts. There again, thought obviously exists outside philosophy, but not in this special form of concepts. Concepts are singularities which react with ordinary life, with ordinary or everyday fluxes of thought.[4]

Philosophy, like painting, is a form of creation, and in this respect it also resembles science, as Deleuze makes clear in a 1985 interview. 'The true object of science is to create functions; the true object of art is to create sensible aggregates; and the object of philosophy is to create concepts'.[5] Truth is 'not something which pre-exists, which must be discovered', but which

> must be created in each domain . . .. There is no truth which does not 'falsify' preestablished ideas. To say 'truth is a creation' implies that the production of truth passes through a series of operations which work and shape a material, a series of literal falsifications.[6]

In these statements, Deleuze delineates specific modes of thought – philosophy, art, science – and their corresponding objects – concepts, sensible aggregates, and functions – but fundamentally thought remains for him both experimentation and creation, something that works and shapes materials and thereby produces truth. Deleuze here attributes a somewhat different role to singularities than he had earlier, but this does not represent a major change in his thought. In his philosophy of difference, Deleuze identifies singularities with the violent forces that impinge on thought, a view that stresses the experiential–experimental dimension of thought. In the 1980 interview, by contrast, he describes singularities as concepts that react with ordinary fluxes of thought, a view that stresses the creative force of difference within thought and that characterizes a particular philosophic practice. Singularity-concepts are such notions as rhizome, abstract machines, and hecceities,[7] paradoxical elements that induce disequilibrium within ordinary thought, and the basic strategy of Deleuze and Guattari is to invent such paradoxical elements and develop their unsettling consequences across various disciplines. But this is also Deleuze's

155

practice in his philosophy of difference, except that there he operates with yet another array of paradoxical elements – aleatory points, incorporeal surfaces, simulacra, the pure and empty form of time, and so on. Thus, singularities may be approached in terms of their passive reception by thought or their active production within thought, but in either case they remain forces of difference that compel thought to move outside a logic of identity.

My primary object has been to describe in some detail Deleuze's philosophy of difference and Deleuze–Guattari's philosophy of desiring-production, but a word should be said about the relation of their thought to that of other French philosophers of the 1960s and 1970s. Deleuze and Guattari have played important roles in the development of French post-structuralism, and it would be impossible to examine here the many lines of exchange that inter-connect their works and those of their contemporaries (for example Jean-François Lyotard, Jean Baudrillard, Louis Marin, Michel de Certeau, Clément Rosset, Paul Virilio, François Laruelle). But perhaps some idea of their position within post-structuralism may be gained through a brief consideration of the affinities between their writings and those of two much-discussed post-structuralists – Jacques Derrida and Michel Foucault. Although I see Deleuze's early writings and his collaborative efforts with Guattari as inspired by a single complex of Nietzschean themes, I would argue as well that *Anti-Oedipus* marks a shift from a philosophy of difference in many ways compatible with Derridean deconstruction to a philosophy of desiring-production closely allied to Foucault's genealogical study of power.

There are a number of striking parallels between Deleuze's philosophy of difference and Derrida's deconstructive philosophy of *différance*. Both writers are intent on disturbing the neat binary oppositions of Platonic idealism and challenging the Hegelian *Aufhebung* of difference, and both find the inspiration for their exploration of difference in Nietzsche and Heidegger. Derridean *différance* resembles Deleuzian difference on a number of points: it is both spatial and temporal, a differing and a deferral (just as Deleuzian difference is manifested in the will to power and the eternal return); it is never present, but always already has been or is about to be (just as Deleuzian difference inhabits the time of *aion*, the past and future with no present); it is both structural and genetic, the space between terms and the movement of spacing that spaces terms (like Deleuze's active self-differentiating difference); it has no stable identity but differs from itself (what Deleuze and Derrida both call a simulacrum, something that defies the logic of model and copy); and it is neither a word nor a concept, since it does not obey a logic of referentiality or identity (what Deleuze calls an aconceptual concept).[8]

In Chapter 3, I indicated that Deleuze, unlike many deconstructionists, does not reduce thought and experience to language. In this, however, Deleuze and Derrida are at one, for neither is a 'textualist' in the sense that the term is often taken. Derrida is famous for his remark that '*il n'y a pas de hors-texte* (*there is nothing outside the text*)',[9] but he does not mean by this that nothing exists other than networks of signs. In *Positions*, Derrida remarks that 'I have often insisted on the fact that "writing" or the "text" are not reducible *either* to the sensible or visible presence of the graphic or the "literal"'; in *Dissemination*, he states that 'a text is never truly made up of "signs" or "signifiers"'.[10] As Rodolphe Gasché has recently argued, the statement 'there is no extra-text' (Gasché's more satisfactory translation of Derrida's phrase)

> means just this: nothing outside the text can, like a last reason, assume a *fulfilling function* (*Erfüllungsfunktion*) of the textual referrals. It certainly does not permit the conclusion that there is nothing else but texts, or for that matter, that all is language.[11]

As Gasché demonstrates, Derrida's 'text' is pre-ontological (neither absent nor present, neither being nor nothingness) and prelogical (neither logical nor illogical). It is neither intelligible nor sensible, and it is 'in excess of the opposition of sense and non-sense, meaning and the absence of meaning'.[12] It is the domain of 'arche-writing', which is 'the quasitranscendental synthesis that accounts for the necessary corruption of the idealities, or transcendentals of all sorts, by what they are defined against, and at the very moment of their constitution'.[13] The Derridean text, according to this description, is largely the same as Deleuze's metaphysical field of difference – a groundless transcendental ground, which is ontologically and logically problematic (an incorporeal materiality possessing extra-being or ?-being, the dimension of a transcendental *sens* that precedes the distinction between sense and nonsense), and which, as the dimension of the disjunctive synthesis, is the condition of possibility of the various foundational dualisms of traditional philosophy, as well as the condition of their possible subversion.

Despite such clear similarities in their thought, however,

157

Deleuze and Derrida differ from one another in at least three important ways: in their conception of philosophy, in their strategies for deploying problematic concepts, and in their understanding of the role of language in thought.

If the world is not simply language for Derrida, it seems that philosophy for him is an essentially linguistic activity. Derrida describes his practice as that of a 'double writing': he isolates within a philosophic text a given binary opposition (for example speech–writing, presence–absence, inside–outside), which is necessarily a hierarchical and biased dualism, and overturns that hierarchy; but he also reinscribes within the philosophic text a problematic term that disrupts the orderly functioning of that text.[14] In 'Plato's Pharmacy', for example, Derrida overturns the Platonic hierarchy of speech and writing, but he also reinscribes within the Platonic corpus the problematic concept of the *pharmakon*, which already exists in Plato but in a repressed form, thereby communicating a subversive violence throughout that text.[15] The second phase of this double writing (the reinscription of a problematic term) is necessary, Derrida believes, since even if one overturns a given hierarchy, 'the hierarchy of dual oppositions always re-establishes itself'.[16] The task of philosophy, then, is to conduct an interminable analysis and subversion of the binary oppositions that structure discourse – and that constantly reassemble to restructure discourse.

Derrida works out of a hermeneutical tradition, in which philosophy is primarily a form of textual exegesis and commentary. He regards the possibility of simply stepping outside philosophy as illusory, since the binary oppositions of metaphysics permeate language and necessarily reappear within any purportedly alternative discourse. He describes a non-linguistic dimension of *différance*, but only as it emerges within philosophical discourse. *Différance*, the ground of metaphysics and of the problematic concepts that undermine metaphysics, is the logical consequence of a rigorous pursuit of Kant's transcendental critique, the result of an immanent self-critique from within the metaphysical tradition. Given the pervasiveness and resilience of metaphysics, the reinscription of problematic terms within philosophy seems the only reasonable strategy for subverting traditional hierarchical dualisms.

Deleuze, by contrast, shows little interest in the hermeneutical tradition. Instead, he follows the example of Spinoza (at least as Deleuze reads Spinoza), creating intricate systems of concepts that are organized according to a self-consistent logic (or anti-logic) of paradoxes. Deleuze, one might say, is a writer of 'science fiction'.[17] On the one hand, he develops concepts in the manner of a theoretical scientist, who explores the logical consequences of such counter-intuitive notions as black holes, n-dimensional space, particle-waves, etc. On the other, he constructs imaginary worlds or alternative universes in the manner of a Borges or a Le Guin, showing what reality would be like if it were made up of simulacra, virtual singularities and anonymous forces, or formless bodies and incorporeal surfaces. He invents paradoxical concepts, which resemble such Derridean notions as *différance*, *pharmakon*, or originary trace, but rather than reinscribe these concepts within traditional texts, he uses them as the building blocks of an alternative world. (It is for this reason that Deleuze's works seem less like logical arguments than extended definitions of terms.) Within this alternative cosmos, he isolates an incorporeal dimension of difference, and he argues for the necessity of such a dimension within any philosophy of language or theory of the proposition; but he asserts as well that difference manifests itself in sub-representative experience (for instance, Proustian reminiscence or Masochian fantasy) and that non-discursive bodies/forces coexist and interact with the incorporeal surface of difference.

Thus Deleuze does not, like Derrida, treat philosophy primarily as a form of exegesis, nor does he believe that thought must remain within traditional philosophic discourse and forever do battle with metaphysics. Some might argue that Deleuze does not question the status of his own discourse, and hence does not confront the inescapable problem of language,[18] but he would respond, I believe, that he is simply adopting a fiction that helps him to avoid some of the pitfalls of deconstruction and to open up other areas of inquiry. If philosophy is restricted to textual commentary, the non-discursive can only emerge within discourse (*différance* as groundless ground of discourse), and hence only as a function of discourse – a position that easily leads to a linguistic or semiotic idealism (everything is text). And if thought must engage in an endless struggle with metaphysical dualisms, it becomes trapped in an agonistic, oppositional, and reactive relationship that *perpetuates* as well as subverts the dualisms it fights. The argument that language and metaphysics are the unavoidable and insurmountable problems of philosophy is itself a fiction (unless, contrary to its stated principles, deconstruction is a new foundationalism), and it is a fiction that often serves a disciplinary function (you *cannot* think outside of philosophy). What Deleuze does is simply create a different fiction that allows him to situate language within a larger non-discursive field of difference and forces.

In his philosophy of difference, Deleuze does not restrict his investigations to language and its groundless ground, yet neither does he examine directly the relationship between discourse and forces. By adhering to a dualism of incorporeal difference and formless forces, he maintains an uneasy alliance with deconstruction, sequestering the (deconstructive) play of difference that permeates rational discourse from the orgasmic play of word-shards and sonic blocks that takes place within the schizophrenic field of body-forces. In Deleuze and Guattari's philosophy of desiring-production, however, the question of the relation of forces to language and signs comes to the fore. By adopting a monism of forces, they are able to explore the materiality of signs and open up an investigation of semiosis as a mode of action. In this regard, Deleuze and Guattari are quite close to the Foucault of *Discipline and Punish* (1975).

Like Foucault, Deleuze and Guattari treat semiosis as practice, as one force among many in a field of power (or, in Deleuze and Guattari's terms, in a field of restricted desiring-production). In *Anti-Oedipus*, Deleuze and Guattari offer a history of representation that is essentially a history of signs as functional components of the social formations that regulate the interrelation of bodies and forces. As I argued in Chapter 4, the power configurations of Deleuze and Guattari's despotic and capitalist machines are broadly similar to those manifested in what Foucault identifies as the *ancien régime's* theatre of punishment and the modern carceral machine of discipline. In *Thousand Plateaus*, Deleuze and Guattari elaborate on this history of representation by expanding their typology of signifying systems (or regimes of signs). They also develop the theoretical groundwork of a pragmatics-oriented linguistics and a material, 'machinic' semiotics, which, among other things, aptly formalizes the detailed analyses that Foucault conducts in his history of the modern prison. The discourse of delinquency traced by Foucault they frame in terms of *mots d'ordre*, speech-acts that impose social obligations by effecting incorporeal transformations of bodies. Foucault's disciplinary technologies of the body they see as indexes of social-technological machines that shape human multiplicities. And Foucault's panopticism they label an abstract machine, an immanent cause that organizes and aligns the two heterogeneous and non-homologous strata of social-technological machines and regimes of signs.[19]

Epilogue

In *Anti-Oedipus*, Deleuze and Guattari playfully speak of their history of representation as a 'universal history', and in *Thousand Plateaus* they often present their theoretical categories as if they were apodictic truths, but it is clear that they regard these schemas as fictions, i.e. as models that have no claim to absolute certainty. These fictions, however, are not narcissistic diversions, but pragmatic interventions in specific historical situations. In essence, Deleuze and Guattari view their diverse taxonomies, maps, and models as Foucault does his histories. In his genealogies of power, Foucault writes what Nietzsche called 'effective history' (*wirkliche Historie*), described by Foucault as history 'without constants' that 'affirms knowledge as perspective'. Such history 'is slanted, being a deliberate appraisal, affirmation, or negation; it reaches the lingering poisonous traces in order to prescribe the best antidote'.[20] Effective history is a 'history of the present',[21] as Foucault describes his *Discipline and Punish*, a history that starts from an intolerable present situation and then invents a genealogy of that situation that serves as a means for transforming the present. His genealogies are often abstract and intensely theoretical in their analyses, but as Foucault insists in a discussion he and Deleuze conducted in 1971, theory for him is practice. It 'is an activity conducted alongside those who struggle for power, and not their illumination from a safe distance. A "theory" is the regional system of this struggle'. 'Precisely', Deleuze responded to Foucault's remark.

A theory is exactly like a box of tools . . . . It must be useful. It must function. And not for itself. If no one uses it, beginning with the theoretician himself (who then ceases to be a theoretician), then the theory is worthless or the moment is inappropriate. We don't revise a theory, but construct new ones.[22]

It is in this sense that Deleuze–Guattari and Foucault subscribe to Nietzschean perspectivism and aestheticism – as theorist-practitioners who create fiction-interventions in order to alter present power structures.

To attempt an assessment of the enduring significance of contemporary philosophers is a hazardous business, particularly when they show signs of having a good deal of interesting work ahead of them. One can safely say, however, that over the last few decades Deleuze and Guattari have emerged as major figures in French intellectual life who have occupied a significant position within post-structuralism. *Nietzsche and Philosophy* and *Anti-Oedipus* especially stand as important turning-points in contemporary French thought, the one signalling the advent of the new French Nietzsche, the other the shift away from the sciences of the signifier, in both their structural and Lacanian guise, and towards the analytics of power, desire, and the body. Deleuze's philosophy of difference, besides articulating an inventive version of the Kantian critique, provides an illuminating alternative to Derridean deconstruction by extending the analysis of difference in philosophical discourse to embrace difference in its physical, biological, mathematical, and psychological manifestations. Deleuze and Guattari's philosophy of desiring-production, as well as challenging Lacanian psychoanalysis at its most fundamental level, serves as an important complement to Foucault's genealogical study of power, one that questions the relationship between desire and power and that underlines the radical theoretical implications of Foucault's Nietzschean stance.

The importance of Deleuze and Guattari as philosophers is clear. But what is the primary significance of their work for the study of literature? Given their opposition to all totalizing theories, it is obviously not that of articulating a unified critical methodology or system, even though one may find in their works many methodological strategies and systematically interrelated concepts of great interest. Nor is it that of exemplifying a model critical practice, at least for the majority of British and American literary critics. Deleuze in his studies of Proust and Sacher-Masoch, and Deleuze–Guattari in their analysis of Kafka, do not write as literary critics, but as philosophers who use other writers for the development of their own ideas. In Proust, Deleuze finds a typology of signs and a theory of differential essences. In Sacher-Masoch, he isolates a philosophy of law, fantasy and the imagination. In Kafka, Deleuze and Guattari disclose a rhizomic writing-practice, a mapping of social networks of desire and power that is itself an experimentation on the real. In all these cases Deleuze and Guattari argue polemically, at times deliberately ignoring the claims of competing interpretations or the difficulties posed by texts that resist their theses. In so doing, they are merely observing the conventions of a rather common form of French philosophical writing, but it is doubtful whether many Anglo-American critics will choose to emulate such practices.

It is at the level of critical theory rather than practical criticism, I would argue, that Deleuze and Guattari have the most to offer students of literature. Deleuze and Guattari's assimilation of sociolinguistics and speech-act theory within a pragmatic theory of language opens up interesting prospects for an extended analysis of discourse as political action and the deployment of force. Their treatment of minor languages and literatures suggests intriguing, if problematic, possibilities for exploring the interrelationship of social and artistic marginality and evaluating the political implications of literary modernism and postmodernism. Their history of representation in *Anti-Oedipus* and their subsequent elaboration of various regimes of signs in *Thousand Plateaus* indicate promising lines of development for a study of orality and literacy within larger patterns of social domination. Finally, and I believe, most importantly, their reading of Foucault points the way toward a historical, materialist study of literature within social configurations of power and desire that is based neither on economic determinism (even in the last instance) nor on psychological universals (be they sexual, familial, or structural).

There are, of course, other reasons for reading Deleuze and Guattari. One need not share their basic stance to profit from their works, for the two are consistently inventive thinkers who, even in their most outlandish or perverse moments, offer striking insights into a wide range of issues – the nature of the close-up in film, the relation of nomads to metallurgy and cities, the coexistence of two qualitatively different forms of capital in capitalism, the opposition between sadism and masochism, the importance of the theory of differential calculus for an understanding of structuralism, and so on. Their writing possesses an engaging intensity and a lively, baroque humour that seldom declines into pedantry or tedious self-indulgence. And there is in their work a refreshing absence of rancour and *ressentiment*, a generous spirit of affirmation in their treatment of others' thought, that I find especially commendable. 'My ideal when I write about an author', says Deleuze,

> is to write nothing which might cause him sadness, or if he is dead, which would make him weep in his grave: to think *about* an author on whom one writes. To think about him so strongly that he can no longer be an object and one can no longer identify with him. To avoid the double ignominy of erudition and familiarity. To give back to an author a little of that joy, of that force, of that amorous and political life which he was able to give, to invent. (D 142)

My effort has been to emulate such a spirit in this book.

Notes

Introduction

1 'Theatrum philosophicum', in *Language, Counter-Memory, Practice*, tr. Donald F. Bouchard and Sherry Simon (Ithaca: Cornell University Press, 1977), p. 165.

2 Alexandre Kojève, *Introduction to the Reading of Hegel*, ed. Allan Bloom, tr. James H. Nichols, Jr. (New York: Basic Books, 1969), p. 71. Kojève's *Introduction*, originally published in 1947, consists of notes and transcripts of Kojève's lectures from 1933 to 1939 collected and edited by Raymond Queneau. For an excellent account of Hegelian studies in France during the 1940s and 1950s, see John Heckman's introduction to the English translation of Jean Hyppolite's *Genesis and Structure of Hegel's Phenomenology of Spirit*, tr. Samuel Cherniak and John Heckman (Evanston, Ill.: Northwestern University Press, 1974), pp. xv–xli. On the centrality of Hegel in French philosophy from 1930 to 1975, see Vincent Descombes' admirable *Modern French Philosophy*, tr. L. Scott-Fox and J. M. Harding (Cambridge: Cambridge University Press, 1980), esp. pp. 9–54.

3 Descombes, *Modern French Philosophy*, p. 14.

4 For a particularly clear statement of Deleuze's understanding of structuralism, see 'A quoi reconnaît-on le structuralisme', in *Histoire de la philosophie: Vol. 8. Le XXe Siècle*, ed. François Châtelet (Paris: Hachette, 1973), pp. 299–335. The introductions to French structuralism are legion, but a useful starting-point in the investigation of this complex phenomenon is Terence Hawkes' *Structuralism and Semiotics* (London: Methuen, 1977). A sound introduction to deconstruction is Christopher Norris's *Deconstruction: Theory and Practice* (London: Methuen, 1982), which explains difference/differance. An incisive reading of Derrida is offered by Rodolphe Gasché in *The Tain of the Mirror* (Cambridge, Mass.: Harvard University Press, 1986).

5 Illuminating accounts of post-war French Marxism include Irwin M. Wall's *French Communism in the Era of Stalin* (Westport, Conn.: Greenwood Press, 1983); Michael Kelly, *Modern French Marxism*

(Baltimore: Johns Hopkins University Press, 1982); Ted Benton, *The Rise and Fall of Structural Marxism* (New York: St Martin's, 1984); and Keith A. Reader, *Intellectuals and the Left in France Since 1968* (New York: St Martin's, 1987). Guattari's political activities during the 1950s and 1960s are detailed in 'Raymond et le groupe Hispano', PT 268–75.

6 Guattari's participation in the institutional psychiatry movement is documented in PT, especially pp. 9–97 and 151–72. His theory of the psychological and political dynamics of groups is outlined in Chapter 4.

7 For a lively account of the formation of France's 'psychoanalytic culture' in the 1960s and 1970s, see Sherry Turkle, *Psychoanalytic Politics: Freud's French Revolution* (New York: Basic Books, 1978). See especially pp. 141–63 on the stir created by *Anti-Oedipus*.

8 Guattari has remained active in political and psychiatric movements during the 1970s and 1980s. He has worked with women's rights and gay rights organizations for several years. In 1975, he helped found the Réseau International d'Alternative à la Psychiatrie, of which he remains an active member. In the late 1970s and early 1980s, he became involved in the 'free radio movements' of France and Italy, reform movements opposed to the current state regulation of the number and kinds of radio stations allowed to broadcast in those countries. Recently, despite threats of physical violence, he has come to the defence of several Italian dissidents (most notably Toni Negri) who have been accused, without proof, of involvement with terrorism.

It should be pointed out that Deleuze has also lent his support to several political causes, including the Groupe d'Information sur les Prisons, which Foucault helped organize in 1971. In 1969 he demonstrated his solidarity with educational reform and leftist dissidence by joining the faculty of the University of Paris's experimental campus at Vincennes, where he taught until 1978, when Vincennes' buildings were razed and the faculty transferred to the Saint-Denis campus.

9 *Empirisme et subjectivité: Essai sur la nature humaine selon Hume* (Paris: PUF, 1953), p. 119.

10 *Le Vent Paraclet* (Paris: Gallimard, 1977), pp. 151–2.

11 Proust, *A la recherche du temps perdu*, ed. Pierre Clarac and André Ferré (Paris: Pléiade, 1954), III, 259.

1. Deleuze's Nietzsche

1 James A. Leigh also accords Deleuze a central role in the reception of Nietzsche in France in his useful study, 'Deleuze, Nietzsche and the eternal return', *Philosophy Today* (Fall 1978) : 206–23.

2 Some students of Nietzsche may be disturbed by Deleuze's casual acceptance of *la volonté de puissance* and *l'éternel retour* as adequate translations of *der Wille zur Macht* and *die ewige Wiederkunft* (or *die ewige Wiederkehr*), particularly when Deleuze plays with the French terms without considering the feasibility of such word-play in German. I believe, however, that despite such liberties, his basic interpretation of the will

to power and the eternal return can be reconciled with the denotative and connotative senses of the German expressions.

3 The obvious exceptions are Heidegger and Fink. The relationship between their work on Nietzsche and Deleuze's *Nietzsche and Philosophy* is problematic, however. Heidegger's *Nietzsche* appeared in 1961, but was not translated into French until 1971. Fink's *Nietzsches Philosophie* was published in 1960, but only translated in 1965. Deleuze clearly absorbed Heideggerian insights from works not devoted exclusively to Nietzsche, and he cites Heidegger's essay 'The word of Nietzsche: "God is dead"' in *Nietzsche and Philosophy*. It seems unlikely, however, that Heidegger's and Fink's books on Nietzsche directly influenced Deleuze's reading of Nietzsche. For a discussion of the relationship between Nietzsche, Heidegger, Fink and Deleuze, see Mihai Spariosu's forthcoming *Dionysus Reborn: Play and the Aesthetic Dimension in Modern Philosophical and Scientific Discourse*.

4 Nietzsche distinguishes linguistically between the 'bad' of the master, *schlecht* (bad, inferior, poor), and the 'bad' of the slave, *böse* (evil). Deleuze similarly distinguishes between the master's categories of *le bon* and *le mauvais* and the slave's categories of *le bien* and *le mal*, associating *bon/mauvais* with an immanent ethics of the body and *bien/mal* with a transcendent morality of religion. See the First Essay of *On the Genealogy of Morals*, tr. Walter Kaufmann and R. J. Hollingdale (New York : Vintage, 1967), and N 123, *139*.

5 Deleuze cautions us that 'we must rid ourselves of all "personalist" references' in our understanding of Nietzsche's method of dramatization. When we ask 'who makes this meaning?' the 'who' 'does not refer to an individual, to a person, but rather to an event, that is to the forces in their various relationships in a proposition or a phenomenon, and to the genetic relationship which determines these forces (power)'. The speaker 'is always Dionysus, a mask or a guise of Dionysus, a flash of lightning' (NP, Preface to the English Translation, xi).

6 'Sur la volonté de puissance et l'éternel retour', *Nietzsche, Cahiers de Royaumont* (Paris: Minuit, 1967), p. 278.

7 *The Will to Power*, tr. Walter Kaufmann and R.J. Hollingdale (New York: Vintage, 1968), # 635, p. 339.

8 *The Will to Power*, # 619, pp. 332–3.

9 Deleuze treats Spinoza's conception of the body at length in *Spinoza et le problème de l'expression* (Paris: Minuit, 1968), pp. 197–203, and *Spinoza: Philosophie pratique* (Paris: Minuit, 1981), pp. 27–43, 164–75.

10 *Ecce Homo*, tr. Walter Kaufmann (New York: Vintage, 1969), p. 295.

11 *Nietzsche, Cahiers de Royaumont*, p. 283.

12 ibid., 283.

13 ibid., 284.

14 *Twilight of the Idols*, '"Reason" in Philosophy', section five, in *The Portable Nietzsche*, tr. Walter Kaufmann (Harmondsworth: Penguin, 1954), p. 483.

15 *Philosophy in the Tragic Age of the Greeks*, tr. Marianne Cowan (Chicago: Gateway, 1962), pp. 62, 67.

16 *Thus Spoke Zarathustra*, III, 'The Seven Seals', in *The Portable Nietzsche*, p. 341.
17 *Ecce Homo*, p. 258.
18 *Modern French Philosophy*, tr. L. Scott-Fox and J.M. Harding (Cambridge: Cambridge University Press, 1980), pp. 156–67.
19 Deleuze attempts to counter the oppositional connotations of mastery in several ways: by characterizing domination as the artistic activity of imposing or creating forms (NP 42, *48*); by including affectivity within activity, and hence positing a kind of 'active passivity'; by including reactive forces within active individuals and positing among the activities of such individuals that of 'acting their reactions'; and by conceiving of activity as a force's going to the limit of its capabilities and by suggesting a possible equality of active forces (NP 61, *69*).
20 For an opposing opinion, see Vincent P. Pecora, 'Deleuze's Nietzsche and post-structuralist thought', *SubStance* 48 (1986): 34–50.

2. Proust and Sacher-Masoch

1 *Proust et les signes* (published in 1964 as *Marcel Proust et les signes*, but as *Proust et les signes* in subsequent editions) has undergone a complicated history of publication. A long Second Part was added in the second edition (1970); the Second Part was divided into chapters in the third edition (1975); and a nèw Conclusion was added in the fourth edition (1976). I will limit my discussion in this chapter to the material included in the first edition.
2 Jacques Bersani, in his collection of Proust criticism, *Les Critiques de notre temps et Proust* (Paris: Garnier, 1971), describes Deleuze's first edition of *Proust et les signes* as one of the three most important studies of Proust in the twentieth century. Deleuze provides, he says, 'a series of analyses which entirely renew our interpretation of the *Recherche* – or at least systematize it as no critic has before' (p. 147). He, like many other Proust scholars, is less positive in his evaluation of the material added by Deleuze in subsequent editions of *Proust et les signes*. What sets Deleuze's study apart from most earlier readings of Proust is his disregard of the personal and autobiographical dimension of the *Recherche*. It is for this reason that he also eschews the techniques of psychoanalytic and phenomenological analysis, which are prevalent in so much Proustian criticism. Robert Mauzi provides a useful synopsis of the first edition of *Proust et les signes* in 'Les complexes et les signes', *Critique* 225 (February 1966): 155–71.
  Literary critics have only begun to explore the many provocative insights offered by Deleuze in his study of Sacher-Masoch. See, for example, Gregory L. Ulmer's 'Fetishism in Roland Barthes's Nietzschean phase', *Papers on Language and Literature* 14 (3) (Summer 1978): 333–55, and Frances L. Restuccia's 'Molly in furs: Deleuzean/Masochian masochism in the writing of James Joyce' *Novel* 18 (2) (Winter 1985): 101–16.

Notes

3 *A la recherche du temps perdu*, ed. Pierre Clarac and André Ferré (Paris: Pléiade, 1954) II: 205. Further citations will be given in the text as *Recherche*. All translations from the *Recherche* are my own.

4 *Spinoza et le problème de l'expression* (Paris: Minuit, 1968), p. 12.

5 ibid., p. 12.

6 For a cogent presentation of those aspects of Leibniz's philosophy which are discussed here, see Nicholas Rescher, *The Philosophy of Leibniz* (Englewood Cliffs, N.J.: Prentice-Hall, 1967), chapters 1, 4, 5, 7 and 9.

7 Deleuze treats Bergson's pure past at length in *Le Bergsonisme* (Paris: PUF, 1966): 45–70. See also DR 108–15.

8 See especially Pierre Klossowski, *Sade, mon prochain* (Paris: Seuil, 1947), Maurice Blanchot, *Lautréamont et Sade* (Paris: Minuit, 1949), and Georges Bataille, *La Littérature et le mal* (Paris: Gallimard, 1957) and *L'Erotisme* (Paris: Minuit, 1957). As late as 1975, Gertrud Lenzer could still remark that Sacher-Masoch is a virtually unknown and undiscussed writer ('On masochism: a contribution to the history of a phantasy and its theory', *Signs* 1 (2) (Winter 1975): 277–324). Lenzer, unlike Deleuze (whom she does not mention), sees Sacher-Masoch as a second-rate writer and a contradictory thinker whose works are of interest primarily as examples of masochistic fantasies.

9 On disavowal and fetishism, see Freud, 'Fetishism', *Standard Edition of the Complete Psychological Works of Sigmund Freud* (London: Hogarth Press, 1953–73) XXI: 149–57. For a concise treatment of the concept of disavowal in Freud, see J. Laplanche and J.-B. Pontalis, *The Language of Psycho-Analysis*, tr. Donald Nicholson-Smith (New York: Norton, 1973), pp. 118–21.

10 In his analysis of the relationship of Sade and Masoch to the Kantian law, Deleuze makes use of some of the ideas put forth by Jacques Lacan in 'Kant avec Sade', *Critique* 191 (April 1963), reprinted in *Ecrits* (Paris: Seuil, 1966), pp. 765–90.

11 *The Ego and the Id* (1923), tr. Joan Riviere, rev. James Strachey, in *Standard Edition* XIX: 28–39 and 54.

12 'If this displaceable energy is desexualized libido, it may also be described as *sublimated* energy . . . . If thought-processes in the wider sense are to be included among these displacements, then the activity of thinking is also supplied from the sublimation of erotic motive forces' (*The Ego and the Id*, p. 45).

13 Several French psychoanalysts follow Daniel Lagache in distinguishing between a narcissistic ego/ideal-ego system and a superego/ego-ideal system. See Laplanche and Pontalis, *The Language of Psycho-Analysis*, pp. 144–5 and 201–2.

14 In *Beyond the Pleasure Principle* Freud characterizes the death drive as, among other things, animate matter's drive to return to an original inanimate state. Deleuze here makes use of this idea, but in *Difference and Repetition* he dismisses it as an unfortunate product of Freud's devotion to nineteenth-century mechanistic thought (DR 147–8). Thanatos, he insists, is the pure form of time, against the background of which

emerges Eros; the biological concept of a drive that compels life to return to an inanimate state, therefore, should be treated simply as a myth. Deleuze uses this myth in his *Presentation of Sacher-Masoch* to delineate the paradoxical relationship between the foundation or ground of the pleasure principle (Eros) and the groundless element from which Eros emerges (Thanatos): Eros distinguishes itself from Thanatos, but Thanatos remains tied to Eros. In *Difference and Repetition*, Deleuze compares this relationship between ground and groundless element to that of lightning against the night sky: the lightning distinguishes itself from the black sky, but the sky remains inseparable from the lightning (DR 43). Deleuze associates the pure form of time with death, it would seem, because the self and identity in general are destroyed, and hence 'die', within the ceaseless becoming of Thanatos.

3. The Grand Synthesis

1 Deleuze so characterizes the difference between these two works and his earlier monographs in a third-person biographical statement on the cover of *Dialogues*. *Sens*, the pivotal word of *Logique du sens*, can mean, among other things, 'sense', 'meaning', and 'direction', and Deleuze plays on the word throughout the book in his discussion of sense, nonsense, good sense, common sense, and the *sens unique* ('single direction', but also 'one-way street'). I have rendered *sens* throughout as 'meaning', but the reader should keep in mind these other senses of *sens*.

The best single study of *Difference and Repetition* and *The Logic of Meaning* remains Michel Foucault's 'Theatrum Philosophicum', in *Language, Counter-Memory, Practice*, tr. Donald F. Bouchard and Sherry Simon (Ithaca: Cornell University Press, 1977), pp. 165–96. Also quite useful are Jean-Jacques Lecercle's extended remarks on *The Logic of Meaning* in *Philosophy through the Looking-Glass* (La Salle, Ill.: Open Court, 1985), pp. 86–117. I have found two essays from the special Deleuze issue of *L'Arc* (1972), no. 49, helpful as well: Jean-Noël Vuarnet's 'Métamorphoses de Sophie', pp. 31–8, and Gérard Kaleka, 'Un Hegel philosophiquement barbu', pp. 39–44.

2 For Deleuze's analysis of the simulacrum in Plato, see primarily 'Platon et le simulacre', reprinted as an appendix to *The Logic of Meaning* (LS 292–307). See also DR 82–95, 165–8, 180–6, 340–1, and LS 9–12. Deleuze indicates as well that Derrida's study of the relationship between logos and writing in 'Plato's pharmacy', reprinted in *Dissemination*, tr. Barbara Johnson (Chicago: Chicago University Press, 1981), pp. 61–171, provides several parallel examples of Plato's efforts to distinguish between false simulations and true imitations of the ideal (good and bad writing, good and bad rhetoric, good and bad rulers, good and bad fathers, and so on). Deleuze's 'Platon et le simulacre', it should be pointed out, first appeared in 1967, Derrida's 'La pharmacie de Platon' in 1968.

3 Deleuze provides a thorough analysis of Kant's critical philosophy in

terms of the doctrine of faculties in his *The Critical Philosophy of Kant* (1963), tr. Hugh Tomlinson and Barbara Habberjam (Minneapolis: University of Minnesota Press, 1984).

4 For Deleuze's characterization of Kantian ideas, see DR 219–20 and *The Critical Philosophy of Kant*, p. 32.

5 See especially Lautman's *Essai sur les notions de structure et d'existence en mathématiques* (Paris: Hermann, 1938). Lautman's arguments are much too complex to be adequately summarized here. My effort is simply to make intelligible the basic metaphor that Deleuze uses to describe the idea as problem, even if at the expense of fidelity to the details of Lautman's analysis.

6 Throughout Deleuze's discussion of being in *Difference and Repetition* one hears echoes of Heidegger. For further clarification of Deleuze's understanding of, and objections to, Heidegger, see DR 89–91, 169 and 384.

7 Saussure says, for example, that 'phonemes are above all else opposing, relative, and negative entities', and that 'in language there are only differences *without positive terms*' (*Course in General Linguistics*, tr. Wade Baskin (New York: McGraw Hill, 1959), pp. 119–20). Deleuze suggests that the work of the linguist Gustave Guillaume might provide an alternative conception of phonology in terms of positive differential elements. For an exposition of Guillaume's theory, see Edmond Ortigues, *Le Discours et le symbole* (Paris: Aubier, 1962), pp. 75–167.

8 Gilbert Simondon, *L'Individu et sa genèse physico-biologique* (Paris: PUF, 1964).

9 'The living individual would be in a certain way, at its most primitive levels, a crystal in a nascent state amplifying itself without stabilizing itself' (*L'Individu et sa genèse physico-biologique*, p. 133).

10 Deleuze cites specifically the work of Jacques Paliard, with reference to certain aspects of the work of Maurice Pradines and Jean Piaget. See DR 295–7.

11 Although Deleuze associates the intensity with energy, the concept of energy as intensive quantity 'is a transcendental principle and not a scientific concept' (DR 310), in that the scientific concept of an empirical energy is that of energy as it is explicated in the *extensio*, not the implicate energy of the *spatium*, which, because it escapes common sense, must be thought of as partaking of the transcendental domain of the idea.

12 The imperative, it should be noted, is the *cogitandum*, the transcendental object of thought that the faculty of thought, when disjoined from the other faculties, alone can think. (Deleuze does not differentiate between the Kantian faculties of understanding and reason.)

13 *Critique of Pure Reason*, tr. Norman Kemp Smith (New York: St Martin's, 1929), pp. 168–9.

14 The primary source for Deleuze's reading of the Stoics is Emile Bréhier's *La Théorie des incorporels dans l'ancien stoïcisme* (Paris: Vrin, 1928). Deleuze also makes use of Victor Goldschmidt's *Le Système stoïcien et l'idée de temps* (Paris: Vrin, 1953) in his remarks on the Stoic theory of time.

15 For somewhat differing accounts of the *lekton*, see A.A. Long, 'Language and thought in Stoicism', in *Problems in Stoicism*, ed. Long (London: Athlone, 1971), pp. 75–113, and Andreas Graeser, 'The Stoic theory of meaning', in *The Stoics*, ed. John M. Rist (Berkeley: University of California Press, 1978), pp. 77–100.

16 Bréhier, p. 12.

17 I base my account of Meinong's objective on J.N. Findlay's *Meinong's Theory of Objects and Values*, second edn (Oxford: Clarendon, 1963).

18 'Introduction à l'oeuvre de Marcel Mauss', in Marcel Mauss, *Sociologie et anthropologie* (Paris: PUF, 1950), p. 50.

19 Deleuze takes this opposition of the nomadic and the sedentary, so crucial in much of his later work, from E. Laroche's *Histoire de la racine NEM – en grec ancien* (Paris: Klincksieck, 1949).

20 Foucault, 'Theatrum philosophicum', p. 169.

4. Anti-Oedipus

1 In *Modern French Philosophy*, tr. L. Scott-Fox and J. M. Harding (Cambridge: Cambridge University Press, 1980), Vincent Descombes correctly notes the Nietzschean appropriation of Freud and Marx in *Anti-Oedipus* (pp. 173–5), and Jean-François Lyotard, in 'Energumen Capitalism', tr. James Leigh, *Semiotext(e)* 2 (3) (1977): 11–26, makes patent Deleuze and Guattari's latent subversion of Marx in their characterizations of desiring-production, capitalism and revolutionary action. The most helpful guides to *Anti-Oedipus*, besides the studies of Descombes and Lyotard, are Jacques Donzelot, 'An antisociology', tr. Mark Seem, *Semiotext(e)* 2 (3) (1977): 27–44; Charles J. Stivale, 'Gilles Deleuze and Félix Guattari: schizoanalysis and literary discourse', *SubStance* 29 (1981): 46–57; Robert D'Amico, *Marx and the Philosophy of Culture* (Gainesville: University Presses of Florida, 1981), pp. 58–74; Jean-Jacques Lecercle, *Philosophy through the Looking-Glass* (La Salle, Ill.: Open Court, 1985), pp. 160–97; and Vincent Leitch, *Deconstructive Criticism: An Advanced Introduction* (New York: Columbia University Press, 1984), pp. 213–23. See also the illuminating essays of Colin Gordon, 'The subtracting machine', *I and C* 8 (1981): 27–40, and Paul Patton, 'Notes for a glossary', *I and C* 8 (1981): 41–8, on general themes in *Anti-Oedipus* and other works of Deleuze and Guattari.

2 'Secheresse de Deleuze', *L'Arc* no. 49 (1972), p. 89.

3 Deleuze and Guattari, 'Entretien: capitalisme et schizophrénie', *L'Arc* 49 (1972): 47–8.

4 Much of Guattari's work from the 1950s and 1960s shows the influence of existentialism, including his distinction between subjected groups and group-subjects, which parallels Sartre's opposition of series and groups in fusion. On series and groups in fusion, see Mark Poster, *Existential Marxism in Postwar France* (Princeton: Princeton University Press, 1975), pp. 287–305. Harold Rosenberg, in *The Tradition of the New* (New York: Horizon Press, 1959), pp. 154–77, offers an example of what Guattari

would call a transitional fantasy in his discussion of the French Revolution, arguing that revolutionaries assumed the archaic masks and poses of Roman republicans, but only so that they could create institutions that broke from the past. (Deleuze comments on Rosenberg's analysis in DR 123.)

5 'Entretien: capitalisme et schizophrénie', p. 47.

6 The notable exception among philosophers is Spinoza, who remarks in the *Ethics* that 'we do not endeavour, will, seek after or desire because we judge a thing to be good. On the contrary, we judge a thing to be good because we endeavour, will, seek after and desire it' (tr. Samuel Shirley (Indianapolis: Hackett, 1982), Pt. III, Prop. 9, Scholium, p. 110). On this point, see Dominique Grisoni, 'Les onomatopées du desir', in *Les Dieux dans la cuisine* (Paris: Aubier, 1978), pp. 137–50.

7 I find decisive Isaac Balbus's argument, in *Marxism and Domination* (Princeton: Princeton University Press, 1982), pp. 11–60, that the explanatory power of a Marxist reading of history depends on the differentiation of production from distribution, exchange, and consumption, and that such a differentiation cannot be maintained in the analysis of precapitalist economic formations, the modifications and emendations of Godelier and Althusser notwithstanding.

8 For an extended analysis of the use-value/exchange-value distinction and its dependence on a presumed foundation of needs, see Jean Baudrillard, *Le Miroir de la production* (Paris: Casterman, 1973). Baudrillard frequently cites Marshall Sahlins's *Stone Age Economics* (Chicago: Aldine Atherton, 1972), especially pp. 1–39, in which Sahlins argues that hunters and gatherers, presumed by most anthropologists to be desperately impoverished and miserable peoples, are actually members of the first affluent societies. Hunters and gatherers, except where marginalized by colonialism, generally lead a leisurely, relatively anxiety-free existence, since their needs and desires are minimal and hence easily satisfied.

9 Samuel Beckett, *Three Novels: Molloy, Malone Dies, The Unnamable*, tr. Patrick Bowles and Samuel Beckett (New York: Grove Press, 1958), pp. 69–74.

10 In identifying the *socius* of the primitive machine as the body of the earth and the *socius* of the barbaric machine as the body of the despot, Deleuze and Guattari are elaborating on Marx's observations in the *Grundrisse* that in primitive societies, assumptions about men's communal relation to the earth serve as the 'natural or *divine* presuppositions' of their understanding of labour, and that in some societies ownership of the land can be seen as residing solely in the despot (K. Marx, *Grundrisse*, tr. Martin Nicolaus (New York: Vintage, 1973), p. 471). Although Deleuze and Guattari initially seem to indicate that the *socius* is a body without organs, speaking, for example, of capital as 'the body without organs of the capitalist' (AO 10, *16*), eventually they discriminate between the *socius* and the body without organs: 'the body without organs is the limit of the socius, its tangent of deterritorialization, the ultimate residue of a deterritorialized socius' (AO 281, *334*). The

difference between the *socius* and the body without organs lies in the different usages of the disjunctive synthesis, whether exclusive (*socius*) or inclusive (body without organs).

11 The designations 'savage', 'barbaric' and 'civilized', by which Deleuze and Guattari at times refer to the three forms of desiring-production, are taken from Frederick Engels's tripartite periodization of history in *The Origin of the Family, Private Property and the State*, tr. Alec West (1884; New York: International Publishers, 1972). I find Engels's taxonomy, however, less significant than Marx's modes of production as a parallel to the Deleuzoguattarian schema.

12 Deleuze and Guattari rely primarily on the work of Pierre Clastres for their conception of a primitive, anti-state political organization. See Clastres's collection of essays, *La Société contre l'état* (Paris: Minuit, 1972), especially pp. 161–86.

13 F.W. Nietzsche, *On the Genealogy of Morals*, tr. Walter Kaufmann and J.R. Hollingdale (New York: Vintage, 1967), pp. 86–7.

14 Deleuze and Guattari base their conception of an axiomatic on Robert Blanché's *Axiomatics* (1962). See MP 568–70 for further elaboration on the capitalist axiomatic.

15 Paul Patton, 'Conceptual politics and the war-machine in *Mille Plateaux*', *SubStance* 44/45 (1984): 61–80.

16 Deleuze and Michel Foucault, 'Entretien: les intellectuels et le pouvoir', *L'Arc* 49 (1972): 12.

17 Despite similarities between *Anti-Oedipus* and the work of Bataille, Deleuze and Guattari differ from Bataille in ignoring his central theme of transgression (as Lyotard notes in 'Energumen Capitalism', p. 25), and in focusing on production rather than consumption as the fundamental aspect of libidinal economics. Closest to Bataille among contemporary theorists is Jean Baudrillard, in his emphasis on consumption, the priority of primitive, symbolic exchange over modern forms of commodity relations, and the centrality of risk and the wager in desire. See especially his *La Société de consommation* (Paris: Gallimard, 1970), *L'Échange symbolique et la mort* (Paris: Gallimard, 1976) and *De la séduction* (Paris: Galilée, 1979).

18 Michel Foucault *Discipline and Punish: The Birth of the Prison*, tr. Alan Sheridan (New York: Pantheon, 1976), p. 28.

19 There is no question here of proving that Deleuze and Guattari influenced Foucault, or vice versa, but of noting a common field of analysis that developed through years of friendly association. There is certainly no evidence to support Frank's characterization of Deleuze and Guattari as 'disciples of Foucault' ('The World as Will and Representation: Deleuze and Guattari's Critique of Capitalism as Schizo-Analysis and Schizo-Discourse', tr. David Berger, *Telos* 57 (Fall 1983): 175), to say nothing of his absurd claim that Foucault, Deleuze, and Guattari should all be lumped together with the 'nouveaux philosophes, and the new right! For a clarification of Deleuze's attitude toward the 'nouveaux philosophes', see his scathing remarks in 'A propos des nouveaux philosophes et d'un problème plus general', *Minuit* supp., no. 24 (June

1977), no pagination. For Deleuze and Guattari's appraisal of the relationship between their work and Foucault's, see MP 175-6.

5. Kafka's Rhizomic Writing Machine

1 *Agencement machinique*, like so many of Deleuze and Guattari's terms, is difficult to translate. For *agencement*, translators of Deleuze and Guattari have suggested 'assemblage', 'arrangement' and 'organization', but no one of these is fully satisfactory. *Agencement* denotes an arrangement resulting from a combination of elements, as well as the action or manner of assembling or combining elements, and may be assimilated to the concepts of both *organization* and *organism*. *Machinique* is a coinage which plays on the words *machine* (machine) and *machin* (thing, whatchamacallit), suggesting both the functional and the whimsical nature of arrangements. In Deleuze and Guattari's later work, 'machinic arrangement' tends to replace 'desiring-machines'. (See D 121, 160 on the abandonment of 'desiring-machines' and the nature of 'arrangements'.)

2 Deleuze and Guattari object specifically to the psychoanalytic readings of Marthe Robert and the religious, allegorical readings of Max Brod. Characterizations of Kafka as the artist of modern *Angst* and alienation, of course, are commonplace in textbooks, anthology commentaries and histories of twentieth-century literature.

3 *Über Franz Kafka* (1937; rpt. Frankfurt am Main: Fischer, 1974), p. 156, my translation.

4 *Dearest Father: Stories and Other Writings*, tr. Ernst Kaiser and Eithne Wilkins (New York: Schocken, 1954), p. 177; hereafter cited as DF. Other works by Kafka cited in the text are *The Trial*, tr. Willa and Edwin Muir, rev. E.M. Butler (New York: Modern Library, 1956), cited as T; *The Penal Colony: Stories and Short Pieces*, tr. Willa and Edwin Muir (New York: Schocken, 1948), cited as PC; *The Diaries of Franz Kafka: 1910-1913*, ed. Max Brod, tr. Joseph Kresh (New York: Schocken, 1948), cited as D1: *The Diaries of Franz Kafka: 1914-1923*, ed. Max Brod, tr. Martin Greenberg with Hannah Arendt (New York: Schocken, 1949), cited as D2; and *Letters to Friends, Family and Editors*, tr. Richard and Clara Winston (New York: Schocken, 1977), cited as LFF.

5 Deleuze and Guattari's handling of *Amerika* is rather sketchy and, I find, somewhat inadequate. Their emphasis falls much more heavily on *The Trial* and *The Castle*.

6 Here one finds a clear indication of the close relationship between Foucauldian power and Deleuzoguattarian desire, and of the similarity between positive desire and Nietzschean will to power: 'What does "will to power" mean? Above all not that the will wants power, not that it desires or seeks power as an end, nor that power is its moving force' (NP 90).

7 It should be evident from Deleuze and Guattari's treatment of Justice as an unlimited rhizome that they object to Max Brod's placement of

K.'s death at the end of the novel. They argue that this chapter is probably a dream interlude. 'To impose the execution of K. as the final chapter seems to us to have an equivalent in literary history: the placement of the celebrated description of the plague at the end of Lucretius' work. In these two cases, it is a matter of showing that an Epicurean near death can only collapse in anguish, or that a Prague Jew can only assume the guilt which troubles him' (K 81).

8 The more conservative critic Ritchie Robertson, in his *Kafka: Judaism, Politics, and Literature* (Oxford: Clarendon, 1985), agrees in many ways with Deleuze and Guattari in their evaluation of Kafka's remarks on minor literature:

> it should be clear by now that by a minor literature Kafka did not just mean a collection of books but was envisaging a society in which literature was intimately connected with popular and political life and had a central place in people's interest . . . . At the same time, we may reasonably infer that Kafka was imagining a society to which he himself would have liked to belong. (pp. 24–5)

9 'To have a style is to manage to stammer in one's own language. This is difficult, since there must be a necessity in such a stammering. Not to be a stammerer in one's speech, but to be a stammerer in relation to language itself. To be like a foreigner in one's own language. To create a line of flight. The most striking examples for me are Kafka, Beckett, Gherasim Luca, Godard . . . . We must be bilingual even in a single language, we must have a minor language inside our language, we must make a minor usage of our own language' (D 10–11).

10 Several critics have recently made use of Deleuze and Guattari's concept of 'minor literature' in a variety of contexts. See especially Louis A. Renza, *'A White Heron' and the Question of Minor Literature* (Madison: University of Wisconsin Press, 1984); Réda Bensmaïa, 'Traduire ou "blanchir" la langue: *Amour Bilingue* d'Abdelkebir Khatibi', *Hors Cadre* 3 (Spring 1985): 187–206; and the special issues of *Cultural Critique* nos 6 and 7 (1987) devoted to minor literature.

11 See, for example, Robbe-Grillet's 'Order and disorder in film and fiction', tr. Bruce Morrissette, *Critical Inquiry* 4 (1977): 1–20.

6. *Thousand Plateaus*

1 Particularly insightful studies of *Thousand Plateaus* include Arnaud Villani, 'Géographie physique de *Mille Plateaux*', *Critique* 455 (April 1985): 331–47; Jean-Jacques Lecercle, *Philosophy through the Looking-Glass* (La Salle, Ill.: Open Court, 1985), Ch. 5; and several articles from a special issue of *SubStance*, no. 44/45 (1984): Charles J. Stivale, 'The literary element in *Mille Plateaux*: The new cartography of Deleuze and Guattari', 20–34; Peter M. Canning, 'Fluidentity', 35–45; Alice Jardine, 'Woman in Limbo: Deleuze and His Br(others)', 46–60; and

Paul Patton, 'Conceptual politics and the war-machine in *Mille Plateaux*', 61–80.

2 Much of Guattari's work on semiotics in *La Révolution moléculaire* and *L'Inconscient machinique*, for example, relies on Peircean terminology, and the two volumes of Deleuze's *Cinéma* are organized along Peircean lines (in conjunction with certain concepts taken from Bergson).

3 Louis Hjelmslev, *Prolegomena to a Theory of Language*, tr. Francis J. Whitfield (Madison: University of Wisconsin Press, 1961), p. 60.

4 *Le Geste et la parole, technique et langage* (Paris: Albin Michel, 1964), 2 vols.

5 In the anthropomorphic stratum, the brain is 'a common external milieu for the entire stratum, grasped in the entire stratum, the cerebral-nervous milieu' which constitutes 'the prehuman soup in which we bathe. We bathe our hands and our faces in it. The brain is a population, a collection of tribes which tend toward two poles [hand and face]' (MP 83).

6 Lynn White, in *Medieval Technology and Social Change* (Oxford: Clarendon, 1962), demonstrates in great detail the extraordinary importance of the stirrup in the formation of feudal society.

7 In a 1980 interview, Deleuze says that 'the idea of a non-organic life is constantly present in *Thousand Plateaus*' (*L'Arc* 49, new edn (1980), p. 101).

8 *Critique* 343 (Dec. 1975), cited in the text as EN. A slightly modified version of this essay is included in Deleuze's *Foucault* (Paris: Minuit, 1986), pp. 31–51.

9 *Spinoza: philosophie pratique* (Paris: Minuit, 1981), p. 165. Further citations are abbreviated as S.

10 Deleuze and Guattari state that the time of hecceities is that of '*Aion*, which is the indefinite time of the event' (MP 320). Hecceities and the plane of consistency, in fact, are similar in most respects to the events and metaphysical surface of *The Logic of Meaning*. See Chapter 3.

11 *La Révolution moléculaire* (Fontenay-sous-Bois: Recherches, 1977), p. 310.

12 There is no good English equivalent for *régime de signes*. *Régime* in French may mean 'political regime', 'system of government', 'mode of living', 'organization', 'administration', 'management', 'regimen', 'diet', 'system of regulations', and 'laws', among other things. Despite its inadequacy, 'regime of signs' is the phrase most translators of Deleuze and Guattari have adopted in rendering *régime de signes* in English; the reader should, however, keep in the mind the much wider range of meanings that the French expression may have.

13 Deleuze and Guattari discuss the face at length in Plateau 7: 'Year zero: faceness'. Deleuze provides a fascinating analysis of the function of the face in cinema in 'L'image-affection: visage et gros plan', Chapter 6 of *Cinéma 1: Image-Mouvement* (Paris: Minuit, 1983), pp. 125–44.

14 Deleuze and Guattari relate the motif of the mutual turning away of man and God to Hölderlin's *Remarks on Oedipus* and to Jean Beaufret's Heideggerian gloss of Hölderlin's difficult comments, 'Hölderlin et Sophocle'. Both Hölderlin's *Remarks* and Beaufret's essay may be found in *Remarques sur Oedipe et sur Antigone*, tr. François Fédier (Paris: 10/18, 1965). Deleuze makes use of the same texts in his explication of

tragedy and the third passive synthesis of time in DR 118–21.

15 Deleuze and Guattari's more detailed reading of the book of Jonah, which cannot be repeated here, is based on Jérôme Lindon's commentary accompanying his translation of *Jonas* (Paris: Minuit, 1955).

16 In *Kafka*, Deleuze and Guattari align Titorelli's ostensible acquittal and indefinite postponement with a simpler opposition of a transcendental paranoiac law of reterritorialization and an immanent schizo-law of deterritorialization. In *Thousand Plateaus*, however, they complicate this schema by isolating forces of absolute deterritorialization which nevertheless remain 'negative and stratified' and 'appear in the process of subjectification (*Ratio et Passio*)' (MP 168). Throughout *The Trial* and *The Castle*, therefore, the line of flight, which deterritorializes the hierarchical, despotic forces of the law of the Castle is always in danger of being reterritorialized within a subjectifying, passionate regime of signs (the unlimited sequence of contiguous but segmentary offices of the lawyers or the Castle bureaucracy).

Epilogue

1 Empiricism itself is misunderstood, Deleuze claims, if it is regarded simply as the view that the intelligible derives from the sensible. The decisive insight of empiricism is that relations are external to their terms. Relations are differences that cannot be subsumed within principles but can only be explored experimentally.

> Relations are in the middle, and exist as such. This exteriority of relations is not a principle but a vital protest against principles. So, if one sees something that traverses life, but that resists thought, then one must force thought to think it, make it the hallucination point of thought, an experimentation that does violence to thought. The empiricists are not theoreticians but experimenters: they never interpret, they have no principles. (D 69)

Hence Deleuze's description of his philosophy in *Difference and Repetition* as a transcendental empiricism.

2 The fluid model of the cosmos is essentially Epicurean, as Michel Serres demonstrates in *La Naissance de la physique dans le texte de Lucrèce* (Paris: Minuit, 1977). Deleuze and Guattari incorporate Serres' analysis within their discussion of 'smooth space' (fluid, Epicurean) and 'striated space' (solid, Euclidean), in MP, Plateau 14 (pp. 592–625). In his 1961 essay on Lucretius (appendix 2, LS 307–24) Deleuze makes several points that coincide with certain arguments in Serres' study.

3 In a review of *Thousand Plateaus*, Arnaud Villani notes the relevance of the pre-Socratic and Heideggerian concepts of *physis* for Deleuze. 'When questioned on this point, Deleuze recognized that *physis* plays a role in his work, but, as is often the case with key problems, an implicit role' ('Geographie physique de *Mille Plateaux*', *Critique* 455 (April 1985), p. 336).

4 'Entretien 1980', *L'Arc* 49 (rev. edn 1980): 99.

5 Interview in *L'Autre Journal* 8 (Oct. 1985): 13.

6 *L'Autre Journal*, p. 16.

7 'There are many experiments in concepts in *Thousand Plateaus*: rhizome, smooth space, hecceity, becoming-animal, abstract machine, diagram, etc. Guattari invents lots of concepts, and I have the same conception of philosophy' ('Entretien 1980', p. 100).

8 Derrida's *Positions*, tr. Alan Bass (Chicago: University of Chicago Press, 1981) provides the most accessible and concise introduction to these aspects of *différance*. On *différance* as differing/deferral, see pp. 8–10; as non–present, p. 45; as structural and genetic, pp. 27–8 and 106–7; as simulacrum, p. 58; as neither word nor concept, p. 40.

9 *Of Grammatology*, tr. Gayatri Chakravorty Spivak (Baltimore: Johns Hopkins University Press, 1976), p. 158.

10 *Positions*, p. 65; *Dissemination*, tr. Barbara Johnson (Chicago: University of Chicago Press, 1981), p. 261.

11 Rodolphe Gasché, *The Tain of the Mirror* (Cambridge, Mass.: Harvard University Press, 1986), p. 281.

12 Gasché, pp. 148–9. For discussion of the pre-ontological and pre-logical nature of the text, see especially pp. 148–53.

13 Gasché, p. 274. Gasché chooses to describe the text in terms of 'infrastructures' which, he says,

> represent a mode of synthesis that is older, or more 'simple', than the mode of uniting that is characteristic of philosophical synthesizing. Synthesis, with respect to the infrastructures, involves a complicity and complication that maintain together an undetermined number of possibilities, which need not necessarily be in a relation of antithetical contrast with one another, as is the case in the classical concept of synthesis. (p. 152)

He also asserts that the infrastructures are not 'deep, as opposed to surface, structures: there is nothing *profound* about them' (p. 155). Deleuze seems to be making similar points when he speaks of an incorporeal surface of singular points structured through the connective, conjunctive, and disjunctive syntheses.

14 Derrida describes this 'double writing' quite clearly in *Positions*, pp. 41–2.

15 See 'Plato's pharmacy', in *Dissemination*, tr. Barbara Johnson (Chicago: University of Chicago Press, 1981), pp. 63–171.

16 *Positions*, p. 42.

17 Deleuze says of Hume that 'his empiricism is, before the term existed, a sort of science-fiction universe. As in science-fiction, one has the impression of a fictive, strange, foreign world, seen by other creatures; but also the presentiment that this world is already ours, and these other creatures, ourselves' ('Hume', in *Histoire de la philosophie: les lumières*, ed. François Châtelet (Paris: Hachette, 1972), IV, 65).

18 Vincent B. Leitch criticizes Deleuze and Guattari on these grounds in *Deconstructive Criticism: An Advanced Introduction* (New York: Colombia

University Press, 1983), p. 223.

19 For an extended analysis of Foucault along these lines, see Deleuze's recent *Foucault* (Paris: Minuit, 1986).

20 'Nietzsche, genealogy, history', in *Language, Counter-Memory, Practice*, tr. Donald F. Bouchard and Sherry Simon (Ithaca: Cornell University Press, 1977), pp. 153, 157. For a discussion of 'effective history' and Foucault's genealogical method, see Hubert L. Dreyfus and Paul Rabinow, *Michel Foucault: Beyond Structuralism and Hermeneutics*, 2nd edn (Chicago: University of Chicago Press, 1983), pp. 104–25.

21 *Discipline and Punish*, tr. Alan Sheridan (New York: Pantheon, 1977), p. 31.

22 Deleuze and Foucault, 'Intellectuals and power', in *Language, Counter-Memory, Practice*, p. 208. It is interesting to note that Foucault credits Deleuze with having thematized the question of power in all his works:

> if the reading of your books (from *Nietzsche* to what I anticipate in *Capitalism and Schizophrenia*) has been essential for me, it is because they seem to go very far in exploring this problem: under the ancient theme of meaning, of the signifier and the signified, etc., you have developed the question of power, of the inequality of powers and their struggles. (pp. 213–4)

Bibliography

Works by Deleuze and Guattari

Articles initially published as separate pieces but later included in books by Deleuze and/or Guattari are not listed. For further bibliographical information, see the special Deleuze issue of *SubStance*, no. 44/45 (1984).

I. Books by Gilles Deleuze

(1952) With André Cresson, *David Hume, sa vie, son oeuvre*, Paris: PUF.

(1953) *Empirisme et subjectivité*, Paris: PUF.

(1953) *Instincts et institutions* [collection of texts edited by Deleuze], Paris: Hachette.

(1962) *Nietzsche et la philosophie*, Paris: PUF. (1983) *Nietzsche and Philosophy*, tr. Hugh Tomlinson, Minneapolis: University of Minnesota Press.

(1963) *La Philosophie critique de Kant*, Paris: PUF. (1984) *The Critical Philosophy of Kant*, tr. Hugh Tomlinson and Barbara Habberjam, Minneapolis: University of Minnesota Press.

(1964) *Marcel Proust et les signes*, Paris: PUF. Rev. edn published 1970, 1971, 1976 as *Proust et les signes*. (1972) *Proust and Signs* [Tr. of the 2nd edn], tr. Richard Howard, New York: G. Braziller.

(1965) *Nietzsche*, Paris: PUF.

(1966) *Le Bergsonisme*, Paris: PUF.

(1967) *Présentation de Sacher-Masoch*, Paris: Minuit. (1971) *Masochism: An Interpretation of Coldness and Cruelty*, tr. Jean McNeil, New York: G. Braziller.

(1968) *Différence et répétition*, Paris: PUF.

(1968) *Spinoza et le problème de l'expression*, Paris: Minuit.

(1969) *Logique du sens*, Paris: Minuit.

(1970) *Spinoza*, Paris, PUF. (1981) Rev. edn published as *Spinoza: Philosophie pratique*, Paris, Minuit.

(1975) *Mémoire et vie* by Henri Bergson [collection of texts edited by Deleuze], Paris: PUF.

(1977) With Claire Parnet, *Dialogues*, Paris: Flammarion. (1987) *Dialogues*, tr. Hugh Tomlinson and Barbara Habberjam, London: Athlone, and New York: Columbia University Press.

(1979) With Carmelo Bene, *Superpositions*, Paris: Minuit. Originally published in Italian (1978), Milan: Feltrinelle economica.

(1981) *Francis Bacon: Logique de la sensation*, 2 vols., Paris: Editions de la différence.

(1983) *Cinéma 1: l'Image-Mouvement*, Paris: Minuit. (1986) *Cinema 1: The Movement-Image*, tr. Hugh Tomlinson and Barbara Habberjam, Minneapolis: University of Minnesota Press.

(1985) *Cinéma 2: l'Image-Temps*, Paris: Minuit.

(1986) *Foucault*, Paris: Minuit. English translation by Seán Hand (1988), foreword by Paul A. Bové, Minneapolis: University of Minnesota Press.

II. Books by Félix Guattari

(1972) *Psychanalyse et transversalité*, preface by Deleuze, 'Trois problèmes de groupe', Paris: Maspéro.

(1977) *La révolution moléculaire*, Fontenay-sous-Bois: Editions Recherches. (1980) Rev. edn, Paris: 10/18. (1984) *Molecular Revolution: Psychiatry and Politics*, tr. Rosemary Sheed, New York: Penguin. [Includes material from *Psychanalyse et transversalité* and *La révolution moléculaire*, as well as one essay from *Les années d'hiver 1980–1985*.]

(1979) *L'Inconscient machinique*, Fontenay-sous-Bois: Editions Recherches.

(1985) With Toni Negri, *Les Nouveaux espaces de liberté*, Paris: Dominique Bedou.

(1985) With Toni Negri, *Les Nouveaux espaces de liberté*, Paris: Dominique Bedou. [Includes three essays: Guattari and Negri, 'Les Nouveaux espaces de liberté; Guattari, 'Des libertés en Europe; Negri, 'Lutte archéologique'.]

(1986) *Les Années d'hiver 1980–1985* Paris: Barrault.

(1986) With Jean Oury and François Tosquelles, *Pratique de l'institutionnel et politique*, Vigneux: Matrice éditions.

III. Books by Deleuze and Guattari

(1972) *L'Anti-Oedipe: capitalisme et schizophrénie I*, Paris: Minuit. (1977) *Anti-Oedipus*, tr. Robert Hurley, Mark Seem, and Helen R. Lane, preface by Michel Foucault, New York: Viking. (1983) reprint, Minneapolis: University of Minnesota Press.

(1975) *Kafka: pour une littérature mineure*, Paris: Minuit. (1986) *Kafka: For a Minor Literature*, tr. Dana Polan, foreword by Réda Bensmaïa, Minneapolis: University of Minnesota Press.

(1976) *Rhizome: Introduction*, Paris: Minuit. 'Rhizome', tr. Paul Foss and Paul Patton, *I and C* 8 (1981): 49–71.

(1977) *Politique et psychanalyse*, Alençon: des mot perdus.

(1978) With François Châtelet *et al.*, *Où il est question de la toxicomanie*,

Alençon: des mots perdus.

(1980) *Mille Plateaux: capitalisme at schizophrénie II*, Paris: Minuit. (1987) *A Thousand Plateaus: Capitalism and Schizophrenia*, tr. and foreword by Brian Massumi, Minneapolis: University of Minnesota Press.

IV. Articles, Prefaces, Interviews by Deleuze

(1946) 'Mathèse, Science et Philosophie', Introduction to Jean Malfatti de Montereggio, *Etudes sur la Mathèse ou anarchie at hiérarchie de la science*, tr. Christian Ostrowski, Paris: Editions du Griffon d'Or, pp. ix–xxiv.

(1956) 'La Conception de la différence chez Bergson', *Etudes bergsoniennes* 4: 77–112.

(1959) 'Nietzsche, sens et valeurs', *Arguments* 15: 20–8.

(1961) 'De Sacher-Masoch au masochisme', *Arguments* 21: 40–6.

(1963) 'L'Idée de genèse dans l'esthétique de Kant', *Revue d'esthétique* 16: 113–36.

(1963) 'Unité de *A la recherche du temps perdu*', *Revue de Métaphysique et de morale* 68 (4): 427–42.

(1966) 'L'Homme, une existence douteuse', *Le nouvel Observateur* (1 June): 32–4 [on Foucault's *Les Mots et les choses*].

(1967) With Michel Foucault, Introduction to Friedrich Nietzsche, *Le gai savoir. Les fragments posthumes (1881–82)*, tr. Pierre Klossowski, vol. 5 of *Oeuvres philosophiques complètes*, Paris: Gallimard: pp. i–iv.

(1967) 'Méthode de dramatisation', *Bulletin de la société française de philosophie* 61 (3): 89–124.

(1967) 'Sur la volonté de puissance et l'éternel retour', in *Nietzsche, Cahiers de Royaumont*, Paris: Minuit, 275–87.

(1969) 'Spinoza et la méthode générale de M. Guerault', *Revue de Métaphysique et de morale* 74 (4): 426–37.

(1969) 'Gilles Deleuze parle de la philosophie', *La Quinzaine littéraire* 68 (March): 18–19 [interview with Jeannette Colombel].

(1970) 'Faille et feux locaux, Kostas Axelos', *Critique* 275 (April): 344–51 [on Axelos's *Vers une pensée planétaire*, *Arguments d'une recherche*, and *Le Jeu du monde*].

(1970) 'Un nouvel archiviste', *Critique* 274 (March): 195–209 [on Foucault's *L'archéologie du savoir*]. Reprinted as separate edn (Montpellier: Fata Morgana, 1972).

(1982) 'A new archivist', tr. Stephen Muecke, in *Theoretical Strategies*, ed. Peter Botsman, Sydney: Local Consumption, pp. 215–30.

(1970) 'Schizologie'. Preface to Louis Wolfson, *Le Schizo et les langues*, Paris: Gallimard, pp. 5–23.

(1972) 'Hume', in *Histoire de la philosophie, Volume 4: Les Lumières (le XVIIIe siècle)*, ed. François Châtelet, Paris: Hachette, pp. 65–78.

(1972) 'Les Intellectuels et le pouvoir', *L'Arc* 49: 3–10 [interview with Michel Foucault]. 'Intellectuals and power', tr. Donald F. Bouchard and Sherry Simon, in Michel Foucault (1977) *Language, Counter-Memory, Practice*, Ithaca: Cornell University Press, pp. 205–17.

Bibliography

(1972) 'Schizophrénie et Société', in *Encyclopédie Universalis* vol. 14, Paris: Editions Encyclopédie Universalis France pp. 733–5.

(1972) 'Qu'est ce que c'est, tes "machines désirantes" à toi?' *Les Temps modernes* 316 (November): 854–6 [Introduction to Pierre Bénichou, 'Saint Jackie, Comédienne et Bourreau'].

(1972) 'Trois problèmes de groupe': Preface to Félix Guattari, *Psychanalyse et transversalité*, 'Three group problems', tr. Mark Seem, *Semiotext(e)* 3 (2) (1977) : 99–109.

(1972–3) 'A quoi reconnaît-on le structuralisme?' in *Histoire de la philosophie, Volume 8: Le XXe siècle*, ed. François Châtelet, Paris: Hachette, pp. 299–335, and in *La philosophie au XXe siècle*, Vevier, Belgium: Marabout (1979).

(1973) 'Lettre à Michel Cressole'. Appendix to Michel Cressole, *Deleuze*, Paris: Editions Universitaire, 'Psychothèque', pp. 107–18. ' "I have nothing to admit" ', tr. Janis Forman, *Semiotext(e)* 2 (3) (1977): 111–16.

(1973) 'Pensée nomade', in *Nietzsche aujourd'hui?*, Paris: 10/18, vol. 1, pp. 159–74. 'Nomad Thought', tr. Jacqueline Wallace, *Semiotext(e)* 3 (1) (1977), and tr. David B. Allison in *The New Nietzsche: Contemporary Styles of Interpretation*, New York: Dell (1977), pp. 142–9.

(1974) 'Préface to Guy Hocquenghem, *L'Après-Mai des Faunes: Volutions*, Paris: Grasset, pp. 7–17.

(1975) 'Ecrivain non: un nouveau cartographe', *Critique* 343 (December): 1207–27 [on Foucault's *Surveiller et punir*].

(1975) 'Table Ronde', with Roland Barthes and Gérard Genette, in *Cahiers Marcel Proust*, new series, no. 7, Paris: Gallimard, pp. 87–116.

(1976) 'Avenir de linguistique'. Preface to Henri Gobard, *L'Aliénation linguistique*, Paris: Flammarion, pp. 9–14.

(1976) 'Entretien avec Gilles Deleuze', *Cahiers du Cinéma* 271: 5–12. 'Three questions on *Six Fois Deux*: an interview with Gilles Deleuze', *Afterimage* 7 (Summer 1978): 112–19.

(1976) 'Gilles Deleuze fasciné par "Le Misogyne" ', *La Quinzaine littéraire* 229 : 8–10 [book review of Alain Roger's *Le Misogyne*].

(1977) 'A propos des nouveaux philosophes et d'un problème plus général', *Le Monde*, 19–20 June, p. 16. Reprinted in *Recherches, Les Untorelli* 30 (November): 179–84, and as a supplement to *Minuit* 24 (5 June): no pagination.

(1977) 'Nous croyons au caractère constructiviste de certaines agitations de gauche', *Recherches, Les Untorelli* 30 (November): 149–50.

(1977) 'L'ascension du social', Postface to Jacques Donzelot, *La Police des familles*, Paris: Minuit, pp. 213–20. 'The rise of the social', tr. Robert Hurley, Preface to Donzelot, *The Policing of Families*, New York: Random House (1979), pp. ix–xvii.

(1978) 'Four propositions on psychoanalysis', tr. Paul Foss, in *Language, Sexuality and Subversion*, ed. Paul Foss and Meaghan Morris, Darlington, Australia, Feral Press, pp. 135–40 [tr. of 'Quatre propositions sur la psychanalyse', in *Politique et Psychanalyse*].

(1978) 'Philosophie et minorité', *Critique* 369 (February): 154–5.

(1978) 'Politics', tr. Janet Horn, *Semiotext(e)* 3 (2): 154–63 [portions of

Chapter IV, 'Politiques', of Deleuze–Parnet, *Dialogues*].

(1979) 'En quoi la philosophie peut servir à des mathématiciens ou même à des musiciens – Même et surtout quand elle ne parle pas de musique ou de mathématiques', in *Vincennes ou le désir d'apprendre*, Paris: Alain Moreau, pp. 120–1.

(1979) 'The schizophrenic and language: surface and depth in Lewis Carroll and Antonin Artaud', in *Textual Strategies: Perspectives in Post-Structuralist Criticism*, ed. Josué V. Harari, Ithaca: Cornell University Press, pp. 277–95 [secs. of *Logique du sens*, ch. 13].

(1980) 'Entretien 1980', *L'Arc* 49 (rev. edn): 99–102.

(1980) Interview, *Libération*, 23 October, pp. 16–17.

(1980) 'Open letter to the Negri judges', *Semiotext(e)* 3 (3): 182–5.

(1981) Interview with Hervé Guibert, *Le Monde* (3 December), p. 15 [on *Francis Bacon*]. '"What counts is the scream"', *Guardian* (10 January 1982).

(1981) Preface to Antonio Negri, *L'anomalie sauvage. Puissance et pouvoir chez Spinoza*, Paris: PUF, pp. 9–12.

(1983) 'L'abstraction lyrique', *change International* 1: 82.

(1983) 'Francis Bacon: The Logic of Sensation', *Flash Art* 112 (May): 8–16 [excepts from chapters 1, 3, 4, 6 of *Francis Bacon*].

(1983) Interview, *Libération*, 3 October, pp. 30–1.

(1983) Interview, *Le Monde*, 6 October, pp. 1, 17.

(1983) 'Le pacifisme aujourd'hui', *Les Nouvelles* (21 December): 60–4 [interview with Deleuze and Jean-Pierre Bamberger].

(1983) '"La photographie est déjà tirée dans les choses": entretien avec Gilles Deleuze par Pascal Bonitzer et Jean Narboni', *Cahiers du Cinéma* 352 (October): 35–40 [on *L'Image-Mouvement*].

(1983) 'Politics', tr. John Johnston, in *On the Line, Semiotext(e)*, New York: Foreign Agents Series, pp. 69–115 [Chapter IV, 'Politiques', of Deleuze–Parnet, *Dialogues*].

(1983) 'Plato and the Simulacrum', tr. Rosalind Krauss, *October* 27 (Winter): 45–56 [excerpt from *Logique du sens*].

(1984) 'Books', *Art Forum* 22 (5) (January): 68–9 [on *Francis Bacon*].

(1984) 'Michel Tournier and the world without others', tr. Graham Burchell, *Economy and Society* 13 (1): 52–71 [tr. of 'Michel Tournier et le monde sans autrui', appendix to *Logique du sens*].

(1985) 'Interview', *L'Autre Journal* 8 (October): 10–22.

(1985) 'Les Plages d'immanence', in *L'Art des confins*, ed. Annie Cuzenave and Jean-François Lyotard, Paris: PUF, pp. 79–81.

(1986) '"Le cerveau, c'est l'écran", entretien avec Gilles Deleuze', *Cahiers du Cinéma* 380 (February): 24–32 [on *L'Image-Temps*].

(1986) Interview, *Libération*, 2 September, pp. 27–8, and 8 September, p. 38.

(1986) 'Sur quatre formules poétiques qui pourraient résumer la philosophie kantienne', *Philosophie* 9 (Winter): 29–34. 'On four poetic formulas which might summarize the Kantian philosophy', Preface to the English translation of *The Critical Philosophy of Kant*, tr. Hugh Tomlinson and Barbara Habberjam, Minneapolis: University of Minnesota Press, 1984, pp. vii–xiii.

(1986) 'La Vie comme une oeuvre d'art', *Le Nouvel Observateur* 1138 (4 September): 58–60 [on Foucault].

(1987) 'Preface to the English Language Edition', *Dialogues*, tr. Hugh Tomlinson and Barbara Habberjam, London: Athlone, and New York: Columbia University Press, pp. vii–x.

V. *Articles, Interviews and Prefaces by Guattari*

(1972) 'Laing divisé', *La Quinzaine littéraire* 132 (1 January): 22–3.

(1973) 'Le Suicide', *Cahiers de l'Herne* (June).

(1974) 'Interview/Félix Guattari', *Diacritics* 4 (3) (Fall): 38–41.

(1975) 'L'Amateur Amaté', Preface to Marc Pierret, *Le Divan romancier*, Paris: Christian Bourgois, pp. 9–15.

(1975) 'La poétique de l'énonciation', *Semiotext(e)* 1 (3).

(1975) 'Sémiologies signifiantes et sémiologies asignifiantes', in *Psychanalyse et sémiotique. Actes du Colloque de Milan*, ed. Armando Verdiglione, Paris: 10/18, pp. 151–63.

(1977) 'La Borde: un lieu psychiatrique pas comme les autres', *La Quinzaine littéraire* 250: 20–21 [discussion with Guattari, Jean Oury, *et al.*].

(1977) 'Everybody wants to be a Fascist', tr. Suzanne Fletcher, *Semiotext(e)* 2 (3): 87–98 [from *La révolution moléculaire*].

(1977) 'Freudo-Marxism', tr. Janis Foreman, *Semiotext(e)* 2 (3): 73–5.

(1977) 'Masses et minorités à la recherche d'une nouvelle stratégie', *Recherches, Les Untorelli* 30 (November) : 113–22.

(1977) 'Psycho-analysis and schizo-analysis: an interview with Félix Guattari', tr. Janis Forman, *Semiotext(e)* 2 (3): 77–85 [from *La révolution moléculaire*].

(1978) 'Psychoanalysis and politics', tr. Paul Foss, in *Language, Sexuality and Subversion*, ed. Paul Foss and Meaghan Morris, Darlington, Australia: Feral Press, pp. 125–33.

(1978) 'Revolution and desire: Interview with Hannah Levi and Mark Seem', *State and Mind* (Summer/Fall): 53–7.

(1979) 'A Liberation of desire: An interview with George Stambolian', in *Homosexualities and French Literature*, ed. George Stambolian and Elaine Marks, Ithaca: Cornell University Press, pp. 56–69.

(1980) 'The Proliferation of margins', tr. Richard Gardner and Sybil Walker, *Semiotext(e)* 3 (3): 108–11 [from *La révolution moléculaire*, 2nd edn].

(1980) 'Why Italy', tr. John Johnston, *Semiotext(e)* 3 (3): 234–7 [from *La révolution moléculaire*, 2nd end].

(1981) 'Becoming-woman', tr. Rachel McComas and Stamos Metzidakis, *Semiotext(e)*, 4 (1): 86–8.

(1981) 'Entretien avec Jack Lang sur les radios libres', *La Quinzaine littéraire* 359: 27–8.

(1981) 'I have even met happy travelos', tr. Rachel McComas, *Semiotext(e)* 4 (1): 80–1 [from *La Révolution moléculaire*].

(1981) 'The Molecular Revolution: A Talk with Félix Guattari', *Tabloid: A Review of Mass Culture and Everyday Life* (Winter): 46–51.

(1981) 'Interpretance and Significance', *Semiotica* special supplement: 119–25.

(1981) Response to the question, 'Quelle est pour vous la cité idéale?', *La Quinzaine littéraire* 353: 39.

(1982) 'Like the Echo of a Collective Melancholia', tr. Mark Polizzotti, *Semiotext(e)* 4 (2): 102–10 [from *La révolution moléculaire*, 2nd edn].

(1983) 'The New Alliance: An Interview with Félix Guattari by Sylvère Lotringer', *Impulse* 10 (2) (Winter): 41–4.

(1983) 'Plaidoyer pour un "dictateur"', *Le Nouvel Observateur* 961 (8 April): 14–15 [in defence of the Socialist Minister of Culture Jack Lang].

(1983) 'Boîte noire: le curseur à zéro' (p. 5); 'boîte noire: le non-retrait' (p. 8); 'la guerre, la crise ou la vie' (p. 50); with Eric Alliez, 'Le capital en fin de compte: systèmes, structures et processus capitalistiques' (pp. 100–6); *change International* 1 (Autumn).

(1984) 'Créativité et folie', *Cahiers Actes Sud* 1 (February): 34–50 [discussion with Jean Oury].

(1984) 'La Gauche comme passion processuelle', *La Quinzaine littéraire* 422: 4.

(1984) 'Boîte noire: La valse à sept temps' (p. 3): interventions in the debate 'L'etat nucléaire: Table ronde' (p. 9); *change International* 2 (May).

(1984) 'Rêves de Franz Kafka', *Avant Scène Théâtre* 755: 4–5.

(1985) 'Cinematic desiring-machines', *Critical Theory: A Review of Theory and Criticism* 3 (7) (Autumn): 3–9.

(1985) Interview, *L'Autre Journal* 5 (May): 6–22.

(1985) 'Les rêves de Kafka', *change International* 3: 32–8.

(1986) 'Genet retrouvé', *Revue d'Etudes Palestiniennes* 21 (Autumn): 27–42. 'Genet rediscovered', tr. Brian Massumi, *The Journal of the Los Angeles Institute of Contemporary Art* (in press).

(1986) 'L'Impasse post-moderne', *La Quinzaine littéraire* 456: 20–1.

(1986) 'Questionnaire 17', tr. Bruce Benderson, *Zone* nos. 1/2: 460.

(1986) 'La Schizoanalyse', *L'Esprit créateur* 26 (4): 6–15.

VI. Articles and Interviews by Deleuze and Guattari

(1970) 'La Synthese Disjonctive', *L'Arc* 43: 54–62.

(1972) 'Capitalisme et Schizophrénie', *L'Arc* 49: 47–55.

(1972) 'Deleuze et Guattari s'expliquent', *La Quinzaine littéraire* 143 (16 June): 15–19.

(1973) 'Bilan-programme pour machines désirantes', *Minuit* 2: 1–25. Published as appendix to rev. edn of *L'Anti-Oedipe* (1976). 'Balance sheet–programme for desiring-machines', tr. Robert Hurley, *Semiotext(e)* 2 (3): 117–35.

(1973) 'Gilles Deleuze, Félix Guattari', in Michel-Antoine Burnier (ed.), *C'est demain la veille*, Paris: Seuil, pp. 137–61.

(1976) Discussions, in François Fourquet and Lion Murard, *Les équipements de pouvoir*, Paris: 10/18, pp. 39–47, 161–95, 212–27.

Bibliography

(1977) 'May 14, 1914. One or several wolves?', tr. Mark Seem, *Semiotext(e)* 2 (3): 137–47 [Plateau 2 of *Mille Plateaux*].

(1978) 'The interpretation of utterances', with Claire Parnet and André Scala, tr. Paul Foss and Meagham Morris, in *Language, Sexuality and Subversion*, Darlington, Australia: Feral Press, pp. 141–58 [tr. of 'L'interprétation des énoncés', from *Politique et psychanalyse*].

(1981) 'How to make yourself a body-without-organs', tr. Suzanne Guerlac, *Semiotext(e)* 4 (1): 265–70 [excerpt from Plateau 6 of *Mille plateaux*].

(1983) 'Rhizome', tr. John Johnston, in *On the Line, Semiotext(e)*, New York: Foreign Agents Series, pp. 1–65 [tr. of modified version of 'Rhizome' in *Mille plateaux*].

(1984) 'Concrete rules and abstract machines', tr. Charles J. Stivale, *SubStance* 44/45: 7–19 [translation of Plateau 15 of *Mille plateaux*].

(1985) 'Nomad art', tr. Brian Massumi, *Art and Text* 19 (October–December): 16–24 [from Plateau 14 of *Mille plateaux*].

(1986) 'City/state', tr. Brian Massumi, *Zone* 1/2: 194–217 [from Plateau 13 of *Mille plateaux*].

Selected books and articles on Deleuze and Guattari

L'Arc (1972; rev. 1980) 49, 'Deleuze':

Berçu, France, 'Sed perseverare diabolicum', pp. 23–30

Clément, Cathérine, 'Les petites filles ou les aventures de la philosophie', pp. 1–2

–, 'Postface 1980: De l'Anti-Oedipe aux Mille Plateaux, Bob Wilson philosophie', pp. 94–8 (rev. edn)

–, 'Entretien 1980', pp. 99–102 (rev. edn)

Fedida, Pierre, 'Le Philosophe et sa peau', pp. 61–9

Gandillac, Maurice de, 'Vers une schizo-analyse', pp. 56–60

Kaleka, Gérard, 'Un Hegel philosophiquement barbu, notes pour un mauvais usage de l'histoire', pp. 39–44

Klossowski, Pierre, 'Digression à partir d'un portrait apocryphe', pp. 11–14

Rosset, Clément, 'Sécheresse de Deleuze', pp. 89–91

Sempé, Jean-Claude, 'Le Leurre et le sumulacre', pp. 70–7

Taat, A. Mieke, 'Les Signes du feu', pp. 78–88

Vuarnet, Jean-Noël, 'Métamorphoses de Sophie', pp. 31–8

Aronowitz, Stanley (1980) 'Anti-Oedipus and molecular politics', *New Political Science* (Fall).

Baudrillard, Jean (1977) *Oublier Foucault*, Paris: Galilée. 'Forgetting Foucault', tr. Nicole Dufresne, *Humanities in Society* 3 (1) (1980): 87–111.

Benoist, Jean-Marie (1975) *La Révolution structurale*, Paris: Grasset, pp. 224–75.

Burchell, Graham (1984) 'Introduction to Deleuze', *Economy and Society* 13: 43–51.

Burger, Christa (1985) 'The reality of 'Machines', Notes on the Rhizome-

Thinking of Deleuze and Guattari', tr. Simon Srebrny, *Telos* 64 (Summer) 33–44.

Callinicos, Alex (1982) *Is There a Future for Marxism?* London: Macmillan.

Caron, Didier (1986) 'Le Cinéma experimental: une ignorance entretenue', *Critique* 469–70 (June–July): 678–91.

Castel, Robert (1976) *Le Psychanalysme*, Paris: 10/18, especially pp. 365–401.

Cressole, Michel (1973) *Deleuze*, Paris: Editions Universitaire, 'Psychothèque'.

D'Amico, Robert (1981) *Marx and the Philosophy of Culture*, Gainesville: University Presses of Florida, pp. 58–74.

Delcourt, Xavier, 'Foucault, par Deleuze' *La Quinzaine littéraire* 470 (16 September): 5–7.

Descombes, Vincent (1980) *Modern French Philosophy*, tr. L. Scott-Fox and J.M. Harding, Cambridge: Cambridge University Press, pp. 152–80.

Dews, Peter (1984) 'Foucault's theory of subjectivity', *New Left Review* 144 (March–April): 72–95.

Foucault, Michel (1977) 'Theatrum philosophicum', in *Language, Counter-Memory, Practice*, tr. Donald F. Bouchard and Sherry Simon, Ithaca: Cornell University Press, pp. 165–96.

Frank, Manfred (1983) 'The world as will and representation: Deleuze and Guattari's critique of capitalism as schizo-analysis and schizo-discourse', tr. David Berger, *Telos* 57 (Fall): 166–76.

Girard, René (1978) 'Delirium as System', tr. Paisley N. Livingston and Tobin Siebers, in *'To double business bound': Essays on literature, mimesis, and anthropology*, Baltimore: Johns Hopkins University Press, pp. 84–120.

Glucksmann, André (1965) 'Préméditations Nietzschéennes', *Critique* 213: 125–44.

Gordon, Colin (1981) 'The subtracting machine', *I and C* 8: 27–40.

Grisoni, Dominique (1978) 'Les onomatopées du désir', in *Les dieux dans la cuisine*, Paris: Aubier, pp. 130–50. 'Onomatopoeia of desire', tr. Paul Foss (1982) in *Theoretical Strategies*, ed. Peter Botsman, Sydney, Australia: Local Consumption, pp. 169–82.

Grossberg, Lawrence (1982) 'Experience, signification and reality: The boundaries of cultural semiotics', *Semiotica* 41: 73–106.

Hans, James S. (1981) *The Play of the World*, Amherst: University of Massachusetts Press.

Holland, Eugene (forthcoming) 'Schizoanalysis: The postmodern contextualization of psychoanalysis', in *Marxism and the Interpretation of Culture*, ed. Cary Nelson and Lawrence Grossberg, Champaign: University of Illinois Press.

Jameson, Fredric (1981) *The Political Unconscious*, Ithaca: Cornell University Press.

—— (1979) 'Marxism and historicism', *New Literary History* 11 (1): 41–73.

Kremer-Marietti, Angèle (1970) 'Différence et qualité', *Revue de metaphysique et de morale* 75 (3): 339–49.

Bibliography

Kudszus, W.G. (1978) 'Reflections on the double bind of literature and psychopathology', *SubStance* 20: 19–36.

Leigh, James A. (1978) 'Deleuze, Nietzsche and the Eternal Return', *Philosophy Today* (Fall): 206–23.

Leitch, Vincent (1984) *Deconstructive Criticism: An Advanced Introduction*, New York: Columbia University Press, pp. 213–23.

Lecercle, Jean-Jacques (1985) *Philosophy through the Looking-Glass*, La Salle, Ill.: Open Court, pp. 86–117, 160–97.

Mattéi, Jean-François (1983) *L'Etranger et le simulacre*, Paris: PUF, especially pp. 73–176.

Mauzi, Robert (1966) 'Les Complexes et les signes', *Critique* 225 (February): 155–71.

Mehlman, Jeffrey (1972) 'Portnoy in Paris', *Diacritics* 2 (4): 21–8.

Metzidakis, Stamos (1985) 'Contra Deleuze: towards a singular theory of reading', *Romanic Review* 76 (3): 316–22.

—— (1986) *Repetition and Semiotics*, Birmingham, Alab.: Summa Publications.

Norton, Theodore Mills (1986) 'Line of flight: Gilles Deleuze, or political science fiction', *New Political Science* 15 (Summer): 77–93.

Patton, Paul (1986) 'Deleuze and Guattari: Ethics and post-modernity', *Leftwright*, 20: 24–32.

—— (forthcoming) 'Marxism and beyond: Strategies of reterritorialization', in *Marxism and the Interpretation of Culture*, ed. Cary Nelson and Lawrence Grossberg, Champaign: University of Illinois Press.

—— (1981) 'Notes for a Glossary', *I and C* 8: 41–8.

Pecora, Vincent P. (1986) 'Deleuze's Nietzsche and post-structuralist thought', *SubStance* 48: 34–50.

Polan, Dana (1984) 'Cinéma 1: L'Image-mouvement', *Film Quarterly* 38 (1): 50–2.

Poster, Mark (1978) *Critical theory of the family*, New York: Seabury Press.

Reader, Keith A. (1987) *Intellectuals and the Left in France since 1968*, New York: St Martin's, pp. 80–91.

Rudnytsky, Peter L. (1987) *Freud and Oedipus*, New York: Columbia University Press, pp. 337–60.

Seem, Mark D. (1973) 'Liberation of difference: Toward a theory of antiliterature', *New Literary History* 5 (1): 119–33.

Semiotext(e) (1977) 2 (3), '*Anti-Oedipus*':

Brinkley, R.A. and Dyer, Robert, '. . . returns home (mythologies, dialectics, structures): Disruptions', pp. 159–71

Donzelot, Jacques, 'An anti-sociology', tr. Mark Seem, pp. 27–44

Hocquenghem, Guy, 'Family, capitalism, anus', tr. Caithin and Tamsen Manning, pp. 149–58

Lotringer, Sylvère, 'Libido unbound: the politics of "schizophrenia"', pp. 5–10

—— 'The fiction of analysis', pp. 173–89

Lyotard, Jean-François, 'Energumen capitalism', tr. James Leigh, pp. 11–26.

Rajchman, John, 'Analysis in power', pp. 45–58

Stivale, Charles J. (1981) 'Gilles Deleuze and Félix Guattari: Schizoanalysis and literary discourse', *SubStance* 29: 46–57.

SubStance (1984) 44/45, 'Gilles Deleuze':

Canning, Peter M., 'Fluidentity', pp. 35–45

Jardine, Alice, 'Woman in limbo: Deleuze and his br(others)', pp. 46–60

Patton, Paul, 'Conceptual politics and the war-machine in *Mille Plateaux*', pp. 61–80

Stivale, Charles J., 'Introduction', pp. 3–6

———, 'The literary element in *Mille Plateaux*: The new cartography of Deleuze and Guattari', pp. 20–34

Turkle, Sherry (1978) *Psychoanalytic Politics: Freud's French Revolution*, New York: Basic Books, esp. pp. 141–63.

Vauday, Patrick (1982) 'Ecrit à vue: Deleuze–Bacon', *Critique* 426 (November): 956–64.

Villani, Arnaud (1985) 'Géographie physique de *Mille plateaux*', *Critique* 455 (April): 331–47.

Wright, Elizabeth (1984) *Psychoanalytic Criticism*, London: Methuen, pp. 159–74.

Index

191